CONTESTED TERRITORY

History, Languages, and Cultures of the Spanish and Portuguese Worlds

This interdisciplinary series promotes scholarship in studies on Iberian cultures and contacts from the premodern and early modern periods.

———

SERIES EDITOR
Sabine MacCormack,
Theodore M. Hesburgh Professor of Arts and Letters,
Departments of Classics and History, University of Notre Dame

SERIES BOARD
J.N. Hillgarth, *emeritus, Pontifical Institute of Mediaeval Studies*
Peggy K. Liss, *Independent Scholar*
David Nirenberg, *University of Chicago*
Adeline Rucquoi, *École des Hautes Études en Sciences Sociales*

RECENT TITLES IN THE SERIES
Upholding Justice: Society, State, and the Penal System in Quito (1650–1750) (2004)
Tamar Herzog

Conflict and Coexistence: Archbishop Rodrigo and the Muslims and Jews of Medieval Spain (2004)
Lucy K. Pick

The Origins of Mexican Catholicism: Nahua Rituals and the Christian Sacraments in Sixteenth-Century Mexico (2004)
Osvaldo F. Pardo

Missionary Tropics: The Catholic Frontier in India (16th–17th Centuries) (2005)
Ines G. Županov

Jews, Christian Society, and Royal Power in Medieval Barcelona (2006)
Ella Klein

How the Incas Built Their Heartland: State Formation and Innovation of Imperial Strategies in the Sacred Valley, Peru (2006)
R. Alan Covey

Pastoral Quechua: The History of Christian Translation in Colonial Peru, 1550–1650 (2007)
Alan Durston

Contested Territory: Mapping Peru in the Sixteenth and Seventeenth Centuries (2009)
Heidi V. Scott

CONTESTED
TERRITORY

*Mapping Peru in the Sixteenth
and Seventeenth Centuries*

HEIDI V. SCOTT

University of Notre Dame Press   *Notre Dame, Indiana*

Manufactured in the United States of America

Library of Congress Cataloging-in-Publication Data

Scott, Heidi V., 1976–
    Contested territory : mapping Peru in the sixteenth and seventeenth
centuries / Heidi V. Scott.
        p.   cm. — (History, languages, and cultures of the Spanish and
Portuguese worlds)
    Includes bibliographical references and index.
    ISBN-13: 978-0-268-04131-1 (pbk. : alk. paper)
    ISBN-10: 0-268-04131-8 (pbk. : alk. paper)
    1. Peru—History—Conquest, 1522–1548.   2. Peru—History—1548–1820.
3. Peru—Discovery and exploration—Spanish.   4. Spaniards—Peru—
History—16th century.   5. Spaniards—Peru—History—17th century.
6. Cultural landscapes—Peru.   7. Human geography—Peru.   I. Title.
    F3442.S36   2009
    985'.02—dc22
                                                                            2009027704

CONTENTS

ILLUSTRATIONS

ABBREVIATIONS

AAL   Archivo Arzobispal de Lima

AGI   Archivo General de Indias, Seville

AGN   Archivo General de la Nación, Lima

ABNB Archivo y Biblioteca Nacionales de Bolivia, Sucre

BNE   Biblioteca Nacional de España, Madrid

BNP   Biblioteca Nacional del Perú, Lima

RG   *Relación Geográfica*

ACKNOWLEDGMENTS

This book has undergone a great many changes and additions since its initial incarnation as a doctoral thesis. The assistance and support that I received from numerous sources and individuals during my predoctoral phase of research played a crucial role both in bringing about the completion of my Ph.D. and in making possible the publication of this monograph.

The doctoral research underpinning this book was funded by the Economic and Social Research Council. I gratefully acknowledge this assistance. I would also like to thank St. John's College, Cambridge, and the Department of Geography at the University of Cambridge for supplementary financial assistance. I am particularly indebted to Sarah Radcliffe and James Duncan, who supervised my Ph.D., for their invaluable guidance, advice, and encouragement over the course of my doctoral research and also beyond it. As a graduate student in the Department of Geography, I benefited from discussions about my research with Philip Howell and Gerry Kearns, and with my fellow graduate students, especially Liz Gagen, David Lambert, Stephen Legg, and Mitch Rose. I am deeply indebted to Newnham College, Cambridge, for providing me with a precious opportunity to carry forward my research at the postdoctoral level in the form of a Junior Research Fellowship. In particular, the archival and library-based research that forms the basis of chapters 5 and 6 of this book was made possible by this fellowship.

The bulk of my archival research for this book was conducted in the Archivo General de Indias, Seville. I am indebted to the director and staff of the archive for their help. I am equally grateful to my fellow researchers at the AGI for the companionship and intellectual stimulation that helped to make my visits to Seville both enjoyable and productive. In Spain, I also made brief visits to the Biblioteca Nacional and the Real Academia de la Historia, and I thank the staff for their assistance.

During my two-month period of research in Lima, I incurred many debts of gratitude. I thank the directors and staff of the Archivo Arzobispal, Biblioteca Nacional, and Archivo General de la Nación for their assistance and for making me feel very welcome. I also thank Hildegardo Córdova Aguilar and Ricardo Bohl Pazos for making me welcome in the geography department of the Pontificia Universidad Católica del Perú, and to Ricardo for his help in finding me a place to stay in Lima. The hospitality and friendship of Karin Mansel and Walter Huamaní Tito and his family ensured that my time in Peru was a thoroughly enjoyable one. Walter generously provided me with secondary materials that I would almost certainly have overlooked without his help, and he showed me around Lima. Thanks to Walter, I was also able to make a brief but unforgettable trip to the Huarochirí province, about which I had read so much in colonial texts. In Sucre, Bolivia, I conducted a few weeks of archival research in the Archivo y Biblioteca Nacionales de Bolivia. Thanks are due to the director and staff for their generous assistance.

In developing the ideas and arguments that form the basis of this book, I have benefited from invitations to present my research at the Latin American Centre in Oxford, at the Department of Geography, University of Cambridge, at the Martin Centre for Urban and Architectural Studies, Cambridge, at the Institute for the Study of the Americas (formerly Institute of Latin American Studies) in London, and at the Institute of Geography and Earth Sciences, Aberystwyth University. Thanks are due to Mitch Rose and John Wylie for inviting me to present my work on the colonial landscapes of Huarochirí in their session "Reanimating Landscape" at the annual meeting of the Association of American Geographers, Philadelphia, 2004. Likewise, I thank Paulo Drinot and Leo Garófalo for giving me the opportunity to contribute to their edited collection *Más allá de la dominación y de la resistencia: Ensayos de historia peruana,* published in 2005.

I am greatly indebted to George W. Lovell, Sabine MacCormack, and an anonymous reviewer for their incisive and encouraging evaluations of my manuscript, as well as to Barbara Hanrahan, Rebecca De-Boer, and other staff at the University of Notre Dame Press for their invaluable help in the process of review, editing, and publication. I also express my gratitude to Ian Gulley of the Institute of Geography and Earth Sciences, Aberystwyth University, for his assistance in preparing the maps that illustrate this book. For their intellectual contributions and encouragement, thanks are due to Daniel Clayton, Tim Cresswell, Linda Newson, Gabriela Ramos, and David Robinson. To Daniel Clayton at the University of St. Andrews I owe a particular debt. Without his initial inspiration and encouragement, I would not have embarked on the research that produced this book.

Some material contained in chapters 2, 3, and 4 of this book has been published previously. I thank Pion Limited, London, for allowing me to use material from two articles that appeared in *Environment and Planning D: Society and Space* in 2004 and 2006. I am grateful to Elsevier for permitting the use of excerpts from an article that was published in *The Journal of Historical Geography* in 2003. I gratefully acknowledge the permission granted by the John Carter Brown Library, Brown University, to reproduce the map that illustrates the cover of this book and that was first published in the 1554 edition of Pedro Cieza de León's *Crónica del Perú*. I also thank the Real Academia de la Historia, Madrid, for permission to reproduce Diego Dávila Briceño's map of the Yauyos province (1586). I am grateful to the Agencia Española de Cooperación Internacional para el Desarrollo (AECID), Penguin Books, and Stanford University Press, respectively, for allowing me to use modified versions of maps that appear in the following publications: Guillermo Lohmann Villena, *El corregidor de indios en el Perú bajo los Austrias*; Edwin Williamson, *The Penguin History of Latin America*; and Karen Spalding, *Huarochirí: An Andean Society under Inca and Spanish Rule*.

Finally, I owe a particular debt to all those who are close to me, and especially my parents, for the ongoing support and encouragement that helped me to bring this book to completion. Thank you, gracias, obrigada.

CONTESTED TERRITORY

ONE

Landscape and the Spanish Conquest of Peru

In 1527, about five years before the conquest of Peru began in earnest, a small band of Spaniards, sailing southward along the Pacific coast in the vicinity of the equator, captured an indigenous seagoing raft bearing trade goods that included, among other things, emeralds and fine textiles. Described in the *Relación Samano-Xerez,* a brief report of uncertain authorship, this event gave the Europeans a first glimpse of the riches that fueled the subsequent exploration and conquest of Peru. The account, however, also provides what may well be the earliest European description of Peru's northernmost coastal settlements, first viewed by Francisco Pizarro and a small group of followers in 1528. Although this text portrays a moment of first encounter, it does not, as one might expect, convey a wonder-filled vision of exoticism and otherness. Instead, it projects an image of a landscape that is startlingly European in nature:

> [T]here are many sheep and pigs and cats and dogs and other animals and geese, and there [in the coastal towns] the blankets of cotton and wool that I mentioned above are made, and [also] the needlework and the beads and objects of silver and gold, and the

people are very rational; they appear to have many tools made of copper and other metals with which they work their fields, and they mine gold and practice all kinds of farming; the streets of their settlements are very well laid out; they have many types of fortresses and they live in a state of order and justice; the women are white and well-dressed and almost all of them are embroiderers; there is an island in the sea near the settlements where they have a temple built in the style of a rustic shelter, hung with very fine embroidered cloth, and where they have an image of a woman with a child in her arms and who is called María Mexía.[1]

This account of Peru's human geographies may be understood as an exceptionally vivid fantasy of familiarity and, by extension, of possession. Only by making the alien known and by forging connections where none existed, could the incommensurable be comprehended and described, and only by description could this new world be transported to Spain and laid at the monarch's feet.[2] By insisting on the familiarity of the yet-to-be-possessed, the account conveys to its royal recipient an ardent plea for his approval of the conquest of this territory: according to the text, this land and its inhabitants are *already almost Spanish,* for all the elements of a civilized Castilian existence — including even a fore-shadowing of Christian knowledge — are identified.[3]

This excerpt, belonging to one of the earliest known European descriptions of what was to become Peru, reveals the powerful role that cultural preconceptions, ambitions, and desires played in shaping early Spanish interpretations and representations of the Americas. In terms of shared language, values, and beliefs, the author of the document was, to borrow a phrase from Mignolo, situated in the self-same "locus of enunciation" as his European audience — a cultural positioning that shaped his account at a profound level.[4] Clearly, however, those early modern Europeans who ventured to Peru and other parts of the New World did not occupy merely linguistic and cultural spaces, exclusively shared with their companions and compatriots in distant Europe. Rather, they also traveled through *real* geographical spaces,[5] traversed physical terrain, and interacted in diverse ways with indigenous peoples.

Just as the Spaniards' perceptions and portrayals of New World landscapes were influenced by their membership in shared cultural communities and by individual interests, so too, their perceptions were shaped, in sometimes unpredictable ways, by the local contexts in which they found themselves, whether as conquistadors, travelers, or residents. In similar fashion, the construction of colonial geographical knowledge about the Americas depended as much on the local and ever-changing conditions in which it was produced as it did on shared cultural assumptions. The emphasis on change is significant, for the ways in which the New World's colonial landscapes were perceived, the meanings that were attached to them, and the manner in which they were portrayed were never constant but were subject to ongoing transformation.

✲   Scholarly interest in the geographical knowledge and writings that took shape in the wake of Spain's conquest of the Americas is by no means a recent phenomenon. It can be traced back to the nineteenth century and earlier, especially in the Spanish-speaking world.[6] Recent years, however, have witnessed a remarkable surge in the publication of studies on colonial Latin America that are concerned more broadly with issues of geography and space. The Columbian quincentenary brought with it a flurry of publications on European visions of the New World in the early years of encounter and exploration.[7] Since then, increasing attention has been paid to the production, use, and representation of colonial (and especially urban) spaces in Spanish America and to the construction of colonial geographical knowledge.[8] Within this growing literature, studies that focus on Peru are not absent. Extensive work exists on Andean concepts of space, territory, and landscape, both prior to and during the colonial era,[9] and on changing post-conquest patterns of landholding and usage.[10] Likewise, a number of scholars have explored the conflicts and differences that emerged between indigenous and Spanish concepts of space and territory, as well as cross-cultural negotiations over territorial control.[11] Others have addressed practices of colonial domination and resistance associated with the creation and use of urban spaces.[12] The geographical dimensions of numerous colonial chronicles, descriptions, and natural histories of Peru have also attracted growing, albeit still limited, scholarly attention.[13]

Colonial negotiations over Peru's landscapes still remain to be explored more fully, especially where the diversity of *Spanish* experiences and portrayals of those landscapes is concerned. It is striking that studies of Spanish visions of Peru, even in the early years of conquest and colonization, are relatively few and far between compared with those that focus on Mexico and the Caribbean—a phenomenon that may be related in part to the lack of wonder that, as Graubart suggests, characterizes many early European accounts of Peru.[14] This book, however, is less concerned with dwelling on expressions of wonder in the fetishized moments of first encounter than it is with drawing attention to the frequently mundane and everyday circumstances that shaped *ongoing* negotiations over landscape and geographical knowledge in Peru, and that may be traced in documentation that goes well beyond explicitly geographical accounts and descriptions.[15]

In placing landscape and geographical knowledge at the center of the study of early colonial Peru, this book explores some of the ways in which the viceroyalty's human and physical landscapes and its Amazon frontiers were experienced, portrayed, and negotiated—both physically and discursively—over the course of the sixteenth and early seventeenth centuries, predominantly from within Peru itself, but also from the geographical location of Spain. In particular, it questions the notion of a unified and homogeneous "Spanish geographical imagination" that was straightforwardly opposed to Amerindian understandings and perceptions of landscape. In doing so, it demonstrates how Peru's landscapes and territories were imbued with meaning by Spaniards and Spanish Americans in diverse, improvisatory, and frequently conflicting ways, and were shaped within shifting networks of power, agency, and interest.

My predominant (but by no means exclusive) emphasis on Spanish and Spanish American experiences and portrayals may appear to go against the grain of much recent scholarship that challenges the marginalization of Amerindian, *mestizo,* and other groups in colonial society. As Elliott observes, however,

> our contemporary discovery of the presumed "otherness" of others has embraced the non-European world to the exclusion of the conquerors, colonists, and chroniclers of the sixteenth century; the observers have been accorded a privileged status that has been denied their observers, whose individual voices, reduced to

an unattractive unison, are dismissed as "the hegemonic voices of the West." But in reality there are many voices, among the conquerors and conquered alike.[16]

In citing Elliott's comments, my intentions are emphatically not to suggest that "the colonizers" should be returned to a privileged location in historical analysis. On the contrary, this study is propelled by a conviction that the adoption of nuanced approaches to the Spaniards' experiences of landscape and their imaginative geographies can contribute to dismantling narratives that aggrandize the coherence and power of European imperialism and perpetuate its binaries. Rather than focus exclusively on dramatic conflicts between Spanish and indigenous groups, this book explores how knowledge of landscape and geography was *negotiated* within colonial networks that frequently confounded clear-cut oppositions between colonizers and colonized.

Within these networks, as I hope to show, Amerindian groups did not merely resist the imposition of alien geographical notions but played an active role in shaping Peru's colonial geographies, as well as Spanish experiences and perceptions of its landscapes. As historians have repeatedly recognized, Spanish colonialism in the New World was heavily dependent on the presence of colonial subjects, in practical as well as ideological terms.[17] Taking account of how Spanish engagements with Peruvian landscapes were molded by native agency is therefore crucial: as the viceroyalty took shape, the beliefs of indigenous people, their settlement patterns and mobility, and their sheer physical presence and absence were all reflected in the diverse ways in which Peru's landscapes mattered for Hispanic populations.

Landscape, Territory, and Colonialism

As Sluyter observes, no significant attempts have yet been made to construct a "comprehensive geographic theory of colonialism and landscape,"[18] despite the dramatic and far-reaching transformations that landscapes have so often undergone as a result of European overseas expansion and colonization. Central to his proposals for developing such a theory is the contention that reciprocal interactions between indigenous populations, Europeans, and material landscape resulted in that landscape's transformation. In outlining his approach, Sluyter decisively rejects the notion that European colonizers were the "ultimate determinant" in the process of transformation[19]—a deeply rooted belief that finds expression in Elliott's suggestion that "America had given Europe space, in the widest sense of that word—space to dominate, space in which to experiment, and space to transform according to its wishes."[20] Although the central purpose of my study is not to contribute to the development of Sluyter's theory, significant common ground exists between his objectives and my own. In exploring colonial negotiations over Peru's landscapes, I seek to convey, like Sluyter, that they were never the product of European agency alone, but emerged from ongoing *interactions* between the material landscape, its indigenous inhabitants, and Hispanic populations.

Before I turn my attention to these negotiations, however, it seems appropriate to explain how I use and understand the term "landscape" in this study of colonial Peru, not least because the historical origins of the term are European. If the term is understood in a narrowly genealogical fashion, centered on particular, elite "ways of seeing"[21] that first emerged in Renaissance Italy with the discovery of perspective, then its use, as Bender suggests, is distinctly limited outside very specific cultural and geographical contexts. Instead of restricting the term to a reduced set of historical, cultural, and geographical associations, I use it, like Bender, in a manner that is intentionally expansive and that has room for diverse ways of experiencing, relating, and giving meaning to places and environments:

> If . . . we broaden the idea of landscape and understand it to be the way in which people—all people—understand and engage with the material world around them, and if we recognize that people's being-in-the-world is always historically and spatially contingent, it becomes clear that landscapes are always in process, potentially conflicted, untidy and uneasy.[22]

By speaking of "landscape" in the context of sixteenth- and seventeenth-century Peru, then, my intention is not to impose on its inhabitants (European or otherwise) a set of alien concepts that they did not possess, but instead to gain insight into an array of experiences, meanings, and embodied relationships that were constantly being reshaped. Indeed, the very value of the term "landscape" may be seen to lie in what one cultural geographer has described as landscape's "duplicity"—its perennial refusal to be pinned to any fixed or unitary meaning.[23]

My explorations of landscape and colonialism in Peru are informed by ongoing endeavors in cultural geography and anthropology to conceptualize landscape as animated rather than static, as process rather than as product, and as embodied experience rather than as disembodied vision.[24] As Rose suggests, landscape does not possess inherent or predetermined qualities, but instead is made to "matter"—to take on diverse meanings and to have effects on people's lives by means of "the everyday practices and activities that surround it."[25] By conceptualizing Peru's colonial landscapes in these ways, emphasis may be shifted away from the analysis of selected representations and toward an exploration of the varied spatial, material, and discursive *practices* that continuously shaped those landscapes and the meanings with which they were imbued. At the same time, the dynamism of landscape may be brought to the fore by treating colonial texts not simply as sources of "finished" landscape representations that are open to critical analysis, but as *resources* that allow valuable insights into ongoing colonial negotiations.

Peru's colonial landscapes were not merely represented in text and image, but were also experienced in corporeal and spatial ways by all those who traveled through, inhabited, and sought to control them. These aspects have not been ignored in work on colonial Latin America: recent studies that highlight the impact of frequently harsh New World environments on explorers' and conquistadors' bodies—and, indeed, on their very ambitions and objectives—provide a clear example of this.[26] Frequently, however, the profound physicality of the Spaniards' experiences has been sidelined by concerns for the cultural (and hence metaphorical) locations from which they perceived and wrote about the Americas, as well as by a tendency to focus on their role as agents who appropriated and transformed America's spaces, while paying scant attention to how they were affected by those spaces.[27] "Negotiations over landscape," therefore, certainly refers to verbal and textual exchanges but also, and no less significantly, to the ways in which landscape was experienced, struggled over, shaped, and used in physical and corporeal ways.

I have also chosen to speak of "negotiation" because it calls forth conditions of contingency, compromise, and modification. Although this choice of terminology may appear to trivialize or sideline the violence and conflict that was ever-present in the colonial world of Peru, this is not my intention: as Bolaños writes, the study of colonialism in Latin America brings with it a responsibility to remember that it was founded on cultures of violence and exploitation.[28] Instead, my use of this term is intended to reflect the ways in which landscape experiences, perceptions, and portrayals were contextualized and subject to change, instead of being rigidly predetermined by cultural origins or the existence of an unbridgeable colonial divide.

This study, although focusing in part on the ways in which colonial negotiations over landscape unfolded within particular localities or regions, is equally concerned with tracing their development at the viceregal and transatlantic level. Locally focused negotiations over landscape and those that extended *beyond* the local sphere were inextricably connected: the discursive and embodied practices that surrounded particular landscapes were never restricted to the local, but always formed part of broader networks of practice and communication that connected them with other, more distant, landscapes and spaces.[29]

The following chapters attempt to convey how Peruvian landscapes and territories were negotiated not just within Peru itself but also from across the Atlantic in Spain. As this study illustrates, particularly in chapters 5 and 6, these negotiations not only focused on clearly demarcated localities or regions but also unfolded around vast and often vaguely defined geographical spaces that extended across and beyond the viceroyalty. By speaking of both "landscape" and "territory," I seek to convey a clear sense of this multiscalar perspective. In using these two terms, I also distinguish between negotiations that revolved, on the one hand, around particular places and regions that were experienced directly by the Spanish, and, on the other, around the representation of frequently extensive geographical spaces that largely lay beyond the realm of the colonizers' experience.

Cartography, Text, and Landscape

Material and discursive struggles over landscape, territory, and space have always been central to the implementation of colonial and imperial ventures. The production of diverse maps and cartographies in and of Spanish America, as in other parts of the world, played a highly signifiant role in the process of conquest and colonization. Besides facilitating America's emergence within an increasingly dominant Western geographical worldview, mapmaking reflected and reinforced the material transformation of New World landscapes and the creation of new, colonial spaces.[30] The intense scholarly interest that has emerged around colonial Spanish mapping practices represents a welcome move away from the once widely held view that imperial Spain contributed little to the development of modern European cartography or geography.[31]

It may be argued, however, that Spain's nascent modern cartography has come to represent an "overdetermined signifier"[32] of Spanish imperialism in the New World. Despite the undeniable role that cartography played in the service of imperialism, it was by no means representative of all Spanish geographical ideas. Indeed, it appears to have been of limited relevance for a majority of the Spaniards and Spanish Americans who experienced, inhabited, and portrayed the New World and its landscapes in the sixteenth and seventeenth centuries.[33] As such, it is important, as some scholars have done, to take account of other, "popular" forms of mapmaking and visual representation that were practiced alongside formal cartography in early modern Spain as well as in the Americas.[34]

The significance of cartography and mapmaking should not be allowed to overshadow the value of written text as a source of insights into colonial negotiations over landscape and geographical knowledge in the New World. As a result of their great scarcity for many areas of early colonial Spanish America, including the Viceroyalty of Peru, extant colonial maps must frequently be considered a supplementary rather than a principal historical source.[35] Overwhelmingly, Peru's landscapes were portrayed and contested through the production of written texts rather than of maps, and it is in written records that the most detailed accounts of everyday, nonrepresentational negotiations over those landscapes may be found. The scarcity of cartographic records for early Spanish

Peru may therefore be regarded not as a disadvantage but as an invitation to explore negotiations over its landscapes and territories in a diverse range of administrative, ecclesiastical, and other documents that fill the colonial archives.

In drawing on these written records, the chapters that follow do not attempt to focus on a comprehensive spectrum of colonial identities. Most notably, perhaps, they do not address the ways in which Peru's landscapes were experienced and perceived by women, for all the texts that I draw on, without exception, were written by men. Neither "colonizing women" nor those women who experienced colonialism ever constituted unitary groups:[36] as recent scholarship shows, however, their spatial practices, perceptions of landscape, and geographical imaginings often differed significantly from those of their male counterparts.[37] Given my concern for bringing to light difference and diversity among "the colonizers," such an omission may strike some readers as puzzling, even inexcusable.

In focusing primarily on the writings of those whose voices are heard more insistently in the colonial archive, however, I believe that these complex entanglements can be most effectively explored. The abundant writings produced by administrators, conquistadors, and ecclesiastics not only shed light on their own engagements with landscape, perceptions, and experiences, but also provide a window onto an array of *other* practices—indigenous as well as Hispanic—that were central to negotiations over landscape. Indigenous-authored sources are not ignored by this study, for they too shed valuable light on how native agency played a key role in shaping Spanish engagements with landscape. Accounts of merits and services, geographical descriptions, and other documents produced by Andean subjects reveal, moreover, that indigenous experiences and portrayals of landscape were no less diverse, improvisatory, or open to change than those of Spaniards or Spanish Americans.

Spatial, Temporal, and Thematic Limits

This study cannot claim, of course, to include every area of the Viceroyalty of Peru or to chart the continuous unfolding of colonial negotiations over landscape throughout a period of more than one hundred years. Inevitably, the study is geographically selective; although commencing on the northern fringes of the Inca empire, it is predominantly oriented toward the central highlands of the *Audiencia* of Lima and the tropical frontiers of the *Audiencia* of Charcas (see figs. 1 and 2). The existence of rich textual records that relate to the colonial provinces of Huarochirí, Jauja, and Huamanga has placed these areas in a particularly prominent position. Materials relating to these provinces have already been extensively studied by Andeanist historians. Rather than seek out new or little-known sources, however, I am more concerned with revisiting those that are familiar and exploring the ways in which they can provide fresh insights into colonial negotiations over landscape and geographical knowledge.

Chapters 5 and 6 also focus on the Amazon frontier regions of present-day Bolivia and southern Peru: above all, the inclusion of these areas is intended to further scholarly efforts to challenge the frequently encountered segregation of the Andes and Amazon in historical studies.[38] Although the Spanish conquest undoubtedly brought about the widespread disruption of cultural and political linkages and networks of exchange between Andes and Amazon—thereby continuing a process that had already been set in motion by the Incas—these linkages did not disappear altogether. Large-scale military expeditions of conquest into the Amazon had largely ceased by the beginning of the seventeenth century, yet Spanish interest in the region did not disappear; indeed, sporadic exchanges and encounters between the highlands and tropical lowlands continued throughout the colonial period.[39] If the Amazon regions are persistently portrayed in colonial texts as spaces that were detached from and in many ways the antithesis of the Andean highlands (whether in a positive or negative sense), many writings also confound this stark dualism. As this book endeavors to illustrate, fascinating textual sources exist that allow the negotiations that took place over Peru's Amazon frontiers in the sixteenth and seventeenth centuries to be explored in considerable depth.

Focusing on petitions and accounts produced by Peru's first conquistadors, chapter 2 traces changes in the Spaniards' experiences and perceptions of landscape as they passed from the exploration of the Pacific coastline to the conquest of the Inca empire. By comparing these

Fig. 1. The Viceroyalty of Peru. Adapted from Edwin Williamson, *The Penguin History of Latin America* (London: Penguin Books, 1992), 610. Copyright © Edwin Williamson, 1992. Reproduced by permission of Penguin Books Ltd.

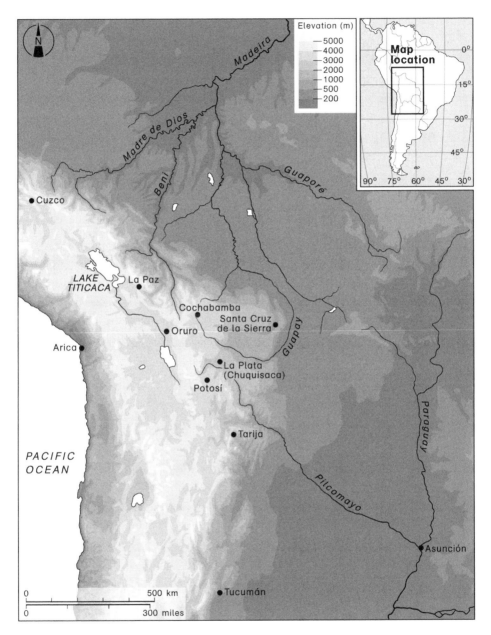

Fig. 2. The *Audiencia* of Charcas.

texts with native testimonies of conquest produced in Jauja, I argue that the conquistadors' physical engagements with landscape, and consequently their portrayals of it, were strongly shaped by the agency of indigenous groups and by their physical presence or absence. A final section examines how, in the wake of conquest, Peru's indigenous populations continued to play a crucial role in shaping the material landscapes of the new viceroyalty and the ways in which Europeans experienced and portrayed them.

Chapter 3 shifts the discussion from the era of conquest to the 1580s. By examining the production of geographical accounts in response to the questionnaires prepared by the Council of the Indies, it questions the notion that indigenous and Spanish geographical representations were always straightforwardly opposed or defined by clear-cut relations of domination and resistance. As well as questioning the suitability of "resistance" as a concept for understanding indigenous participation in this process, this chapter illustrates the point that Spanish portrayals of landscape produced in Peru were far from homogeneous and were often at odds with the "official" geographical notions embedded within the questionnaire.

Whereas chapter 3 focuses predominantly on the colonial provinces of Jauja and Huamanga, chapter 4 traces Spanish negotiations over the landscapes of Huarochirí between the 1570s and the 1630s. Beginning with a dispute over jurisdictions that took place between two parish priests, it goes on to explore the ways in which the landscapes of the province were experienced and represented by Jesuit missionaries, a crown official, and seventeenth-century extirpators of idolatry. In doing so, it draws attention to the significance of travel in shaping these diverse individuals' experiences of Huarochirí, but also foregrounds how their portrayals of travel in the province were influenced by the nature and extent of their involvement in local affairs, as well as by their personal and professional objectives.

In chapter 5, the focus shifts from descriptions of Huarochirí produced in Peru to portrayals of the viceroyalty's Amazon frontiers produced in early-seventeenth-century Madrid by a Spanish officer, a *maestre de campo* named Juan Recio de León. By tracing the ways in which his portrayals of Amazonia and of his proposed colonizing venture were continually revised, I demonstrate that Recio, far from merely succumbing to "contagious" tales about Paititi, El Dorado, and other mythical locations, opportunistically tailored his reports and petitions to suit the ever-changing context of prominent royal interests and concerns. In addition, then, to questioning the homogeneity of colonial Spanish portrayals of Amazonia, this chapter examines how the material and social spaces of the royal court played a crucial role in influencing the ways in which Recio chose to represent the tropical lowlands to the east of the Andes.

The subtropical frontier regions of Charcas that connected the Andean highlands to Amazonia are central to chapter 6. Here, I aim to call into question the notion that clear-cut divisions between Andes and Amazon were common to all Spanish and Spanish-American geographical portrayals in the early colonial era. By examining texts produced by conquistadors, missionaries, and royal officials between approximately 1550 and 1650, I show that stark binary divisions were frequently moderated by the perceived existence and functions of an "in-between space" that connected or separated the Andes and Amazon. Once again, this chapter conveys how colonial negotiations over landscape unfolded through the unpredictable interactions of discursive and embodied practices that were performed at local, regional, viceregal, and transatlantic scales. In a brief concluding section I draw together the themes outlined above and reflect on the insights that they collectively provide on the entanglements between landscape and colonialism in early Spanish Peru.

TWO

Beyond Textuality

Landscape, Embodiment, and Native Agency

In May 1532 a small group of Spaniards disembarked at the port of Túmbez, in the far northwestern reaches of the Inca empire, known to its native inhabitants as Tawantinsuyu. Of the men who came ashore, some had been newly recruited in Spain by their leader, Francisco Pizarro, but most had come from Central America, where they left behind recently established livelihoods to go in search of an empire that lay far to the south. Since Pizarro's first visit to Peru's northern coast in 1527–28, conflict had erupted between Atahualpa and Huascar, sons of the recently deceased Inca Huayna Capac, who now struggled for control of Tawantinsuyu. As a result of the so-called civil war, the once-splendid settlement of Túmbez, which Spanish eyewitnesses described with admiration, had been laid waste and abandoned.[1] The Spaniards' suspense turned to skepticism at the sight of such desolation and, above all else, the absence of the promised wealth. It would not be long, however, until their hopes were amply fulfilled.

The story of the Spanish conquest of Peru is one that has been told many times. As Restall shows so eloquently, tales of Spanish conquest have overwhelmingly celebrated the actions and deeds of a handful of intrepid Europeans.[2] In striking contrast to the dynamism of these individuals, the non-Europeans who participated in the events of conquest, together with the physical environments of the New World, frequently appear as little more than an inert canvas on which the Spaniards went to work. Since the 1970s, however, accounts of conquest have increasingly been told in new ways. Although initial endeavors to recover "the vision of the vanquished" were sympathetic to Amerindian peoples, they accorded them little more in the way of agency than did the celebratory tales of European prowess.[3] More recent studies suggest that the arrival of the first Europeans, far from being perceived by indigenous groups as a momentous occasion or dramatic point of rupture, was often of scant significance for Amerindians and was experienced, to highly variable degrees of intensity, as an event woven into a network of processes and practices that were established well before the Spanish set foot in the Americas.[4]

The task of demystifying conquest, however, must involve more than conceptualizing it as a process or series of events that was imagined and represented in distinct ways by two "sides"—the Spaniards and the Amerindians. It requires, in addition, that the Europeans are understood as individuals, whose actions are closely intertwined with and affected by the agency of other, non-European actors, as well as by the physical environments with which they came into contact. Making important moves toward such an approach, Pastor Bodmer draws attention to the corporeality of early Spanish explorers, their contact with and exposure to frequently harsh New World environments, and the manner in which this embodied contact shaped their perceptions and writings.[5] Other Latin Americanists, looking beyond the Spanish deeds portrayed in colonial accounts, have shed light on the highly significant role of non-Europeans in shaping the trajectories of conquest, either as opponents or as collaborators of the Spaniards.[6] Geographers, although often focusing on other times and places, have increasingly drawn attention to the corporeality of European colonizers and travelers, to their presence *in* the landscapes that they sought to possess, and to the ways in which their textual and visual representations of landscape were shaped by the particular material context in which they found themselves, as well as by the agency of non-Europeans.[7]

Building on these foundations, this chapter endeavors to show how, in the early years of exploration and conquest in Peru, Spanish experiences of landscape were shaped not only by the aims, ambitions, and worldviews that tied them discursively to Spain, but equally by their embodied experiences of American environments and the agency of Amerindians and other non-Europeans. The discussion begins with a comparison of portrayals of conquest contained within petitions for royal reward, which were submitted both by conquistadors and by Andean leaders from Peru's central highlands. It then briefly focuses on early Spanish histories and chronicles. In contrast to the royal petitions, or so-called accounts of services, the histories and chronicles provide detailed descriptions of the architectural and agricultural landscapes of the Inca empire and reveal how, in the wake of conquest, these landscapes underwent destruction but were also reshaped. Because these texts shed light on the ways in which geographies of conquest and emergent colonial landscapes were molded, through ongoing, often mundane, labor and practices, their analysis may usefully contribute to unsettling the notion of conquest as a dramatic and exceptional "moment."

Before exploring the conquistadors' encounters with the Andean world, I first take a brief look at the pre-conquest phase of exploration along the Pacific coast. The surviving descriptions are of particular value for understanding the nature of ensuing Spanish portrayals of the Inca empire and, particularly, the active role of non-Europeans—and the effects of their presence or absence—in shaping the experiences and mobility of the Spaniards.

Suffering as Service: Spanish Accounts of the Pacific Coast

The expedition that arrived at Túmbez in 1532 was preceded by a preliminary phase of reconnaissance that led the conquistadors south-eastward from Panama along the Pacific coast. The first of three expeditions organized by Francisco Pizarro and Diego de Almagro, two wealthy veterans of the Indies, sailed from Panama in November 1524: barely four hundred kilometers from their point of departure, the men were forced to return, defeated by hunger, exhaustion, and hostile indigenous groups, and with scant sign of riches or land suitable for settlement.[8] Two years later, the second southbound expedition left Panama, resulting in the capture of a raft carrying goods from the Inca empire and, by the end of 1527, the first view of the Peruvian coastline. In December 1530, following Pizarro's visit to Spain (where he obtained the governorship of this barely-glimpsed territory), the third voyage left Panama. Less than two years later, in November 1532, the Inca Atahualpa was taken hostage by the Spanish at Cajamarca in the northern highlands (see figs. 3 and 4).[9]

Despite the tantalizing first encounters that the second voyage yielded, the Spanish participants' descriptions of events leading up to their arrival in Túmbez in May 1532 are predominantly characterized not by visions of future conquest but by an all-pervading discourse of physical suffering. The slow process of exploration along the coasts of present-day Panama and Colombia brought the participants of all three expeditions into contact with a harsh equatorial environment, which claimed the lives of hundreds of Spaniards, not to mention those of the many Amerindians and black slaves who had been taken along to serve them.[10] Fringed by dense forest, mangroves, and swamps, the coastal lands offered precious little in the way of food to the Spaniards and their auxiliaries, who, in contrast to the indigenous populations, had no knowledge of how to obtain it. Acute hunger and thirst were compounded by the ceaseless discomfort caused by plagues of insects, the humidity that rotted the clothes on the men's backs, and the diseases to which many fell victim.

An account by the chronicler Cieza de León of the discovery and conquest of Peru provides a vivid description of the conquistadors' suffering during the first voyage of 1524–25:

> And the Spaniards, due to the trials they had undergone, were very thin and yellow, to such a degree, that it was greatly distressing for them to look at one another. And the land which lay ahead of them was infernal because even the birds and the beasts avoid inhabiting it. They could see nothing but tangled thickets and mangroves and the water that fell from the sky and that which constantly lay on the ground, and the sun was so obscured by the clouds' density that on some days they could not see its light at all. And on finding themselves in the midst of these forests, they expected only death.[11]

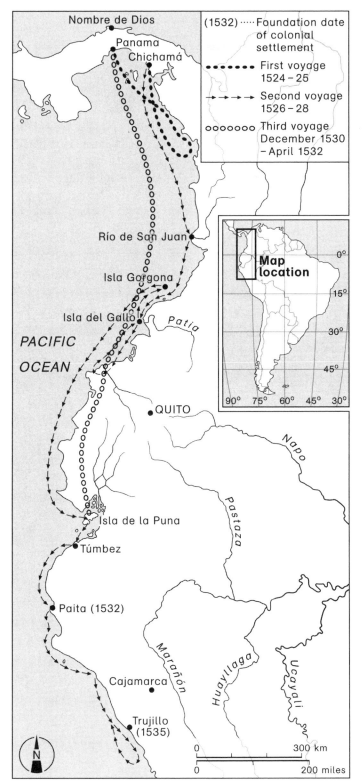

Panama
Chichamá

(1532) ·········· Foundation date
of colonial
settlement

●●●●●● First voyage
1524–25

→·→·→·→ Second voyage
1526–28

ooooooo Third voyage
December 1530
– April 1532

Río de San Juan

Isla Gorgona

Isla del Gallo

Patía

PACIFIC
OCEAN

Map
location

0°

15°

30°

45°

90° 75° 60° 45° 30°

● QUITO

Napo

Pastaza

Isla de la Puna

● Túmbez

Paita (1532)

Marañón

Huayllaga

Ucayali

Cajamarca

Trujillo
(1535)

N

0   300 km

0   200 miles

Fig. 3.
Spanish voyages
to Peru, 1524–32.
Adapted from
John Hemming,
The Conquest of the Incas
(London: Abacus,
1972).

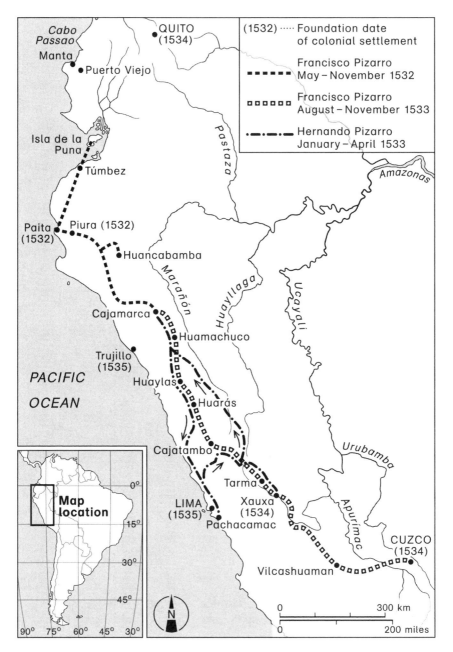

Fig. 4. The Spanish conquest of Peru: Routes taken by Francisco and Hernando Pizarro. Adapted from John Hemming, *The Conquest of the Incas* (London: Abacus, 1972).

Conditions did not improve on the second voyage. In 1527, finding themselves stranded without supplies on the Isla del Gallo, an island off Colombia's southern coast, a number of the expeditionaries sent a desperate request for help to the governor of Panama: of the three hundred men who left Panama in 1526, as many as two hundred and twenty had succumbed to hunger, disease, or native attacks. While the majority of the survivors returned directly to Panama in ships sent by the governor, Pizarro remained behind to lead a small group of men toward Peru.[12]

✸   Drawing on participants' accounts of disastrous expeditions of the early sixteenth century to Honduras, Florida, and the central North American plains, Pastor Bodmer identifies in these texts what she terms the "discourse of failure." These undertakings, like Pizarro's initial exploration along the coast of northern South America, resulted in an exposure to extreme environmental conditions that forced the participants to channel all their energies into struggling to stay alive. The texts that record these expeditions are wholly pervaded by the eyewitnesses' contact with the environment. Nature, asserts Pastor Bodmer, takes center stage: "at first no more than an obstacle to be overcome in the course of reaching an objective, [it] gradually becomes a central focus of the text, shifting the reader's attention away from everything else. The ceaseless struggle against it, as it assaults the members of the expedition in a thousand ways and increasingly threatens their survival, comes to be the organizing purpose of their daily activities."[13]

In the absence of glorious conquest—rendered impossible by the ferocity of American nature—the narratives center on the details of the struggle for survival: wandering in search of food replaces exploration and the aims of conquest, while food replaces gold as a substance of inestimable value.[14] In the accounts of survivors who have nothing tangible to offer their monarch, misfortune and suffering come to be presented as forms of service worthy of reward.[15] The petitioners' descriptions of their struggles to satisfy basic physiological needs contradict the fiction of the infallible and virtually superhuman conquistador that pervades accounts of successful conquest.[16]

On their return to Panama in 1528, Pizarro's companions presented their official testimonies, or *relaciones de servicios,* with the aim of obtaining royal recompense for their efforts.[17] Because the petitioners were able to return to Panama with eyewitness accounts of a wealthy empire, the documents that they presented do not wholly correspond to Pastor Bodmer's discourse of failure. Nevertheless, it was impossible for them to speak of conquest. The encounter of a tiny handful of men with Peru's coastal peoples was necessarily of a peaceful nature. Moreover, in order to set themselves apart from those expeditionaries who had returned to Panama from the Isla del Gallo, the petitioners sought to emphasize the hunger, disease, and exhaustion that they had willingly endured by continuing the venture to the coasts of Peru.[18] In conveying this physical suffering, however, their accounts of services—unlike some of the accounts described by Pastor Bodmer—do not offer detailed portrayals of the coastal jungles and mangroves in which they had spent so many months. These documents were intended to make known the deeds and qualities of men rather than to offer geographical descriptions. References to landscape are extremely brief and reductive: the joint petition of 1528 asks witnesses to confirm that three years were spent "wandering . . . in this said journey and discovery across extremely rough and disorienting terrain and with great suffering to our persons."[19] One witness, confirming the testimony, stated that he too was present when they "encountered and came ashore on land that was very rough and encumbered by water and mountains, where the said [men] and this witness and the other participants faced many difficulties and troubles."[20]

In the Spaniards' accounts of this episode, nature itself and the human suffering it caused are inextricable—one is tied so closely to the other that to describe the landscape in any other terms would probably have been impossible. The debilitating heat and humidity, insects, and apparent lack of food forced the expeditionaries to focus obsessively on their own bodies and on the physiological effects that were produced by their immersion in the forest environment. Unlike the open expanses of Spain's central plateau or, indeed, the plains of New Spain (which Cortés likened to the landscapes of his own country), this world of dense equatorial forests was *ciego*—literally translated, blind—for it could not be visually surveyed or kept at a distance, but had to be negotiated step by step as it physically engulfed those who ventured into it.[21] The physical landscape, therefore, rendered impossible the construction of a triumphant discourse of conquest. Pizarro and his companions quite literally became mired in the coastal swamps and forests, barely able to look forward or to progress.

It would be a mistake, however, to understand the Spanish portrayals of this coastal expedition purely in terms of an encounter between its members and the physical environment. What the *relaciones de servicios* most forcefully and unanimously reveal — and present to the king, moreover, as a worthy form of service — is the suffering that the conquistadors endured as a result of direct and unmediated contact with the landscape. The questions contained in the 1528 accounts of services pay particular attention to the hardships that the petitioners underwent in their arduous search for food during their ill-fated stay on the Isla del Gallo. As no food sources were available in the littoral zone, the men were obliged to venture upstream in canoes to look for native maize plantations and, if any grain was found, to transport it to the island, each man carrying a load on his back. A witness named Ambrosio Monsalve described his experience of these events in the following manner:

> he knows and saw that to go in search of the said maize that they needed to eat, the said men went along the rivers in canoes, and at times they sank and lost what they were carrying and they escaped by swimming . . . and that when they carried the maize, at times they traversed the mountains and mangroves loaded with it, and *they themselves* made the shelters in which they had to take refuge, and if they did not do this they remained outside in the downpours.[22]

The need to offer up such tasks as a worthy form of service was partly determined by the environmental conditions that had sabotaged the original aim of conquest; but this was not all, as the words "they themselves" (*ellos mismos*) suggest. Monsalve goes on to answer affirmatively the next question, which asked if he knew that the "Indian men and women and negroes" who had been taken along to serve the Spaniards died because they were "unable to withstand the great difficulties and hunger."[23]

Mentioned only in their absence, the indigenous servants and black slaves whom the Spaniards brought with them from Panama are suddenly forced into view. It was this absence, after all, that obliged the would-be conquistadors to search for food themselves, carry it on their backs, and, wherever necessary, construct shelters in which to spend the night or protect themselves from the torrential rain. The fact that they were compelled to carry their own supplies caused the Spanish expedition members particular distress, a feeling that is most clearly conveyed in a number of letters written in 1527 on the Isla del Gallo. A joint letter sent by Pizarro's companions to Pedro de los Ríos, the governor of Panama, laments that they were "very weakened by this epidemic, for we have not rested for three years, *carrying the maize we need to eat on our backs,* because over five hundred domestic Indians that we brought from back there [Panama] have died, for which reason many Christians have died, because they have no one to serve or look after them."[24]

Both the *relaciones de servicios* and the letters of 1527 suggest that, more than the nature of the environment itself, the loss of indigenous and black slaves was identified by the Spaniards as the primary cause of their own death rate. Deprived of that human barrier which effectively kept nature at bay, the explorers were thrown into direct contact with its ferocity and forced to provide for their own needs.[25] And, as the would-be conquistadors themselves admitted, their attempts to do so were little less than disastrous.

The Broad Horizons of Conquest

One of the few men who took part in the first two Pacific voyages of exploration and the ensuing conquest was Nicolás de Ribera, a well-placed individual who had close ties with both Francisco Pizarro and his partner, Almagro.[26] In 1553 he presented a *relación de servicios* to the king, highlighting the importance of his role in both stages of the venture. Despite the strong emphasis on his active contributions to the process of exploration and conquest, Ribera's petition paints a picture of misery and physical suffering which, like other accounts of services, is studded with the words "hunger," "necessity," and "difficulty." The eighth question, which relates to the last phase of coastal exploration preceding the Spaniards' arrival in Peru, requests the witnesses to confirm that "because of the great necessity and lack of food that we endured a number of us went . . . in search of habitation and some food, and we were in the mangroves and swamps for eight or nine days until we found some dwellings with a little maize . . . and from there we came with the said don Diego de Almagro to the settlements of Pasao, where we spent many days searching for food for the people and horses."[27]

The entire answer to the eighth question focuses on the search for food, and all movement is directed toward this sole objective. Movement, moreover, is erratic and slow; eight or nine days, Ribera claims, were spent among the mangroves and swamps until the expedition succeeded in finding some grain. In the absence of conquest, Ribera presents the daily struggle for survival and his stoically endured suffering as a worthy form of service to God and king. His response to the next question, which deals with the beginnings of conquest in Peru, could hardly be more different. It states:

> From the said settlements of Pasao we went to the Bay of los Caraques, and from there we went conquering and pacifying the land, and we made great haste until we reached Cajamarca where, with our arrival, the territory was secured, because we were one hundred and fifty men, eighty of us on horseback, from where the said captains don Françisco Piçarro and don Diego de Almagro and I with them went conquering the land until we arrived in the valley of Xauxa [Jauja] where the governor don Françisco Piçarro founded a town.[28]

The pace, the breadth of vision, and the geographical scope undergo a remarkable transformation: suddenly, and without explanation, the struggle for survival is transformed into rapid and relentless conquest. With apparent effortlessness, the Spaniards sweep across the territory, taking possession of it as they progress. The landscape and its physiological impact on the conquistadors fade into the background, giving the impression that the invaders' journey takes them across an unobstructed and homogeneous plain. The replies to questions continue in this vein through the events of Manco Inca's siege of Cuzco in 1536 and the eventual victory of the Spaniards, which, for Ribera, clearly marks the end of conquest. From Jauja, said Ribera, Pizarro dispatched him

> with provision of captain and lieutenant to this coast of Pacha-cama in order to take possession of its government in the name of Your Highness, and he gave me licence to found a settlement and I did this in Pachacama, and I assembled all the Spaniards who were arriving and sent them to the said Governor, and I went along taking possession of the land as far as the valley of Hacari and from there as far as the valley of Guarmey, and I returned to give an account to the said Governor of what I had done.[29]

Although action provides the foundation for responses to questions cited above, it undergoes a qualitative change when the fight for survival gives way to conquest. Among the mangroves, the Spaniards become defenseless recipients of nature's aggressive agency: as Pastor Bodmer puts it, "the Europeans are victims who 'receive' the aggression . . . without being able to defend themselves or avoid the 'trouble' inflicted."[30] On their arrival in Peru, however, they appear to become the masters of their own actions, and therefore of the landscape; the circular wanderings of the tropical coast are left behind and the purposeful linearity of the process of conquest regained.

The conquistadors' relentless forward motion is punctuated by the performance of heroic acts at certain key sites of conquest. The experience of the journey itself, and of the physical territory through which the Spaniards travel, is replaced by a chronology of conquest in which the sites where those acts are performed are linked only by the barest of narrative threads.[31] Most significant among those sites were Jauja, Cuzco, and, above all, Cajamarca in Peru's northern highlands, where on November 16, 1532, the Inca Atahualpa was captured. Other, lesser sites of conquest included Túmbez and San Miguel on the northern coast and the temples of Pachacamac located just to the south of modern-day Lima. These places and the deeds that took place in them became the principal focal points of the conquistadors' petitions to the king.[32] Occasionally, the petitioners drew brief attention to the nature of the land that they had traversed between one site of conquest and the next, usually to emphasize its harshness. Luis Maça, for example, who took part in a four-month expedition led by Hernando Pizarro to Pachacamac and Jauja, declared that over the course of this journey, "we traversed over three hundred leagues of great snows and dangers that were caused by rivers and rope bridges."[33]

Such references to the difficulties posed by the physical terrain, however, bear little relation to the intense suffering conveyed in accounts of the coastal voyages. The environmental conditions are not projected onto the human body as they are in testimonies of the Isla del Gallo: in the coastal forests, landscape and the physical experience of and contact with it were one and the same, but in petitioners' accounts of Peru's conquest there exists a clear boundary between the human subject and the land that is observed and described. Undoubtedly, these accounts describe hostile landscapes, but that hostility now emanates from Peru's human inhabitants rather than from the physical environment or terrain. Petitioners took pride in emphasizing the enormous number of adversaries whom they faced as well as the number they managed to kill: just one and a half leagues outside Cuzco, at a place called Jaquijaguana, said Maça, he and his companions were confronted with a force of over twenty thousand native warriors. Nevertheless, within a short space of time, he claimed, the Spaniards had defeated them and killed at least five hundred men.[34]

What brought about this transformation in the conquistadors' perceptions and modes of portrayal—this shift from suffering to an easy mobility and glory that resulted, above all, from the successful "negotiation" of human adversaries? As historians recognize, the success of Pizarro's venture in Peru was largely due to internal conflicts at the time of the Spaniards' arrival—a situation which they were quick to exploit. The physical landscape also played an important role. It is probable that the expedition members felt great relief on emerging from the equatorial forests and swamps and regaining solid ground in the mountains and coastal deserts of Peru. However, neither the deserts nor the highlands were benign environments for those who lacked provisions and shelter. Despite the triumphant and somewhat exaggerated tone of his words, Cieza de León's description of the new viceroyalty successfully conveys the hostile nature of Peru's natural environments. It was, he claimed, precisely as a result of this environmental hostility that "the natives could be conquered so easily: and why they serve us without rebelling, because if they did they would all die of hunger and cold. Because (as I have said), apart from the land that they inhabit, the rest is all wilderness, filled with snow-covered sierras and extremely high and terrible mountains."[35]

From this author's point of view, conquest was easy because the indigenous population was constrained by the natural environment and, in consequence, was transformed into a vulnerable target for the conquering ambitions of the Spaniards. Here, as in many more recent discussions of pre-Hispanic landscapes, the forces that shape Peru's human geographies appear to emerge exclusively from the physical environment.[36] Undoubtedly, the physical landscape *did* partially shape Peru's human geographies, by presenting Amerindian societies with an array of both constraints and possibilities. Their lived-in landscapes, however, were neither predetermined nor ready-made but emerged, as Raffles suggests with reference to sixteenth-century Guiana, from a continuous input of indigenous labor that ensured the conquistadors' access to nourishment, shelter, and other vital resources.[37] By helping the intruders to negotiate Peru's landscapes, indigenous groups played a central role in shaping the geographies of conquest and, more fundamentally, helped to create the physical and mental conditions that made conquest possible. In what follows, I illustrate this by reading the Spaniards' own accounts alongside those presented by native Andean leaders from the colonial province of Jauja.

Re-presenting the Landscapes of Conquest: The View from Jauja

The *curacas* or lords of Jauja, whose testimonies of service were presented to the Spanish crown in the early 1560s, belonged to the Huanca ethnic group. A powerful and warlike group of polities, the Huancas occupied the most fertile and productive region of the central Andes, known in Inca times as Huanca Huamaní (valley or region of the Huancas) and, during the colonial era, as the Jauja valley. During the rapid expansion of the Inca empire roughly one hundred years before the arrival of the Spanish, the Huancas fought tenaciously to resist the invaders from Cuzco. With their traditional intra-ethnic conflicts over land and power apparently pushed aside in the face of the common enemy, they rejected Capac Yupanqui's offers of peace and engaged in a war that was both long and severe.

Around 1460, however, the Huanca communities were finally forced to surrender, and the region was brought under Inca control.[38] The news of Atahualpa's capture at Cajamarca presented the Huancas with a sudden opportunity to free themselves of Inca dominance. Their principal leaders, the first major group to seek an alliance with the Spaniards,[39] hurried to Cajamarca to offer their support to Francisco Pizarro. Not only did they bring word of their allegiance, however, but they also came with "three hundred Indians loaded with maize and potatoes and clothing and female llamas and male llamas and gold and silver and other things listed in the inventory."[40]

This was only the beginning. On Pizarro's request, the *curacas* returned to Jauja to prepare for the Spaniards' arrival. Before beginning the march to Cuzco, the band of several hundred conquistadors, along with Amerindian and African auxiliaries, stayed in Jauja for about two weeks, where the indigenous community supplied them with huge quantities of food and other provisions, such as firewood and hay for bedding and horse-feed. All items given to the Spaniards were meticulously listed and inventoried in the communities' *quipus,* then transcribed into Spanish and included in their *curacas'* accounts of merits and services. Under the leadership of the royal treasurer Riquelme, thirty Spaniards stayed behind in Jauja to guard the booty that had been seized in Cajamarca and to prepare the ground for what was to become, briefly, the colonial capital of the Peruvian territories.[41] The human landscape, as mentioned above, was portrayed by the Spaniards as a thoroughly hostile one: consequently, the site of Jauja was consistently represented not as a place of refuge but as one of extreme peril. Undoubtedly, the Spaniards fought off a series of Inca attacks on the valley, which were described by Sebastián de Torres:

> we had armed encounters with the Indians and afterward the said Governor founded a settlement where, on his orders, I stayed to help in maintaining it, and . . . afterward Captain Quizquiz came

with a large force with the intention of burning the said settlement and of killing those who were in it, and I and the rest of us
who found ourselves there rendered a great service to His Majesty
and we labored greatly to defend the settlement, keeping watch
and patrolling every night and fighting battles with the Indians
until the Governor returned from the city of Cuzco and sleeping
with our weapons throughout the whole duration of the war.[42]

The testimony of this conquistador and those of his companions, however, thoroughly efface the Huancas' participation in these events and
even their very presence in the Jauja valley. During the months that
Riquelme and his men spent in Jauja, the Huancas continued to look
after their needs, not only providing them with food but also taking part
in battles against the forces of Atahualpa's captain, Quizquiz. The petition presented by the *curaca* don Gerónimo Guacra Paucar, leader of
the Lurin Huanca *repartimiento*,[43] declared that, when the Spaniards first
arrived in Jauja, he

worked hard to build houses for them and serve them with every
kind of food during the six months that they were there, which
caused him considerable harm because, given that the Spaniards
were without servants until that point, they availed themselves
of all the 1500 Indians that the said don Gerónimo had brought to
the governor to carry the loads and so these Indians became *yanaconas* [servants], and they took from the said don Gerónimo, as well
as from other *caciques* of the said valley, many women and girls.[44]

The testimony presented by the Huanca lord Francisco Cusichaca,
meanwhile, bears witness to his active participation in battle against the
Inca force of ten thousand: "while the said treasurer was in the said valley
of Xauxa, the Inca captains Quizquiz and Urcogualca and Chucali came
with ten thousand warriors whom the treasurer and Spaniards went to
do battle with, accompanied by the said *cacique* don Francisco Cusichaca,
and don Xpoual [Cristobal] Canchaya with many Indians, and in the
battle that they fought with them they defeated and put the said Incas
to flight, in which the said Indians of Xauxa served his Majesty."[45]

As the conquest progressed, the leaders of Jauja seemingly maintained this high level of commitment to their new allies. From the time of the Huancas' first encounter with Pizarro at Cajamarca until the end of the civil wars, Cusichaca's community supplied the Spaniards with a total of nearly 17,000 llamas and about 75,000 *fanegas*[46] of maize, as well as vast quantities of other goods, including not merely foodstuffs but also firewood, clothing, footwear, and cooking vessels.[47]

The alliance, however, cost the Huancas dearly in human as well as material terms. Of the many thousands of men and women who accompanied the Spanish during the conquest as warriors and porters, most were destined never to return to their homes. The few who survived the perils of disease and battle became the Spaniards' personal servants. One expedition alone, led by Captain Mercadillo, claimed the lives of all but four of the 379 indigenous men and women who carried the conquistadors' loads to the subtropical eastern frontier of the Jauja province.

On accepting the Huancas' support, the Spaniards, from an Andean viewpoint, had entered into a reciprocal relationship that obliged them, in turn, to provide the Huanca communities with resources or gifts.[48] As the *curacas*' testimonies make clear, however, their assistance to the conquistadors was largely reciprocated with the violent appropriation of further people and goods. The *quipus*—and the Spanish transcriptions of their contents—meticulously recorded not only the goods that were given to the Spaniards but also those that they seized, thereby undermining the aura of rectitude, honor, and justice that the first conquistadors constructed around themselves. When Pizarro first arrived in Jauja, Cusichaca stated, the Indians of Hatun Xauxa "*gave* him for the sustenance and provisioning of the soldiers whom he brought with him a large quantity of llamas and maize and Indian men and women and other things and in addition to this the said soldiers *seized* a large quantity of llamas and the things contained in the inventory."[49]

An inventory included in Cusichaca's petition provides further detail of the resources appropriated by the Spaniards during their initial two weeks in Jauja. This specifies, for example, that in addition to the 12,500 *fanegas* of maize that were given to Pizarro and his men— equal to about 20,000 bushels or 728,000 liters—the Spanish and their auxiliaries seized a further 21,563 *fanegas,* or 1,255,829 liters, of maize.[50]

As Espinoza Soriano points out, the Spaniards' consumption of resources was extravagant as well as destructive. The Huanca leaders, reluctant to lose the female llamas that were needed to maintain the herds, provided the conquistadors with about 12,000 male llamas but only 1,275 females. The Spaniards, however, rounded up over 29,000 females, many of which were slaughtered merely to obtain the prized brains and neck meat.[51]

Coupled with the Huanca testimonies, the inventories forcefully reveal a pattern of plunder and exploitation that remains hidden in Spanish accounts of services. Functioning on the one hand as denunciations of the Spaniards' destructive actions, on the other hand they demand royal reciprocation, in the form of material restitution and legal privileges, in recognition of the Huanca communities' vital role in contributing to the successful outcome of conquest. In striking contrast to the accounts of merits and services presented by Spanish conquistadors, the Huancas' documents animate the geographies of conquest with indigenous agents who are allies and providers as well as enemies.

Like the Spaniards' testimonies, the Huancas' *relaciones de servicios* have to be read with caution. Although the geographies of conquest they portray are more inclusive than those of the conquistadors, they too, inevitably, are partial and selective. Neither the Spaniards' black and Amerindian auxiliaries brought from beyond Peru, nor other indigenous groups from within the Inca empire who allied themselves with the Europeans, appear as agents in Huanca portrayals of the conquest. Indeed, the testimonies presented by don Gerónimo Paucar and Cusichaca mention only the military assistance and resources that were provided by their own *repartimientos,* thereby marginalizing the agency of neighboring Huanca communities and enhancing that of their own. As chapter 3 illustrates in greater depth, the internal rivalries and motivations that underlay the production of these and other documents that were at least partially authored by Andeans mean that they cannot be understood as straightforward expressions of opposition or resistance to a homogeneous Spanish mentality or worldview.

Despite these differences and possible exaggerations, however, the Huancas' testimonies indicate that their communities, along with other indigenous groups who allied themselves with the Spaniards, not only acted as a defense against Peru's hostile human geographies but also provided a protective buffer between the conquistadors and the land itself.[52] The vast quantities of resources that were supplied or surrendered to the European allies permitted the fulfillment of physiological needs to be moved to the margins of the Spaniards' experiences and to be replaced with mobility and the aims and ambitions of conquest.

The relentless mobility that characterized many Spanish accounts of services in Peru, such as the testimony presented by Nicolás de Ribera, must therefore be understood, at least in part, as a product of indigenous agency that shaped Spanish experiences in profoundly corporeal ways. This agency included not only the material and military assistance proffered to the conquistadors by Andean groups, but equally the ongoing practices of cultivation, settlement, and construction that preceded the Spaniards' presence and guided the geographies of conquest once they had arrived. A comment made by Doña Leonor, one of don Gerónimo's witnesses, highlights the way in which the Spaniards were often shielded on their journeys from the physical rigors of traversing the Andean territories. When the *curaca* arrived in Cajamarca and offered his allegiance and resources to the Spaniards, she said, Francisco Pizarro received him favorably and "sent the said don Gerónimo with his Indians to prepare the pathways on their return to Xauxa."[53]

Not only the Huancas' preparations, however, but also the Inca roads—which the conquistadors' petitions consistently fail to mention—smoothed out the ground beneath the Spaniards' feet.[54] If, on the one hand, Cieza de León's chronicle portrayed Peru's human geographies as passive products of the natural environment, on the other hand it acknowledged the transformative effects of Andean road-building technologies that had removed the conquistadors' need to negotiate the harshest physical terrain and thus facilitated their movement across it. The land, said Cieza de León, "is very rugged, with high sierras that appear to reach the clouds and descend infinitely to the deep valleys. And this being the case, the royal highway of the Incas who were so powerful, is so well constructed and laid along hillsides and other parts, that the harshness of the land is hardly felt."[55]

An account of Almagro's expedition of 1535 to Chile suggests that, at times, the Spaniards' feet literally did not touch the ground, for they were carried over it by native servants.[56] Such occasions were the exception, however, rather than the rule: as Taussig comments, "It was not Indians who carried the conquistadors across the Andes, but horses."[57]

Nevertheless, the agency of Peru's native peoples frequently enabled the Spaniards to distance themselves in less literal but equally significant ways from the physical environment. In the account of conquest written by Pizarro's secretary, Francisco de Xerez, the language of bodily suffering, long since abandoned in the swamps of the Pacific coast, resurfaces with the disappearance of the Spaniards' native auxiliaries. Of those who left Cajamarca immediately after Atahualpa's treasure had been distributed to return to the coast and from there to Spain, some were robbed and then abandoned by the indigenous porters. As a result, said Xerez, they suffered "great hunger and thirst and difficulty, and a lack of people to carry their belongings for them."[58] In the absence of the Huancas and other native allies, embodied Spanish experiences of Peru's landscapes and, by extension, their portrayals of those landscapes, would surely have been very different.

The Familiar Landscapes of Conquest

As the brief quotation above from Cieza de León's text suggests, Spanish histories and chronicles of conquest conveyed visions of Peru that were often strikingly different from those encountered in the accounts of merits and services. Whereas the latter are reductive to the extreme, concerned almost exclusively with recalling actions and events at key sites of conquest, most histories, chronicles, and other written accounts provide a far broader descriptive panorama.[59] Like the accounts of services, they frequently served as vehicles for the pursuit of personal interest,[60] but many were also written on the basis of genuine curiosity about the New World and its inhabitants.[61]

The need to render the New World accessible to a distant European readership undoubtedly played a significant part in creating textual landscapes that conveyed a surprising sense of familiarity and ease of comprehension. Just as Columbus's acts of possession were performed "entirely *for a world elsewhere*,"[62] so too, the texts generated by the conquest of Peru were written for consumption in a distant world, and usually with very particular aims in mind. For those aims to be ful-filled, they had to be written within the boundaries of the cultural un-derstandings and logic that both writers and recipients shared, despite the vast physical gulf that separated them. In other words, these writ-ings had to be *comprehensible* to the European recipient in order to be per-suasive. In this sense, as Fossa argues, the recipient played a significant part in shaping the text, and therefore might be said to be present within it.[63]

Spanish portrayals of the New World, however, cannot be under-stood solely as the products of preexisting discursive and cultural ties with Europe. The varied indigenous practices—including the construc-tion of roads and houses and the cultivation of the land—that aided the mobility of conquest through the provision of shelter, food, and other necessities, also facilitated conquest by producing landscapes in some ways comprehensible to the Spaniards and reminiscent of those that were already well known: "By planting and burning, by flood-control and earthworking, by attracting game animals such as deer, by concen-trating valued plant species in accessible sites, native Americans created a landscape that Europeans were able to recognize and understand, a place that offered the sudden sensation of being at home in the world."[64]

Raffles's observations in the preceding quote, although made with reference to the impact of indigenous practices on early European ex-periences of Guiana, concur with a striking sense of familiarity that is often conveyed in early Spanish accounts of Peru. I do not wish to sug-gest that the Spanish regarded the Andean world with which they were confronted as identical to the one that they had left behind in Europe. Nevertheless, the lived-in Andean landscapes of towns, roads, and cul-tivated fields appeared—at least at a superficial level—commensurable with the landscapes of home. A sense of familiarity was conveyed, to some extent, through repeated and often positive comparisons with Spain: comparison led, of course, to the identification of difference, but the fact that comparison was at all possible illustrates that these Andean landscapes, unlike the dense forest environments of the equatorial Paci-fic coast, were able to evoke in the Spanish a sense of "being at home in the world."

Even those commentators who focused most narrowly on describing events of conquest did not fail to comment, however briefly, on the magnificent feats of engineering and architecture that so visibly marked the face of the Andean landscape. The Inca roads of the mountains and coast elicited particular admiration, but in the native settlements the Spaniards' eyes were frequently drawn upward to marvel at the fortresses, temples, and dwellings. The recently founded town council of Jauja declared in a letter to the king that Cuzco "is the best and the largest [city] that has been seen in this land, and even in the Indies; and we say to your Majesty that it is so beautiful and well-constructed that it would be a great sight even in Spain."[65]

The attention of Xerez was similarly drawn to the physical structures — the walled dwellings, temples, and fortifications — that marked the journey from Túmbez to Jauja, where his account is cut short. On arrival in San Miguel (the present-day town of Paita), Pizarro sent a messenger to Atahualpa to discover his intentions and, from there, says Xerez, "he continued his journey through those valleys, every day coming across a settlement with a dwelling that has defensive walls like a fortress."[66]

Xerez's description of Cajamarca portrays an architectural landscape of particular splendor: a place of vast squares, larger than any seen in Spain, of enormous walled dwellings supplied with piped water, of spiral staircases, fortifications, and an abundance of temples. Although visual description attains a prominence in his text that is wholly absent in the accounts of merits and services, the desire for mobility that characterized conquest remains the dominant structuring theme. Here, however, the indigenous presence and assistance that facilitated conquest steps emphatically to the fore, continuously dictating the rhythm of travel, easing its hardships, and, in doing so, producing a sense of mundane familiarity.

The indigenous impact on embodied experiences of travel is strikingly apparent in Miguel de Estete's description — more reminiscent of a monotonous travel account than of a tale of conquest — of Hernando Pizarro's journey to the ceremonial center of Pachacamac on Peru's central coast. On January 5, 1533, the conquistador left the town of Cajamarca with twenty horsemen and a certain number of musketeers; and on the same day he went to spend the night in some country houses that are five leagues from this settlement. On the next day he went to eat in another place called Ichoa, where he was well received and they gave him the things that he and his people required. On that day he went to sleep in another small settlement called Guancasanga, which is subject to the town of Guamachuco. In the morning of the following day he arrived in the town of Guamachuco, which is large and situated in a valley amongst the mountains; it is attractive and has good places to stay.[67]

The sense of familiarity that pervaded many Spanish accounts of the New World cannot be equated, of course, with genuine cultural comprehension. In Xerez's history, as in other early accounts of Peru, the frequent reference to native sites of worship as mosques, or *mezquitas,* provides just one of many pertinent examples of the cultural, linguistic, and experiential distance that separated Spanish commentators from the Amerindian worlds to which they made reference in their texts: given that the prime objective of most conquistadors was to return to Spain as rich men,[68] it is not surprising that their writings display a distinct lack of concern for overcoming that distance. Nevertheless, as Graubart observes, the very persistence of a "proto-orientalist vocabulary" did not indicate dismissal or a sense of alienation from indigenous culture on the part of Spanish writers, but instead "marked its identifiability for Europeans."[69] These writings, then, reveal evidence of a sense of familiarity that permitted Spanish conquest to become a practical possibility and that, most importantly, was primarily the outcome of ongoing indigenous practices of cultivation and construction.

✳   Spanish accounts of conquest such as those written by Xerez and Cieza de León vividly convey what D'Altroy terms the "imperial imprint" of the Incas on the face of the Andean landscape.[70] However, the impact of this "imperial imprint" on the invading Spaniards was not simply visual, although the infrastructure of roads, storehouses, cities, temples, and strongholds presented them with a spectacle that they described with admiration and at times with awe. Instead, as we have seen, the Inca networks of settlement, communication, and resource provision that stretched from Chile to highland Ecuador dramatically facilitated the Spaniards' mobility and their ability to focus on the aims of conquest rather than on the struggle for survival in a hostile physical environment. Although closer scrutiny soon revealed cultures and world-views that in many respects the Spanish found profoundly alien, they were able to envisage the Inca realms as spaces that could comfortably be inhabited and, moreover, that could at least be partially remade in the image of the European landscapes that they had left behind.

As MacCormack observes, the degree of admiration that the Span-iards expressed for the material and social structures of the Inca do-mains greatly overshadowed their appreciation of neighboring indige-nous societies.[71] Nevertheless, it was not only within the heartlands of the Inca empire that the conquistadors could imagine being at home in the world. Far to the north of the Inca realms, in the tropical lands of the Isthmus and the adjoining territories of northwestern Colom-bia that were explored and partially settled by the Spanish prior to the conquest of Peru, the conquistadors frequently commented on the in-habitability and beauty of the lands they encountered. Just as changes in the physical environment partly explain the shift in Spanish mobility as they moved from the rain-drenched coastal forests of western Co-lombia and Ecuador to the parched terrain of northern Peru, so too, the existence of drier, less densely forested regions within the Isthmus allowed the invaders to negotiate the landscape with relative ease. Once again, however, the sensation of being in an environment that was both inviting and at least superficially comprehensible to the Europeans was intimately linked to the presence and activities of native populations, who, through forest clearance and crop cultivation, created landscapes of game-rich savannah and agriculture.[72]

Pascual de Andagoya, who took part in and wrote about Pedrarias Dávila's early-sixteenth-century exploratory ventures in the Panamanian regions, repeatedly expressed his admiration for the open landscapes of rivers, fields, and grasslands that the expedition encountered on its journey from Comogre on the Caribbean coast to the western province of Coiba. All these lands, he declared, "are fine and level and very beautiful, and abundant in food, for there is maize and chili peppers and melons that are different from those found here [in Spain], and grapes, yucca, and many fish in the rivers and sea and large numbers of deer, and the provinces of Coiba and Cueba have all these things as well."[73]

Andagoya's descriptions of these well-populated lands are at times strikingly reminiscent of Estete's account of the journey to Pachacamac in the heart of the Inca dominions. Like Estete, Andagoya frequently portrays the forward motion of the expedition as an uneventful and somewhat mundane passage through a landscape that is exclusively defined in his description by its human presence and its linguistic and cultural geographies:

> from Chiman we went to the province of Pocorosa, and two leagues westward from there we came to that of Paruraca, where the Coiba province begins, and four leagues further on from there along the same route we came to that of Tubanamá, and eight leagues from there still following the same path we came to that of Chepo, and six leagues from there we came to that of Chepobar, and two leagues further on we came to that of Pacora, and four [leagues] from there we came to that of Panamá, and another four [leagues] from there we came to that of Periquete, and another four [leagues] further on we came to that of Tabore, and another four [leagues] further on to that of Chame, which marks the limits of the language and province of Coiba.[74]

It would be wholly misleading to suggest that Spanish experiences of traversing the Andean heartlands and of traveling through the Panamanian interior were interchangeable. To view them as such would be to disregard the profound differences in human and physical geography that separated these regions, as well as the variability of Spanish experience and perception. Nevertheless, the presence of sizeable, sedentary indigenous populations in the Isthmian regions, just as in areas under Inca control, contributed to the production of Spanish accounts of exploration that called forth images of sedate journeys through seemingly familiar landscapes rather than of hazardous ventures that required constant struggle against a hostile and threatening environment.

My intention in this brief discursive return to regions beyond the northern limits of the Andean world is by no means to cast doubt on the distinctive ways in which the geographies of the Inca empire shaped Spanish mobility and experience. Rather, it is to insist upon the fundamental importance of indigenous populations throughout the New World—whether in the humid tropics or in the Andean regions—in permitting the European invaders not only to look beyond the immediate struggle for survival in unknown environments, but to experience the landscapes through which they passed as comprehensible and even as familiar.

Landscapes in Transformation

In the wake of conquest there followed a process of disintegration of many of the architectonic and agricultural landscapes that feature so prominently in early Spanish accounts of Peru. Physical destruction of infrastructure was accompanied and hastened by rapid depopulation, above all in the fertile river valleys of the coast. The destruction of indigenous sites of worship was undoubtedly celebrated by colonial commentators,[75] but otherwise, the decline of Peru's indigenous populations, together with the lived-in landscapes they had forged, was viewed with marked anxiety. Writing to Charles V, the bishop of Cuzco warned that, without protection, Peru's native peoples would soon disappear. With perceptible regret, he described the physical decline that the country had witnessed, and declared that if he were unable to recall Cuzco's location, the present city would now be unrecognizable to him. When Pizarro first arrived,

> this valley was so beautiful in terms of the buildings and the population that lay around it, that it was something to marvel at, because although the city itself had no more than three or four thousand houses, there were almost forty thousand in its vicinity. The fortress that stood above the city looked from a distance like one of the great fortresses of Spain. Now most of the town is all ruined and burnt. The fortress barely rises above the ground. All the

surrounding settlements consist of nothing but walls; it is a miracle to find a house that possesses a roof.[76]

By midcentury, Spanish experiences of travel in Peru were strongly pervaded by a sense not only of ruin and physical destruction but of encroaching wilderness.[77] Traveling through Peru's coastal valleys between Trujillo and Lima in the late 1540s, Cieza de León recorded a landscape that had been emptied of its human presence. Each new valley he entered seemed to bear the scars of irreversible decline, which had allowed the forces of the physical environment to carry out its own conquest of a once carefully tended agricultural landscape. Ironically, the events of conquest brought the nonhuman world back into view: whereas the attention of earlier writers was once drawn to a continuous succession of prosperous settlements and abundant crops, now, "as there are so few Indians . . . most of the fields are uncultivated, converted into woods and scrub: and they are so full of thickets that in many parts it is difficult to make one's way through."[78]

In the absence of native populations that had once labored to ensure the continued existence of these landscapes, the work of non-human forces—largely overlooked in early accounts of conquest—assumed a more prominent position in Spanish consciousness. Sites of cultivation were abandoned and swallowed by tangled scrub and thickets. The Inca highway that connected the coastal settlements was encroached upon in many parts by the desert expanses that stretched between one river valley and the next. Writing about his travels in Peru at the very beginning of the seventeenth century, the Spanish friar Lizárraga described coastal landscapes strikingly similar to those evoked just over half a century before by Cieza de León. Although the coastal valleys were extremely fertile, that fertility was reduced to a mere potentiality: "we passed through six valleys, all [of which would have been] extremely productive in all kinds of food, if the natives who used to work them had not been missing, with sufficient water for irrigation: the channels were dug, but by now they have been lost."[79]

Lizárraga mourned not only the disappearance of productive landscapes. In some places, he remarked, it was no longer even possible to travel along the coastal route because the native inhabitants, who once provided supplies and kept the paths free of undergrowth, had all but disappeared: "one no longer travels along the coast, because the disappearance of the Indians caused it to become choked with reeds."[80] Here again, it is possible to glimpse how the decline of indigenous populations affected Spanish corporeal experiences of Peru's landscapes and, where the production of textual landscapes was concerned, how it permitted the forces of the natural environment to come back into view.

❀   Despite the process of demolition that is captured so vividly in these early colonial texts, new layers of cultural sediment were beginning to settle on the landscape's ravaged surface. As Rabasa comments with reference to the work of Durán, Peruvian writings of the 1550s likewise bear witness to "semantic and material transformations, quite literally layers of stones and words that have accumulated on and around New World phenomena."[81] Gradually, a new colonial geography was emerging in the form of Spanish settlements, places of worship, and European crops. In contrast to his sorrow at the decline of native populations and agriculture along Peru's coast, Cieza de León envisaged with pleasure the materialization of the Hispanicized landscape of desire that was projected on the eve of conquest. Not only had two hundred towns already been founded,

> in some areas of this kingdom . . . there is great fertility, for wheat grows so beautifully, and in great abundance: the same applies to maize and barley. There is no small number of vines around San Miguel, Trujillo, and Los Reyes [Lima]: and in the cities of Cuzco and Guamanga, and in other highland towns they are beginning to appear: and there is great hope that good wines will be produced. Orange groves, pomegranates, and other fruits — all those that have been brought from Spain can be found, as well as the native ones. There are vegetables of every kind. In short, Peru is a great kingdom: and as time goes by it will become greater: because great settlements will have been founded in those places that are convenient. And by the time our own era has ended, it will be possible to export from Peru wheat, wine, meat, wool, and even silk.[82]

The sense of satisfaction and aesthetic pleasure afforded to the author by means of visual encounters with increasingly Europeanized landscapes is difficult to overlook. In focusing on these visual encounters, the passage may be understood as a triumphant discourse that celebrates Spanish colonial achievements by making apparent the striking visual congruencies between the landscapes of Spain and those of Peru. However, the passage also points toward ongoing processes of production and everyday experience, which, when brought to the fore, relegate celebratory discourse to a position of secondary importance.

Like the precolonial landscapes that preceded them, these Hispanicized scenes were tangible products of predominantly indigenous corporeal labor, combined with the forces of environment and climate that permitted their emergence.[83] The material phenomena within Cieza de León's field of vision simultaneously hint at and conceal a never-ending succession of everyday actions that brought them, and the landscape of which they form a part, into being. The author himself was at pains to point out that mundane labor alone would assure the continued transformation of the landscape: chiding the conquistadors and settlers for whiling away the hours with tales of battle and conquest, he exhorted them instead to "concern themselves with planting and sowing, for it is this which will bring greatest benefit."[84]

Whereas Cieza de León emphasized for his European readership the mundane labor that the emergence of Hispanicized landscapes required, royal ordinances on discovery and settlement, issued in 1573, conveyed a desire to *conceal* this process from future colonial subjects. When new colonial settlements were under construction—a task that was largely carried out by non-Europeans—the colonists should do their best "to avoid communication and dealings with the Indians . . . nor [allow] the Indians to enter the circuit of the settlement until it is completed and given defenses, and the houses [are finished]; so that, when the Indians see them, they feel admiration."[85] Here, the down-to-earth activities of construction were purposely to be kept from view in order to ensure that, once the labor was complete, unsubjugated indigenous groups would be witnesses to a dramatic, seemingly ready-made representation of the Spaniards' might and, overawed by the spectacle, would willingly submit to their rule.[86]

Needless to say, the establishment of colonial settlements rarely corresponded to this vision projected by officials in Madrid. Spanish towns were frequently "founded" on the sites of existing native settlements, and the process of construction usually relied on the assistance of native inhabitants as well as on the labor of black and Amerindian auxiliaries who accompanied the conquistadors.[87] My intention here is by no means to suggest that the Spanish played a negligible part in the material emergence of Peru's colonial landscapes. After all, the introduction of Mediterranean biota as well as of agricultural practices and other technologies from Spain played a fundamental role in the shaping of those landscapes. Rather, my point is to suggest that colonial texts can be read, not only to gain access to discursive worlds that evoke European conquest and the establishment of colonial rule as extraordinary "moments" of unparalleled significance, but also to glimpse an array of ongoing *processes* and *practices* that, precisely because of their continuity, repetition, and "everydayness," are an important means of revising our understanding of early European encounters with the New World.[88]

❈   In reading and considering Spanish accounts of conquest, it is unquestionably important to acknowledge the powerful cultural and linguistic forces that, together with culturally situated motivations and ambitions, bound their authors to Europe. Further chapters in this book explore the intersection of various interests, ambitions, and concerns in shaping portrayals of Peru's Amazon regions. The construction of the conquistadors' texts clearly involved the suppression, to varying degrees, of native voices and agency. Nevertheless, it is necessary to recognize the limits to which these texts, in all their diversity, represented "a continuation of Spanish writing in, to, and from the center."[89]

Rather than focusing primarily on textual strategies of silencing and erasure, this chapter has addressed what Spanish accounts of conquest— juxtaposed with Andean perspectives on the same events—can tell us about their authors' embodied engagements with landscape and, above all, how the agency and practices of non-European groups played a role in shaping the nature of those engagements. The sudden shift to easy mobility and the reemergence of wealth, honor, and glory as the central focus in Spanish accounts of Peru's conquest was not only facilitated by a return to landscapes that, for the Spaniards, were more familiar than the equatorial forests of the Pacific coast. Nor was the sense of easy mobility and disconnection from the corporeal challenges of traversing and surviving among harsh mountains and deserts simply a discursive strategy; it was not, as suggested by Bunn (who identifies a similar sense of mobility and "buoyancy" in a nineteenth-century depiction of the French explorer François le Vaillant surveying the distant clutter of his African campsite), merely the product of "a conventional form of staging" that could be employed "for different political effects."[90] Rather, it must also be regarded as the result of embodied experiences of landscape that were shaped by the products of past and ongoing indigenous labor—the roads, settlements, and food supplies.

Alongside indigenous accounts of merits and services, Spanish-authored histories and chronicles of the conquest and early colonial period bring these indigenous practices into view and shed further light on the ways in which they shaped European experiences and, both materially and conceptually, helped to make conquest possible. They also reveal how, in some areas, the suspension of indigenous practices that resulted from population decline affected the ways in which Spanish inhabitants and travelers experienced the landscape and described it in their writings. These same accounts document the emergence of colonial landscapes that, much like conquest itself, were primarily the outcome of *ongoing* labor in which both Europeans and non-Europeans participated, albeit to varying degrees. It bears emphasizing that this practice-oriented approach is not intended to "normalize" the landscapes of conquest and colonization by brushing aside the violence and exploitation that were inherent in their creation. Both the testimonies of the Huanca elite and Spanish evocations of destruction and decline following the initial phase of conquest bear witness to the violence endemic to colonial life.[91] Instead, this chapter has attempted to reconnect the Spaniards and their experiences of the New World with the physical landscapes and human practices from which they are frequently distanced in contemporary critical analyses of their writings.

A few decades after presenting their accounts of services to the Spanish crown, members of the Huanca elite, along with many other inhabitants of late-sixteenth-century Peru, were involved in the production of documents of a very different type. These were intended, by the Spanish authorities who requested them, to provide detailed geographical information about the settlements and provinces of Spain's overseas possessions. The Peruvian *Relaciones Geográficas,* or geographical accounts, like their better-known Mexican counterparts, shed valuable light on the ways in which diverse groups participated in and negotiated the production of colonial geographical knowledge.

THREE

Landscapes of Resistance?

Peru's Relaciones Geográficas

In the late sixteenth century, fifty-point geographical questionnaires, designed by the Council of the Indies' chief chronicler and cosmographer, López de Velasco, were sent to colonial officials throughout Peru and other parts of the New World, along with instructions on how to complete them. Described by Mignolo as "one of the most impressive moves in the colonization of space,"[1] they were intended to permit the creation of a comprehensive and accurate picture of Spain's overseas possessions and facilitate good government of those territories by means of detailed geographical knowledge.[2] Ultimately, the aims of the project remained unrealized, for precious little, if any, of the information obtained from the New World was used "to be better able to attend to its good government," as the introductory letter to the fifty-point questionnaire declared.[3] In terms of its sheer scale, however, it was undoubtedly one of the most ambitious geographical projects to be conceived in sixteenth-century Europe, and reflected the vigorous flourishing of geography in Philip II's Spain.[4]

Although primary responsibility for the completion of the questionnaires lay with colonial officials in the New World provinces and cities, the responses—now known collectively as *Relaciones Geográficas* '(henceforth *RG*s)—were to be compiled on the basis of information supplied not only by other Spaniards but also by indigenous communities. Indeed, written responses were often based overwhelmingly on answers provided by indigenous informants and, in the case of the Mexican *RG*s, many incorporated maps that were created by native painters.[5] In Peru, Altuna suggests, participation in the creation of the responses would have been perceived as an event of great importance by Andeans and Spaniards alike. For the latter it was conceptualized as a means of reinforcing their possession of Peru's territories, but for the former, she argues, it signified a means of reanimating or even re-creating their memories of the past. Given that the production of responses involved the transformation of indigenous oral memory into written text, "it must have held significance for them [the Andeans] as a gesture that affirmed modes of conceptualizing space, time, and ethnicity that contested the occidental parameters expressed by the questionnaire."[6]

For Altuna, therefore, the responses from Peru reveal unequivocal traces of indigenous resistance to Western epistemologies that were contained within and represented by the questionnaire. Several Peruvian *RG*s indeed appear to provide glimpses of resistant tactics on the part of indigenous informants. The very process by which the accounts were produced—as colonial responses to an official order that came from Madrid[7]—also appears to evoke a binary relationship of domination and resistance. As this chapter seeks to demonstrate, however, the closely intertwined nature of indigenous and Spanish life in sixteenth-century Peru makes it impossible to regard the Peruvian *RG*s as vehicles of a rigidly defined resistance to an opposing set of ideas and imaginative geographies that was uniformly shared by all Spaniards, whether in Spain or the New World.

At this point, it is appropriate to acknowledge my indebtedness to Gruzinski's work on the Mexican corpus. With particular subtlety, his study foregrounds the unpredictable, varied, locally determined nature of the Mexican responses, and although it focuses predominantly on indigenous engagements with the questionnaire, it also hints at the variability of Spanish reactions to this document.[8] In the context of the Peruvian *RG*s, I draw on Gruzinski's insights, not only by attending to the varied intentionalities that may have underlain Andean responses, but also by suggesting that *Spanish* engagements with the questionnaire were ambivalent, unpredictable, and connected in complex ways with indigenous "resistance." Following a rereading of the geographical account from Jauja in the light of other documents that reveal the ambiguous and shifting nature of Huanca-Spanish relations, my discussion then highlights forms of "resistance" to the questionnaire that are also conveyed by Spanish voices within certain Peruvian responses. In doing so, it unsettles the frequently encountered notion of a homogeneous "Spanish" vision of colonial geography and spatial order in the New World, and interrogates how—and indeed whether—the concept of resistance can be usefully employed in analyzing the *RG*s that were produced in the Peruvian viceroyalty.

Revelation and Concealment in Peru's Relaciones Geográficas

Metropolitan anxiety over unreliable reports undoubtedly played a part in bringing about the creation of the questionnaires. They were designed to provide a truthful and accurate picture of the Indies, free of the distortions that so many unsolicited accounts were suspected of containing. Their questions covered an extraordinary breadth of topics, which encompassed topography, the location and characteristics of settlements, demographic trends, agriculture, natural history, commerce, and precolonial native customs, to name just a few. Because the questionnaires' content and the assumptions about the New World embedded within them were drawn from a body of information contained in existing encyclopedias of America, Rabasa has conceptualized the creation of the *RG*s as a key moment in Europe's invention of America.[9] Native informants were faced with questions that forced them to describe themselves and their past within alien parameters, which linearized time, secularized space, and historicized indigenous forms of political organization and belief. The conquest, meanwhile, was forced upon them as an all-important moment that provided the explanation for all change, naturally dividing native experience into a "before" and an "after."[10]

Just as the questionnaires' comprehensibility was taken for granted, so too was their authority, for they conveyed the voice of a physically distant king and represented the power of the metropolitan center.[11] In extensive areas of the Spanish empire, however, the level of colonial control that the questionnaires presupposed was at best tenuous and at worst nonexistent. The liberty that many *corregidores* enjoyed, thanks to the vast distances separating these crown officials from the higher echelons of colonial government, meant that royal authority was by no means sufficient in persuading them to comply by responding to the questionnaire.[12] It is no coincidence that the vast majority of responses received by the Council came from areas where the networks of control were most firmly established. Whereas 166 in total were received from Mexico, only about 15 are known to have been returned from Peru, including the *Audiencia* of Charcas, and a mere handful from the remaining peripheries and extremities of the empire.[13]

Of the responses that the Council of the Indies received from Peru, all were created in the central and southern Andes (see fig. 5 for geographical distribution). Within this area, four were returned from the province of Huamanga—one from the colonial city of Huamanga and the remaining three from the surrounding rural districts. The fragmentary nature of the Peruvian corpus has contributed to the fact that the Mexican *RG*s have received far greater attention as documents to be studied and interpreted in their own right.[14] Quantitatively, the Peruvian corpus of *RG*s is undoubtedly meager; qualitatively, however, these documents are no less fascinating or deserving of attention than their better-known Mexican counterparts, for they too provide valuable insights into their authors' geographical ideas and the relations between indigenous and Spanish members of colonial society.

Interpreting these texts, as Gruzinski has shown, is no easy matter.[15] Constructed on the basis of multiple testimonies, many responses were also the product of interpretation that involved, first, the translation of Spanish questions for native informants, and second, the translation of the responses before these were relayed back to the Spanish interlocutors and written down by a scribe. Already products of multiple mediations, the answers were again modified when they came to be edited by the district's *corregidor*. Distinguishing native from Spanish voices is not always possible; no more straightforward is the task of determining the informants' intentions, or interpreting not only what was said but also

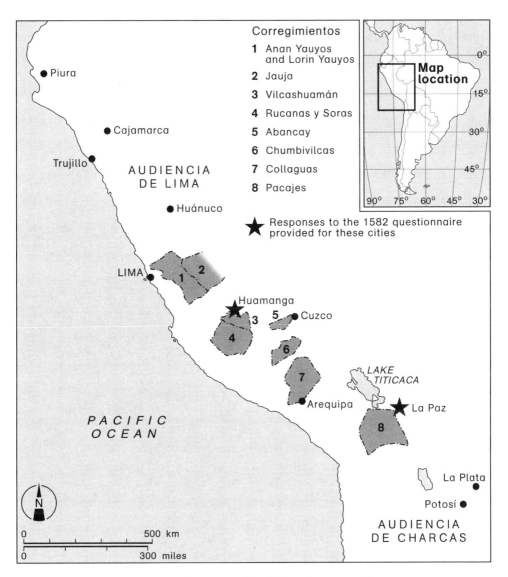

Corregimientos

1 Anan Yauyos
   and Lorin Yauyos
2 Jauja
3 Vilcashuamán
4 Rucanas y Soras
5 Abancay
6 Chumbivilcas
7 Collaguas
8 Pacajes

⭐ Responses to the 1582 questionnaire
   provided for these cities

Fig. 5. Corregimientos in the Viceroyalty of Peru that returned responses to
the Council of the Indies' geographical questionnaire of 1582. Adapted from
Guillermo Lohmann Villena, *El corregidor de indios en el Perú bajo los Austrias*
(Madrid: Ediciones Cultura Hispánica, 1957). Reproduced by permission
of the Agencia Española de Cooperación Internacional para el Desarrollo
(AECID).

the silences and absences. When do the answers reflect ignorance or a simple lack of interest in completing the questionnaire, and when, and for what reasons, are they products of intentional concealment? If the responses are read alongside other texts that shed further light on local circumstances, the motives that persuaded participants to answer in the way they did appear more ambiguous still. Rather than attempting to provide conclusive answers to such questions, however, my aim instead is to draw attention to those very ambiguities.

An initial reading of certain responses, notably those that describe urban centers such as Huamanga and La Paz, seems to confirm the implantation of a colonial order that is more or less congruent with that envisioned in the questionnaire. The landscapes that surround these towns are not only described in a profusion of detail; they are also effortlessly assigned to the questionnaire's utilitarian categories, which separate native crops from Spanish ones, wild animals from domestic livestock, and notable physical features from the everyday. Compartmentalized and described, the unruly landscape is reduced to a set of particulars that, on arrival in Spain, may easily be slotted into place in the Council of Indies' image of America. The colonial town is the axis around which all these particulars revolve, drawing in toward it those which are mobile and useful, including the native people; on the margins of Huamanga, they have been assigned two parishes where they live "for the service of the town."[16] Around La Paz, the indigenous communities now live in a permanent state of Hispanic order, thanks to the efforts of the viceroy Toledo, who moved them out of their scattered, precolonial dwellings and gave them "settlements laid out in an orderly manner, with streets and squares, where they have their churches and parishes, and their mayors and aldermen and their own municipal government."[17]

In the eastern valleys immediately below La Paz, bountiful landscapes filled with diverse fruit trees and vines brought from Spain appear to confirm and celebrate Cieza de León's earlier predictions of an inexorable process of Hispanicization. The detailed descriptions of indigenous crops, plants, customs, and beliefs convey a pronounced sense of certainty and of authoritative knowledge on the part of don Diego Cabeza de Vaca, *corregidor* of La Paz, who was responsible for compiling the account. The preamble to the *RG* draws attention to the legitimacy of Cabeza de Vaca's responses by emphasizing that the information was obtained from one of the first citizens and *encomenderos* of the city, and from two other individuals "who have walked and traversed every part of the region that belongs to this city and they are well-informed about the customs and rituals of the land."[18] The fullness and detail of the answers bear witness, it seems, to a striking congruence between the Council of the Indies' desire for particular types of information and the respondent's ability and desire to provide it.

By contrast to these responses, many *RG*s, especially those that describe remote rural districts, convey a curious sense of vagueness and detachment, and of a fundamental inability on the part of the Spanish investigators to determine the "truth" about these landscapes. In part, the incongruity of the details sought by the questionnaire and the physical nature of the territory produced this sense of absence: the high, harsh mountain landscapes that dominated *corregimientos* such as Collaguas in the southern Andes lacked a significant proportion of the features that, within the utilitarian framework of the interrogatory, brought the territory into existence and rendered it knowable. On the other hand, the often limited nature of many *corregidores'* knowledge and personal experiences of the territories under their jurisdiction may also have played an important role. As Mundy comments with reference to crown administrators in Mexico, the typical brevity of their terms of office in any one jurisdiction prevented many of these men from attaining in-depth knowledge of the districts to which they were posted, let alone a sense of connection or belonging.[19]

The answer provided by the *corregidor* of Collaguas and his native informants in response to the fourth question, which inquires about the physical characteristics and fertility of the territory, is principally expressed in negative terms. Many of the Collaguas people live on the high *puna,* where they herd livestock; further downstream,

> the remaining Collaguas Indians are settled, who grow food, maize and *quinoa* and potatoes; the land is poor, with few crops, and provides very little food, and for this reason they lack sustenance; and the land is bare, sterile, and with little water and no trees, and in the years that bring little rain, they have great difficulties with

irrigation because there is little water. They cannot make use of
the main river for making irrigation channels nor drink from it
nor use it for any other purpose, because it is very shallow and
runs in furrows.[20]

The feeling of lack that pervades this response runs through much
of the remaining text. Not only are there no trees, there are no "useful
plants" except for thistles, and vegetables are absent with the exception
of "plants that appear in the rainy season, that are well known and possess names among them [the Indians]."[21] Even the mountains and rivers
seem strangely insubstantial and elusive. The river that runs through
the valley has no certain name; likewise, where the mountain range that
extends across the province is concerned, the *RG* declares that "[t]he
name of this mountain range is not known."[22] The source of this name-
less river, meanwhile, is to be found thirty leagues distant in the *puna,*
"without it containing anything of note."[23] Like water vapor, these features could be seen but not grasped, and could be known only in terms
of what they were not.

Individually named in the document, the local Andean leaders of
Collaguas who acted as informants must also be regarded as key agents
in determining the content and emphasis of the answers. As Altuna suggests, the sense of vagueness and detachment that pervades some of the
Peruvian responses may reflect the alienating effects of the Toledan
resettlement program, which brought about the physical dislocation of
native populations from their lived-in landscapes.[24] However, the intentional concealment of knowledge by native informants also appears
to have contributed to this phenomenon. This involved the withholding
of information about local resources such as ore or medicinal plants[25]
and also, it seems, about the meaning and origin of indigenous place-
names, possibly because of their connections to non-Christian beliefs
and practices that continued to animate Andean landscapes.[26] In more
than one document, it is repeatedly asserted that indigenous place-
names have no meaning, or that settlements were simply named after
nearby landscape features or vegetation types. In response to a question
about indigenous toponymy, an *RG* from the Huamanga province asserted that the Andeans "took the old names that they [the places] pos-

sess from the trees, stones, and plants that are most abundant in each one, without there being any other mystery or meaning of note."[27] The landscape and the features that provided the settlements with their names were thereby reduced to an innocuous backdrop, divested of any meanings that could challenge the authority of the hagiographic prefixes that now adorned the Andean names.

Although the *corregidor*'s view of his informants' assertions cannot be separated from native voices with any certainty, his additions are more clearly identifiable in another document that he edited. Following the explanations of the meaning and origin of place-names undoubtedly supplied by Andean informants, he occasionally added, "and they give no other reason." The settlement of Santo Tomás de Guanca, for example, possessed this name "because there are many boulders on the plains, for *guanca* means large stones, and they give no other reason."[28] This added comment appears to transmit an undercurrent of suspicion—or an uneasy awareness—that much has been left unsaid. It is difficult to imagine that this would have been otherwise where a village called San Pedro de Songonchi was concerned. The settlement had received the name of Songonchi—meaning "place of the heart"—because of the presence of a large, heart-shaped stone on top of which now stood the bell tower of the chapel. Not only were such large, distinctively shaped stones frequent objects of worship, it was also common practice for churches to be built on top of sites of veneration that could not be physically destroyed.[29]

The *RG* produced in Jauja in 1582 provides another tantalizing glimpse of possible manipulations and tactical suppressions of knowledge. Throughout the text runs an anxious insistence on the wholly Christianized and Hispanicized nature of the province and the native communities that inhabited it. The informants were clearly at pains to emphasize that only the Christian prefixes of the region's place-names held any meaning: whereas the names of the saints were introduced by the friars who first preached in Jauja, "the other old names have no meaning nor [do they know] what they mean, except that they are very ancient names, and they do not know who gave these names."[30]

Having dismissed the indigenous place-names as relics of a distant and barely known past, the informants reinforced this historicization in response to the question that followed, which solicited details about precolonial forms of worship. They have heard, they replied, "that their ancestors said that they had come from and emerged out of caves and lagoons and springs and mountain peaks, and that they told them that they should worship the creator of man and of the earth and the sky and of the waters and mountains and other things."[31] At the end of their reply they added, unsolicited, that "they have converted to our Holy Catholic Faith, and the priests who have instructed them removed the stones and *huacas*[32] and sites of worship." By suggesting that their knowledge of non-Christian practices was based not on firsthand experience but on the words of their ancestors ("their ancestors *said* that"), and by declaring that all physical markers of such activity had been destroyed, the respondents kept all forbidden practices at arm's length.[33]

In the early 1580s a priest named Cristóbal de Albornoz put together a summary, probably at the viceroy's request, of the principal sites of worship that he had found and recorded in the provinces that lay between Cuzco and Quito.[34] Entitled *Instrucción para descubrir todas las guacas del Pirú* (Instructions for Discovering All the *Huacas* of Peru), the document included a section on the *repartimiento* of Hanan Huanca in the Jauja province. Despite its brevity, it provides a glimpse of a physical landscape that was animated by a plethora of deities, who resided in mountain peaks and boulders that lay strewn across the land. Listing seven sites of worship of particular significance, Albornoz warned that these were a mere handful of the *huacas* that existed in the area; "it is inevitable that there are many more in the manner that I have outlined in my instruction, for these are the general ones."[35]

One of the *huacas* mentioned by Albornoz was Guarivilca, "a stone like an Indian"[36] that stood on a plain near the *tambo* of Huancayo and that was venerated by the people of Hanan Huanca. Interestingly, the *RG* from Jauja also mentions a boulder "in the form of a man"[37] that, likewise, was situated on a flat area of land. It is probable that both documents refer to the same object, yet in the Huancas' testimonies it is wholly desacralized, mentioned only to explain that, on entering the valley for the first time and seeing the distinctive stone, the Inca Capac Yupanqui named it Guanca Guamaní.[38]

Enough has been said, I think, to argue persuasively that Andean informants, in Jauja and elsewhere, at times employed a conscious tactic of concealment when giving their replies to the questionnaire. At the very least, they actively seized the opportunity that, as Gruzinski makes clear, was provided by the questionnaire to consign certain practices and beliefs to a distant past.[39] In seeking to keep Andean spiritual practices and beliefs from view, they denied knowledge of such practices and gave credence to a geography of Peru as a Christianized territory that no longer provided space for beliefs and practices of precolonial origin.[40]

The absences and silences implied in the Peruvian *RG*s may be understood, Altuna argues, not only as the product of communication difficulties but also as expressions of "active resistance, at a linguistic level, against yielding to the reductionism of a questionnaire that was based on the particular administrative understandings of the colonizer."[41] The dynamics of a process whereby colonial subjects supplied evasive answers in response to questions sent from Madrid[42] are undoubtedly suggestive of a reactive and oppositional form of resistance. Through the withholding of oral information about existing non-Christian sacred geographies, native informants actively contested the European geographical assumptions contained within the text of the questionnaire.

Such an interpretation, however, divides indigenous and Spanish participants into two neatly separate and homogeneous camps, leaving little room for the ambivalent, creative, and transformative activities that Ortner regards as integral to resistance.[43] It presupposes, moreover, static and inflexible understandings, on the part of both Andeans and Spaniards, of the landscapes and geographies that the responses seek to describe, and overlooks the everyday contexts within which these participants were situated and interacted. As diverse studies of colonial life and belief in the Andes illustrate, Andean people did not simply oppose, in unitary fashion, the new colonial geographies and spatial orders that emerged with the establishment of Spanish rule.[44] At times, indigenous communities may have actively opposed Spanish efforts to Christianize and physically reorganize their lived-in landscapes, but they also embraced elements of Christianity and, in juxtaposing these with elements of modified Andean religious practices, created something new.[45]

Rejecting the notion of a binary opposition between domination and resistance, Sharp and her co-authors insist that these categories not only are "always implicated in, and mutually constitutive of, one another," but also are "played out in, across and through the many spaces of the world."[46] Rose, however, takes this argument further and suggests that the concept of resistance be abandoned altogether, on the grounds that it can only *react* to a system of domination that is always already in existence, thereby reinforcing—rather than undermining—that system's power.[47] Rejecting the notion of a coherent, preexisting system of dominance, he conceptualizes acts of domination and resistance as qualitatively indistinguishable strategies that are deployed in order to "fulfil desires in diverse contexts."[48] Drawing on these ideas below, I highlight the entangled nature of dominant and resistant practices that provided the context for the production of the Jauja *RG,* and, finally, question whether the concept of resistance is at all adequate as a means of comprehending the complex web of activities and relationships that provided that context.

Colonial Jauja: A Landscape of Huanca Resistance?

The intentionalities of human actors, Ortner argues, "evolve through praxis, and the meanings of the acts change, both for the actor and for the analyst."[49] The intentions that underlie particular acts and utterances cannot be taken for granted or assumed to be constant or uniform. Ortner's insight, expressed as a note of caution for those seeking "a fixed box called resistance,"[50] is essential to bear in mind when interpreting the Huancas' contributions to the *RG* of Jauja.

Profound ambivalence characterized the Huancas' relationship with the Spanish from the time of the conquest onward. The accounts of merits and services that were presented by Huanca leaders in the aftermath of the conquest conveyed with unmistakable pride the prominent role that their communities played in these events, and also communicated their desire to maintain prestige and status within the context of an emergent colonial society.[51] At the same time, however, these documents constituted, and were intended to convey to their royal recipient, unequivocal condemnations of the abuses that the Huanca communities experienced at Spanish hands throughout the conquest and ensuing factional conflicts.[52]

Both elements are clearly reflected in the *RG* of 1582. In a generous and opportunistic interpretation of question 20, which requests details of "noteworthy lakes, lagoons, or springs that may exist within the jurisdictions of the towns, together with any notable things that they contain,"[53] the text declares one of the notable features of the Jauja valley to be that "in this valley Francisco Hernández Girón was captured, in the location that will be shown on the map, and these Indians served His Majesty in the said capture, and they have done so in other things, such as in maintaining the armies of His Majesty which have regrouped here, and which were here for many days at the cost of the said Indians."[54]

In response to a request for information about notable features of the physical landscape, the respondents drew attention to the Huanca deeds that marked this landscape and that, at a wider scale, also influenced the histories and geographies of conquest and colonization. The site where the capture of Hernández Girón took place, moreover, was to be marked on an accompanying map of the province, which unfortunately has been lost or was never actually made. Elsewhere in the *RG,* echoes of the condemnations of Spanish actions that run through the accounts of services also make an appearance; responding to a question on demography in the province, the informants took the opportunity not only to point out that the population declined sharply following the arrival of the Spaniards, but also that this was because, at the time of the factional conflicts, "the Spaniards took many Indian men and women as *yanaconas* and servants, and they remained and died outside this valley."[55]

The ambiguities of the Huancas' relationships with the Spanish, however, went beyond a conflict between the desire of the ethnic lords to protect their status within colonial society and the urge to demand restitution for the past actions of the conquistadors. Notwithstanding their role as allies to the Spanish crown, the Huancas had attracted the wrath of the colonial government in 1565: as rumors circulated about their involvement in a planned uprising against the Spanish, the president of the viceroyalty, García de Castro, reported to the king that the Huancas were found to be secretly manufacturing weapons for the purpose of rebellion. The *cacique principal* of Lurin Huanca was arrested in connection with these rumors, but was freed in the night by Franciscan friars.[56]

Just one year later, in striking contrast to these tensions, the Huanca communities addressed to the monarch a set of letters that conveyed a humble endorsement of the colonial order. Whereas other Andean communities signed a lengthy petition requesting the removal of the recently appointed *corregidores de indios,* Jauja's native leaders expressed unstinting praise for this system—or, at least, for the merits of their own *corregidor.* The Hanan Huancas' description of Juan de Larrinaga, the man who had been appointed to this post in Jauja, was nothing less than a rapturous eulogy. Larrinaga, they assured the monarch, was received by them "no less as a father than as a *corregidor* who has guided and guides us as minors, enlightening us and freeing us from our ignorance and inappropriate customs; he has founded and tended town councils in this valley, [which are] necessary and convenient for looking after the common good of the republic and for ensuring civility and order; for everything he has given us laws and a way of life."[57]

Even more startlingly, the letter went on to declare that the people of Hanan Huanca were so honored by the appointment of Larrinaga as *corregidor* that "we almost accept it as a payment and honor in return for the special service that we, the natives of this valley, gave to your Majesty by capturing in it Francisco Hernández Girón . . . as well as having provided for all your Majesty's royal armies and shown great care and loyalty in your royal service."[58]

Their only request was that the monarch continue to favor the members of the newly created native council with special privileges and, in addition, that he pay the salary of the *corregidores,* given that "it is your Majesty's privilege and duty to preserve us in a state of justice."[59] If there was some truth in the accusations made against the Huancas in 1565, then these letters would seem to indicate a sudden shift from intentions of armed rebellion to a position of subjugation vis-à-vis the colonial authorities. More probably, however, they reflect the adoption of astute tactics designed to deflect the growing hostility of Peru's colonial government by taking advantage of a political situation as it unfolded. If by the mid-1560s the government regarded the Jauja valley with suspicion, as a site at which weapons intended for rebellion were secretly fabricated and concealed, the letters sought to renegotiate it as a landscape inscribed with memories of the Huancas' acts of loyalty and service to the crown.

Nonetheless, the Huanca leaders' enthusiastic acceptance of Larrinaga as *corregidor* may have contained some sincerity. Appearing as a witness in support of don Gerónimo Guacra Paucar's account of services, described in chapter 2, Larrinaga confirmed in his testimony that he had already known the *curaca* for about fourteen years. In contrast to many acerbic Spanish portrayals of *curacas* that emerged in the 1560s, Larrinaga had nothing but praise for don Gerónimo, who, he insisted, governed "his Indians and populace very well and with great prudence" and was also generous, charitable, and a good Christian.[60] The positive nature of Larrinaga's long-term relationship with the wider Huanca community was also affirmed in a letter submitted by the *repartimiento* of Lurin Huanca: throughout the turbulent times of the civil conflicts, they declared, Larrinaga always favored them and came to their aid.[61]

At least for the Huanca leaders, the appointment of Larrinaga as *corregidor* may have signified a valuable alliance at a time when their relations with the higher echelons of colonial government and, moreover, with the religious clergy who worked in Jauja were particularly strained.[62] The picture that emerges from this brief sketch is of a set of shifting, unstable relationships that were continuously renegotiated as circumstances changed. These glimpses serve as an eloquent reminder that Andean contributions to the creation of the *RG*s should not be narrowly conceived as reactive practices that were straightforwardly determined by entrenched oppositions. By taking a closer look at colonial negotiations over Jauja's native sacred geographies between the 1550s and 1570s, I suggest that the concealment and historicization of these geographies in the *RG*s were often the product of unpredictable and ambivalent intentions that confound the boundaries between "domination" and "resistance."

✳ Several years before the creation of the Jauja *RG*, royal attention had been drawn to the landscapes of the Jauja valley by a map sketched by a Franciscan friar. According to its maker, the map marked the location of an important *huaca,* "where the Indians used to have their place of worship and make offerings to their idols."[63] It was imperative, the monarch declared, that native idolatries be eradicated: moreover, because it was likely that the *huaca* contained items of material value, the viceroy should organize a search for this site—"which may easily be located with the map"—and, following its discovery, have it destroyed.[64] Any riches that the site contained, meanwhile, were to be treated as royal property and dispatched to Spain at the earliest opportunity. In Peru, the excavation of Amerindian sites of burial and worship by individuals in search of riches had taken place since the early colonial period.[65] In the 1570s, however, following the arrival of the viceroy Toledo, official interest in recovering material goods from sites of burial and worship as a means of boosting royal revenue appears to have intensified. Partway through his five-year general inspection of the Viceroyalty of Peru, Toledo informed the monarch that over the course of this inspection, "many idols and sites of worship which were still concealed by the natives have been and are being discovered, as well as much livestock and goods that were dedicated to the sun and to their *huacas* and Inca burials . . . which was not known about until now, nor could it have been known without the territories being inspected."[66]

Responding to the viceroy's doubts about the ownership of such items that were discovered by royal officials, the monarch stipulated in no uncertain terms that they were the sole property of the crown.[67] Formally establishing laws on ownership was considerably easier, however, than the process of locating and excavating the hoards that lay concealed beneath the surface of the landscape. Royal correspondence expressed anxiety over the intentional concealment of these sites by Peru's indigenous inhabitants. In a letter to his viceroy, Philip III stated that he had received reports that many unexcavated *huacas* still remained in Peru, because the native people had not revealed them: many of those who knew about their whereabouts had died, and of those who were still alive, many refused to reveal their knowledge because they wished to protect their ancient places of worship.[68] The geographical questionnaire contained no specific question about the existence of pre-Hispanic sites of worship or burial that contained items of material value to the crown.[69] Nevertheless, the intensification of official interest in excavating such sites in search of treasure, together with the recent experience of Toledo's tour of inspection, may have added to the desire of Andean informants to conceal their knowledge of sacred geographies when responding to the interrogatory.

In the early 1560s, the son of don Gerónimo, one of the three Huanca leaders who presented accounts of services rendered in the conquest and civil wars,[70] was entrusted with the task of traveling to Spain in order to present the three petitions to the Council of the Indies. Raised and educated by the Franciscan friars who worked in the Jauja valley, Felipe de Guacra Paucar was no doubt chosen for this task because of his intimate familiarity with Spanish language and practices. Once in Spain, don Felipe petitioned the monarch—with remarkable success—for a substantial list of honors and privileges.[71] Successfully passing himself off in Spain as the *cacique principal* of Jauja (the title belonged to his father), he returned to Peru in 1565 loaded with royal privileges, which included a yearly pension of six hundred pesos and a coat of arms that memorialized his father's services to the crown.[72] He also succeeded in obtaining a royal letters patent that permitted him, along with other native leaders of Jauja and their subjects, to excavate not only mines but also old sites of burial and worship in search of the offerings "that in ancient times his ancestors used to make."[73]

In Jauja, the king was informed, only Spaniards were permitted to excavate such sites, and as a result many remained hidden and concealed. While drawing attention to the injustice of this situation for his own community, don Felipe was careful to emphasize that, because of the inevitable loss of revenue, it also caused "injury and harm"[74] to the royal patrimony of the crown. No doubt moved as much by don Felipe's financial arguments as by his appeal for justice, the monarch consented to his request that the natives of Jauja be authorized "to discover the said things and that, with regard to whatever they find, they have entitlement to the same share as Spaniards."[75]

Like many *indios ladinos,* Felipe de Guacra Paucar's relationship with members of the Spanish community and government in Peru was often fraught. In 1570, five years after he returned to Peru, the *encomendero* of Lurin Huanca accused him of being the region's greatest *pleitista* (litigious person), who, for the purposes of engaging in legal disputes, exploited his own people by making them run back and forth to Lima and by spending all the community's funds in the process. The result of this case was a ten-year sentence of exile from Jauja and the removal of his right to participate in any further judicial proceedings.[76] In an era when the viceregal government was striving to suppress the power and influence of Peru's ethnic lords, don Felipe's identity as a highly ambitious, astute, and Hispanicized member of Jauja's native elite inevitably earned him numerous enemies.

Fascinatingly, don Felipe was back in the Jauja valley by 1582, at the time the Council of the Indies' questionnaire was received, and he also played an important role as interpreter in the production of the responses. Translating the questionnaire into Quechua for the assembled informants, he then relayed their answers in Spanish to the scribe. He is described in the introduction to the *RG* as an "*indio ladino* who has been to Spain,"[77] and his intimate knowledge of Spanish practices appears, once again, to have placed him in the role of mediator between the crown and colonial authorities, on the one hand, and his native community, on the other. The fact that by 1582 don Felipe was again acting as mediator in the creation of the *RG* bears witness to the profound ambivalence of his position. Clearly feared and distrusted by many Spaniards (and, perhaps, by many Andeans), he was also indispensable to the functioning of colonial society and intimately connected with the social and cultural practices of its rulers.[78]

In consequence, it is impossible to view the nature of don Felipe's bonds with Jauja's landscapes, along with his involvement in the production of the *RG,* in terms of a restrictive binary framework that presents his actions — and those of other Huancas — as predetermined *re*actions to a colonial adversary. In petitioning the crown for the right to excavate *huacas* (and to register mining sites), he undoubtedly may have been motivated by a desire to safeguard his community's control over the sacred sites of burial and worship that connected the people with their ancestors and with the physical landscapes in which they lived.[79] However, as a highly Hispanicized member of the Huanca elite who possessed high ambitions within colonial society, he may also have had a genuine interest in exploiting these sites for material gain.[80] Despite his success in obtaining royal confirmation of his community's rights to excavate *huacas,* the intense official interest in appropriating the contents of such sites probably resulted in these rights being threatened or ignored. If this was the case, members of the wider Huanca community may well have considered the discursive and physical concealment of native sacred geographies as the only effective strategy for protecting these rights. However, the meaning that these geographies held for don Felipe, and the significance of their loss to him, are likely to have been rather different from the meaning for other, less Hispanicized community members.

Precisely because of the particularities of his experiences and background, it is also impossible to use don Felipe's story as a template for understanding the perceptions and intentionalities of other Andeans in Jauja when they were presented with the interrogatory and responded to its questions. Indeed, it is very difficult to determine the perceptions and intentionalities of don Felipe himself. Nevertheless, by being attentive to the particular lives and activities of such individuals—as far as the available documentation allows—it becomes easier to recognize that the questionnaires could take on varied and ambiguous meanings for indigenous respondents, as well as to apprehend that the production of responses took place in varied contexts of geographical location and of social, cultural, and political networks. The history of Huanca-Spanish relations from the time of the conquest onward was one of continuous improvisation and negotiation, as well as of outright conflict and struggle; inevitably, the creation of the *RG* was situated within, rather than beyond, these entangled narratives.

The story of the *huaca* from the Franciscan friar's map of the Jauja valley, the *huaca* so anxiously sought by the Spanish crown, deserves completion. In 1586 the viceroy reported to the monarch that nothing had been found, despite his interrogation of *curacas* and other natives of the Jauja valley, and despite the local *corregidor*'s efforts to locate the site.[81] While these interrogations were underway, the Franciscan friar who had submitted the map and report to the monarch was on his way from Seville to Lima, under orders to identify the location of the *huaca*. Obliged by the viceroy to lead a search party to Jauja, Fray Francisco del Castillo led his companions on a wild goose chase through the valley that yielded no sign of the burial. Back in Lima, he finally confessed to his superior "that there was no *huaca,* nor did he know about it; rather, his dealings with your Majesty were [carried out] so that he would be given permission to return to Peru."[82] En route to Lima, he apparently confided to a fellow traveler that his plan was "to search for a cave or grotto and say that this was the *huaca* and that the Indians had removed the treasure."[83]

This brief cameo helps bring to light the intertwining of dominant and resistant practices in struggles over the landscapes of Jauja and its precolonial geographies. Fray Francisco del Castillo and his actions are impossible to separate from the ambitions of the crown and colonial government to extract and take possession of the subterranean wealth that Peru's landscapes concealed, from mineral deposits to buried offerings. His report led to the formal interrogation of Jauja's *curacas* and, during his own "search" for the *huaca,* to native inhabitants of the valley being forced to dig at scattered locations in the hope that the sacred site and its contents would be revealed. Had the friar's plans succeeded, the valley's indigenous inhabitants would have been the primary victims of his plot, for they would have carried the blame for the "disappearance" of the treasure. At the same time, however, his actions constituted an opportunistic move that was calculated to restore his liberty, by means of a canny appeal to royal interests in Peru's subterranean landscapes. Francisco del Castillo had been to Peru earlier. According to an individual named Joan Saborido, who informed the king about the affair, he had spent between one and two years in the city of Trujillo in northern Peru, where he falsely claimed that he had been granted a bishopric and, for a time, enjoyed the lifestyle and honors of a prelate. After his fraud was discovered, he was sent back to Spain and imprisoned. If Saborido's testimony is reliable, del Castillo was not even a bona fide friar. On account of a string of misdemeanors, he had been expelled from the Franciscan order while he was still a novice in Valencia. Somehow he obtained a passage to Panama and, once there, passed himself off as a friar before continuing his journey to Trujillo. In addition, Saborido exclaimed in his letter, the man could barely even read, but thanks to his audacity he succeeded in carrying out an impressive series of deceptions. For del Castillo, the restoration of liberty meant, first and foremost, release from prison. However, it also meant a return to Peru. Without doubt, the expansive territories of the New World offered far greater opportunities than Spain for a disgraced and illegitimate friar to evade the control of the secular government and the church.[84] Unfettered mobility, which came within tantalizing reach of del Castillo on his return to Peru, was regarded by the royal and viceregal authorities as deeply threatening to the maintenance of colonial order.

The unequal distribution of power relations between colonial government and the native inhabitants of Jauja was undoubtedly part of this story, for it was on the exploitation of inequality that the implementation of del Castillo's plans partially depended. However, just as the indigenous participants in the creation of the Jauja *RG* were neither uniformly nor exclusively concerned with resistance to the colonial order, so too, this disruptive friar was not primarily—or even partially—motivated by a will to colonial domination. Qualitatively, the Franciscan's efforts to regain his freedom are difficult to distinguish from the Huancas' responses to the geographical questionnaire, for both creatively negotiated Jauja's landscapes in pursuit of particular interests and desires.[85]

Spanish *"Resistance"* and the Reducciones

The *reducciones*—colonial towns that were created on a large scale in Peru under the rule of the viceroy Toledo, and to which indigenous populations were forcibly relocated—represent one of the most potent material expressions of the new colonial spatial order. Their implementation, moreover, brought about dramatic changes to Peru's human geographies. They reflected a powerful desire to arrest uncontrolled indigenous mobility and to make native populations visible and easily accessible, as well as to initiate them into a life of *policía*[86] that would ensure their obedience to the twin authorities of government and church. Not all Spaniards, however, were in favor of the *reducciones*; many perceived them as a threat to their access to indigenous labor and hence to their livelihoods. Although the widespread lack of Spanish enthusiasm for Toledo's resettlement scheme has been noted by numerous scholars,[87] it is often overshadowed by a portrayal (albeit unintentional) of the *reducciones* as powerful manifestations of an almost instinctive colonial desire that was shared by all Spaniards.[88]

Some of the Peruvian *RG*s enthusiastically endorsed the vision of colonial spatial order embedded in the questionnaire's inquiry as to whether the native people "are settled in organized and permanent towns."[89] Indeed, the majority of responses affirmed that the reductions had been carried out and claimed that they were still intact. The tone in which these statements were delivered, however, was sometimes strangely detached and ambiguous. The textual gloss that may be attributed to the varied Spanish, *mestizo,* and *ladino* editors (principally the *corregidor* Luis de Monzón) who compiled the responses that describe Huamanga's rural provinces, conveys a curious sense of indifference toward the fate of the *reducciones.* While one of the three texts suggests "*it seems* they will be permanent,"[90] another indicates that "*it is understood* they will be permanent,"[91] as if their destiny were to be left to chance or, perhaps, to the will of their inhabitants.

The tone of these comments may have reflected, on the one hand, a human landscape that was far from permanently "reduced" and, on the other, a veiled opposition to the *reducciones* that could well have included the *corregidor.* This may be inferred from the *RG* that was produced in the city of Huamanga. Here, the informants' portrayal of the state of the *reducciones* in the countryside around Huamanga and, moreover, of the damage they had inflicted, is uncompromisingly clear and direct:

> The Indians who live here are settled in planned towns . . . and although before they were settled in planned towns they lacked the civil order of streets and squares that they were given in the last *reducción* . . . as a result of having been moved to areas with a different climate, together with the causes declared above [mining], a great number of Indians have died; and so, *the recently reduced towns are not permanent for the most part,* because, after the said *reducción,* seeing the inconveniences of being moved to different climates and insalubrious places that are distant from their fields, they have returned to settle in many of the settlements where they had previously lived and to other areas, *with the permission of*

the governors and opinion of the corregidores *of their districts,* who will
be able to provide a more detailed account of this.[92]

Laying bare the realities that the "rural *RG*s" of Huamanga appear to
keep hidden, this response questions the very spatial order upon which
the crown and viceregal government had constructed its vision of a
well-regulated colonial society. Although recognizing the inherent *policía*
of the streets and squares that the Andeans had been made to inhabit,
the commentary reveals the ruptures within what is so often implicitly
portrayed as a unified vision of colonial order innate to all Spaniards,
and indicates that this order was contradicted through everyday practice by Andeans and Spaniards alike.[93]

By the turn of the century, many of Peru's *reducciones* were descend-
ing into disarray as their native inhabitants fled, either to return to their
previous places of habitation, or to take up residence in other areas in
the hope of freeing themselves from the burdens of labor and tribute
that weighed on them in their assigned settlements. The repeated attempts made by Peru's seventeenth-century viceroys to return Andean
migrants to their *reducciones* was construed by a substantial sector of the
Spanish population, however, as a direct threat to their own interests.[94]

In early-seventeenth-century Huamanga these interests were represented and energetically defended at a high level by the bishop of the
province, who engaged in a lengthy and somewhat heated exchange of
correspondence on this matter with the viceroy. On the one hand, the
viceroy insisted on the need to return to their towns the large numbers
of Andeans who had taken up residence in and around Huamanga, on
the grounds that they evaded their obligations of paying tribute and
participating in the labor draft in the nearby mercury mines of Huancavelica. On the other hand, the bishop declared that the town's Spanish inhabitants were heavily dependent on the overwhelmingly Andean population of tradesmen, as well as on the army of *yanaconas* who worked as
agricultural laborers in the Spanish-owned lands that surrounded the
settlement. Arguing that the Andeans residing in and around Huamanga
actually paid their tribute and participated in the Huancavelica draft more
readily than those in the *reducciones,* he predicted that the removal of the
forasteros, or migrant Andeans, would bring "poverty and detriment to

the cities."[95] A comparable point was made rather more bluntly by Hua-manga's *corregidor,* don Luis de Oznayo, who on being accused of concealing a number of Andeans to prevent them being sent to the mercury mines, allegedly declared that "the resettlement . . . was a joke and served no purpose but to rob people of their wealth."[96]

Although the *corregidores de indios* bore principal responsibility for ensuring the establishment and preservation of the *reducciones,* they appeared to play a significant role in hindering these objectives, often in collusion with native leaders, local priests, and other Spaniards who were resident in and around the *reducciones.*[97] The possibility cannot be ruled out, of course, that genuine concern over native well-being played a part in some *corregidores'* rejection of the colonial towns.[98] Personal gain, however, was the principal motivating factor: one royal official, reporting on the difficulties of reestablishing the *reducciones* in the *Audiencia* of Charcas, commented that the priests impeded the expulsion of *forasteros* from their districts in every way they could, for they regarded these people as their own personal property.[99] Such disregard for royal and viceregal legislation regarding the *reducciones* surfaced in many areas of the viceroyalty and was endlessly lamented in seventeenth-century administrative correspondence.[100]

Despite the fact that Spanish endeavors to hinder the *reducciones* were overwhelmingly inspired by personal interests, native movement out of the Toledan settlements was closely interwoven with those actions. The undermining, by means of mobility, of the colonial spatial order as envisaged by successive viceroys as well as by the Council of the Indies' questionnaire was not the product of Andean agency alone. It also resulted from the actions of Spanish individuals for whom the resettlement represented a threat. The degree to which Spaniards were implicated in what is generally understood to be "resistant" indigenous mobility was clearly articulated by officials of the *Audiencia* of Charcas. Informing the monarch about the fierce opposition to the *reducciones* displayed by owners of agricultural plots, farms, and vineyards, they declared that these Spaniards "not only . . . give shelter to those [Indians] who go to them [the Spanish-owned lands] and offer them comforts but, using sophisticated methods, endeavor to bring them from other regions, and they marry them with their Indian domestic servants and allow them to cohabit."[101]

As these sources indicate, the unraveling of the Toledan spatial order was not brought about by a straightforward indigenous opposition to the reductions, though strong indigenous opposition did exist. Instead, it was fomented by the closely enmeshed spatial practices of Spaniards and Andeans, exemplifying the entangled spatiality of power to which Sharp and her co-authors refer.[102] Spanish landowners, *corregidores,* and priests may have wished to exploit Andean labor, but achieving this required not only compromise and concessions vis-à-vis those whom they hoped to exploit, but also an active involvement in violating the ideal spatial order envisaged by the monarchy and viceroys. In terms of their impact upon government attempts to reinstate the *reducciones,* Spanish efforts to hinder this objective cannot be distinguished in any meaningful way from indigenous acts of resistance to resettlement. By reading the *RG*s alongside other documents that deal with disputes over the Toledan *reducciones,* it becomes clear that the *RG*s emerged from processes more complex than indigenous contestation and Spanish affirmation of the assumptions and ideals contained within the questionnaire. The *RG*s from Huamanga are particularly suggestive of "resistant" attitudes toward the *reducciones* that emanated from colonizers as well as colonized. As Cresswell proposes in a very different context, it is pointless to map categories of domination and resistance neatly onto pairs of social groups—in this instance, colonizers and colonized—since they are simultaneously experienced and practiced by both.[103]

By attending, even in a limited fashion, to Ortner's insistence on filling in the "ethnographic black hole" that characterizes many studies of colonialism, it soon becomes apparent that manifestations of resistance are inherently diverse, intertwined with domination, and entangled with desires and objectives that have little or nothing to do with reactive opposition.[104] As Rose suggests, however, the preservation of these categories, even where they are reimagined as diverse and entangled, results in the preservation of a relationship in which resistant agency is inevitably secondary to, and defined by its opposition toward, a preexisting system of domination.[105] With the suppression of these categories, the assumed primacy of acts that have been associated with domination is removed, together with the temptation to portray them as expressions of an inevitably powerful and coherent system. In untying the study of the *RG*s from the conceptual framework of domination and resistance, it becomes easier to acknowledge that their creation involved the pursuit, by all those involved in this process, of diverse desires and interests that were shaped and reshaped in unpredictable contexts.[106]

✴   This chapter has demonstrated that the creation of the *RG*s took place, not as an expression of dualistic struggle between neatly opposed worldviews, but within the context of participants' interests, experiences, and relations with other groups and individuals in colonial society. The interpretation of the *RG*s requires a recognition not only of the ambivalent ways in which Andean informants participated in colonial society, but also of the fact that the interests and geographical visions of *Spanish* contributors did not always coincide with those of the crown and viceregal government. If any further evidence of this is required, it may easily be found in the failure of most *corregidores* in Peru to comply with royal instructions to respond to the questionnaire either adequately or at all. As Mundy points out, López de Velasco's consternation on receiving indigenous-authored maps that bore no relation to the formal cartographies he had requested undoubtedly hastened the fading of his ambition to map the New World.[107] More fundamentally, however, his project was fatally undermined by the fact that so many *corregidores* and other crown officials throughout Spain's overseas territories simply ignored the questionnaire.

FOUR

The Mobile Landscapes of Huarochirí

By the latter half of the sixteenth century, the turbulence of the initial period of conquest and ensuing civil conflicts in Peru had begun to subside, giving way to a new and, in many ways, more grounded colonial society. By the 1570s the age of large-scale expeditions of exploration and conquest that forcibly uprooted thousands of indigenous people, most of whom never returned to their homes, was coming to a close. Under the government of Toledo and his immediate successors, emphasis shifted away from territorial expansion and toward the consolidation of control over territories already under colonial rule. Within the viceroyalty and along its frontiers, the strategic foundation of new towns, the resettlement of indigenous populations into *reducciones,* and increasing concern for eliminating those deemed to be vagrants or vagabonds all reflected the "official" desire to create a sedentary and rooted society.

The society that emerged, however, was in many ways no less mobile than that of the conquest era. On the fringes of the viceroyalty, exploratory, punitive, and missionary expeditions continued throughout the seventeenth century, albeit on a smaller scale than before. In the colonial heartlands of the Andes, new movements of peoples took place under Toledan rule. Some, including the regular migration of *mitayos* to and from the mines of Potosí, were determined by the colonial officials, while others, like the flight of Andeans from the *reducciones,* were unanticipated but no less dramatic in scale.[1] Constant journeying of a more mundane kind also marked the everyday lives of many inhabitants of the viceroyalty. Given the vastness of the territory as a whole and the distances that separated Peru's principal cities, this was inevitable and, of course, necessary for the functioning of commerce and administration.[2]

Even within *corregimientos* and parishes, distances were often considerable. Especially in parts of the highlands, travel was often extremely slow and difficult because of the challenges of the terrain. Of those colonial travelers who made the long journey between Lima and Cuzco and other parts of the central-southern highlands, the majority passed along the well-maintained royal highway that traversed the colonial province of Huarochirí (see fig. 6), which comprised a section of the precipitous western ranges of the Andean mountains and lower-lying river valleys due east of the viceregal capital. For some members of the church and the lower echelons of the colonial administration, however, experiences of the province's mountainous landscapes were much more common. For parish priests in particular, but also for missionaries, ecclesiastical inspectors, and *corregidores,* traveling along the often vertiginous pathways came to be a central part of everyday life, if only, for many, on a temporary basis.

Physical movement along pathways, rather than detached observation, defined the relationship of such individuals with the Peruvian landscape—a situation that was succinctly captured decades ago by Gerbi's felicitous phrase, "Peru is a pathway."[3] The theme of travel along roads and pathways as a principal mode of experience in colonial Spanish America has attained considerable prominence in recent studies.[4] Such experience, some scholars argue, may have produced or at least reflected the perpetuation of imaginative geographies that were shaped by time and motion rather than by atemporal conceptions of space, and thus were distinct from those fostered by the development of modern cartographies.[5] Building on such work, this chapter traces how the landscapes of Huarochirí were experienced and portrayed by a number of men who, between about 1570 and 1630, worked in the province and traveled its pathways. I seek to show that, well into the colonial period, travel along pathways not only continued to shape the ways in which Huarochirí's landscapes were imagined and described, but also contin-

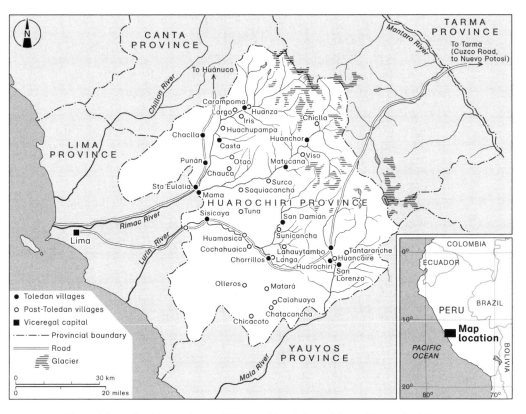

Fig. 6. The colonial province of Huarochirí. Adapted from Karen Spalding, *Huarochirí: An Andean Society under Inca and Spanish Rule* (Stanford: Stanford University Press, 1984). Copyright © 1984 by the Board of Trustees, Leland Stanford Junior University. All rights reserved. Used by permission of Stanford University Press.

ued to be regarded by many as crucial to the maintenance of colonial order and control. As the first chapter of this study illustrates, however, the spatial trajectories of the Spanish in the early years of conquest were guided not only by their own objectives but also by the physical terrain and the agency of indigenous groups. Elaborating on this theme, I examine how, despite the dramatic physical transformations that the *reducciones* brought to Huarochirí's lived-in landscapes, Andean agency continued to affect colonial representatives' spatial practices and hence their experiences of the landscape.

The ways in which landscapes took on significance for the ecclesiastics and administrators who worked in Huarochirí varied, as did their circumstances. The personal and professional objectives that brought these individuals to Huarochirí undoubtedly played a central role in determining how they came to know the province and how they chose to represent it. No less important, however, was the duration of their stay in Huarochirí and the nature and extent of their involvement in local affairs. In some cases, their perceptions and portrayals varied dramatically. As we will see, the representations produced between the 1570s and the 1630s reveal little sign of a coherent linear progression from a landscape that was generally perceived as alien and little-known to one that was regarded as thoroughly familiar, mundane, and domesticated. In tracing these ruptures and contradictions, it is possible not only to highlight the absence of a "master-plan" of colonialism,[6] but also to show that the emergence of Lima-based anxieties over the landscapes of Huarochirí and other rural provinces were in large part the product of colonialism's own agents.

After focusing on two priests' struggles over the human and physical landscapes of their respective parishes in the 1630s, I shift back to the sixteenth century to explore portrayals that were made of the Huarochirí landscapes, first by Jesuit missionaries, and second, by a *corregidor* who — very unusually — spent over ten years working in the region. Last, I return to the early seventeenth century to consider how the landscapes of Huarochirí, together with those of neighboring provinces, came to matter for the prelates, priests, and ecclesiastical inspectors who were involved in the extirpation of idolatry.

Priestly Pathways

In the 1570s the human landscapes of Huarochirí, like those of other Andean provinces, were thoroughly transformed by the creation of the *reducciones*. The inhabitants of over two hundred scattered settlements were "reduced" into just thirty-nine colonial towns. Two of these, San Mateo de Huanchor and San Gerónimo de Surco, became neighboring parish seats, which were occupied several decades later by the priests

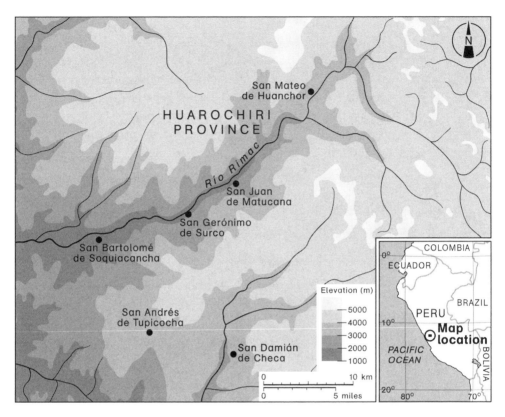

Fig. 7. Map showing the area of Antonio de Guerrero's and Andrés de Mojica's neighboring parishes.

Andrés de Mojica and Antonio de Guerrero, respectively (see fig. 7). From these bases, the two priests were obliged to venture out on muleback, and sometimes on foot, to minister to parishioners in other settlements that fell within their jurisdictions. Without doubt, the relocation of native populations had made this task considerably easier, and also marked the introduction of a colonial spatial order that was imposed from above by means of Toledan legislation.

Nevertheless, just as the colonial reordering was necessarily carried out within the range of possibilities offered by a vertical landscape that presented fairly little in the way of flat, cultivable land, so too, this physical landscape, a steep and often difficult surface to be crossed and recrossed on parish circuits, continued to shape the priests' day-to-day experiences. For Guerrero and Mojica, the mundane experiences of traversing Huarochirí's mountainous landscapes emerged as a central point of contention in a legal dispute that erupted between them in 1630.[7] Revolving around the priests' everyday routines and pastoral labors, the documentation that the case produced reveals how the priests' perceptions of their lived-in landscapes were shaped as much by the temporal rhythm and embodied experience of travel around their parishes as by a detached "cartographic" vision. In addition, it provides a fascinating insight into how the meanings that they attributed to these landscapes were primarily woven and negotiated through the petty intrigues and activities of parochial life.

After years of what appears to have been a peaceful coexistence,[8] Guerrero brought a case against his neighbor over the Andean parishioners of San Juan de Matucana, a settlement lying on the road between San Gerónimo and San Mateo. Jurisdiction over the population, which was divided into two lineage groups or *parcialidades* known as Caionas and Quichas, was shared between the two priests, the Caionas being assigned to Guerrero's parish and the Quichas to that of Mojica. Guerrero, however, demanded that the Quichas be taken out of Mojica's hands and incorporated into his own parish, for Mojica, he claimed, was unable to attend to the spiritual needs of these people in a satisfactory manner. In the first place, San Mateo, the seat of Mojica's parish, was four leagues distant from San Juan de Matucana, "along a pathway so harsh and dangerous that many people traveling to Cuzco and elsewhere in the highlands consider it a lesser inconvenience to make a long detour than to face the dangers and risks of the said four leagues."[9]

Guerrero claimed that this unfavorable situation had caused one of Mojica's parishioners to die without Christian confession, for the priest, being based in San Mateo, was too far away to be summoned in time.[10] Second, Guerrero argued, Mojica possessed far more parishioners than the maximum of 250 permitted by ecclesiastical legislation, for his parish incorporated approximately 400 tribute-paying adults.[11] By contrast, he insisted, his own parishioners were far fewer in number—less than 150 in total—while the seat of his parish was only one league distant from San Juan along a level and easy path.

Mojica, however, was quick to counter these charges. Insisting that pastoral care of the San Juan population had been divided between the two parishes ever since their creation, he denied that he was unable to fulfill his professional obligations and rejected the claim that the pathway along which he was obliged to travel was difficult and dangerous. On the contrary, he said, it was "very well-trodden and busy and may be traveled along easily and quickly without encountering the [said] inconveniences."[12] San Mateo, moreover, was only three leagues distant from San Juan, not four as stated by Guerrero. Not content with rejecting the accusations, Mojica turned the argument against his neighbor by identifying the geographical challenges that allegedly prevented the adequate performance of religious duties in Guerrero's own parish. Not only was the seat of his parish one and a half leagues from San Juan (instead of one as he had claimed), Guerrero was also responsible, Mojica revealed, for administering a third population that resided in a settlement called San Bartolomé de Soquicancha: "that [settlement] of San Bartolomé is three leagues distant from that of San Gerónimo and four and a half from that of the said *parcialidad* [the Caionas of San Juan], as it is one and a half leagues further on from San Gerónimo along an extremely bad path, and the said Bachelor [Guerrero] can barely fulfill his obligations, or provide the Indians with the necessary pastoral care."[13]

Indeed, Mojica insisted, if any changes were to be made to current arrangements, then the Caionas of San Juan should be taken out of Guerrero's hands and incorporated into his own parish, alongside the Quichas.[14] Somewhat predictably, Guerrero responded by contesting Mojica's calculations of the distances between the three settlements and by reiterating his initial claims about the terrible state of the pathways in his rival's parish, which were, he said, "the worst that are to be found in the world, for the difference between those of one and the other [parish] is well known to all."[15]

In defense of their respective claims and counterclaims, each priest presented witnesses, many of whom drew on their own personal experience of these routes in responding to questions regarding the state of the parish pathways and the logistics of traveling along them from one settlement to another. Presented as a witness in support of Guerrero's case, the priest Andrés Sánchez stated that, having worked in Mojica's parish in the past, he knew that the journey from San Mateo to San Juan was a great inconvenience. In fact, he said, the distance and dangerous state of the path caused him to arrive very late in San Juan whenever he traveled there to hold mass.[16] On the contrary, Mojica's witnesses insisted, his parish itinerary—unlike Guerrero's—was very gentle and could be effortlessly managed, allowing ample time for celebrating mass in both settlements on the same morning. These testimonies became a further point of contention for the priests in their struggle over the lived-in landscapes of Huarochirí: while Guerrero insisted that his geographical claims were proven by his witnesses' unanimous replies, Mojica retorted that "most of them have not seen the village of San Mateo nor have they traveled along the path that leads from this town to that of San Juan."[17]

The dispute not only triggered contradictory claims about the state of the parish pathways and the distances between settlements, but also brought to light subtle conflicts of opinion with regard to how the geography of a parish should be understood. Whereas Mojica portrayed the extent of Guerrero's parish in terms of the total number of leagues that the priest was obliged to travel in order to visit all three settlements in one day, Guerrero and his legal representative portrayed it as determined by the distances that separated the seat of the parish from its two satellites. In his concluding summary, Guerrero's representative insisted that his client's parish was "the most compact and short [in distance] of all those in the archbishopric that have more than one settlement," given that San Gerónimo was only two leagues distant from San Bartolomé and only one league from San Juan.[18]

Although a modern cartographic view was emerging in the New World (and Europe), alongside it—and often intertwined with it—were surviving medieval notions of geography and space, defined by mobility and distance.[19] Unquestionably, the latter notions dominated the testimonies of the two priests. The two litigants may have produced startlingly contradictory assertions about the nature of their respective parishes; nevertheless, their modes of geographic portrayal also shared a significant common ground. Both men, along with their respective witnesses, utilized a language of time, distance, and corporeal encounter that was founded, not on an incipient cartographic vision, but on the mobile, embodied, and local experiences of traveling the pathways of the parish. Padrón argues that the production of itinerary maps in colonial Spanish America may not have been stimulated by the specific experience of New World travel, for they carried forward a considerably older medieval tradition that had its roots in Europe.[20] In the production of their textual "itinerary maps," however, the priests' everyday experience of travel in their Huarochirí parishes played a vital role, for it was on this place-specific experience that each litigant ultimately staked the authenticity and validity of his claims.

✷   At its most fundamental, the dispute between Guerrero and Mojica involved a struggle over *people*—over the native parishioners who, for their priests, represented economic resources as well as souls in need of spiritual nourishment. Because ecclesiastical salaries increased in relation to the number of parishioners within each jurisdiction, parishes with large populations were the most lucrative and, inevitably, the most desirable.[21] From the priests' point of view, therefore, the indigenous inhabitants imbued the landscapes of Huarochirí with value, making the priests' lives there both possible and worthwhile through their presence as parishioners and by means of their productive labor.[22]

The decline of population in the San Gerónimo parish—as Mojica very pointedly commented—almost certainly underlay Guerrero's anxiety over his control of the San Juan population and persuaded him, after having spent numerous years in Huarochirí, to voice sudden concerns over the pastoral care of his neighbor's parishioners.[23] Guerrero, Mojica insisted, only had himself to blame for this demographic decline, for by treating his parishioners badly he had encouraged them to flee.[24] Reiterating this point more forcefully at a later stage in the proceedings, he argued that his neighbor's efforts to compel fugitives to return had proven impossible, "because they do not wish to return to the said parish, nor do they dare to do so." Moreover, he added, the Quichas of San Juan "are so fearful of coming under the authority of the said Antonio de Guerrero that they say and affirm that, if the said annexation were to be carried out, they would all flee like the rest have done."[25] The claims that Mojica made about the state of his rival's parish involved, then, the portrayal of landscapes that were the outcome of deficient priestly morality as well as of physical geography, for he interpreted the demography and spatial practices of its populations as direct consequences of Guerrero's abusive behavior.

Although Mojica portrayed the spatial practices of parishioners as a function of their priest's moral comportment, both his statements and those made by Guerrero reveal that the geographies of the parishes—and consequently the priests' own spatial practices and day-to-day experiences of landscape—were subtly yet significantly shaped by their parishioners' agency. A particularly striking example of such influence is provided by San Bartolomé, the third community for which Guerrero was responsible. Unlike the remaining settlements that featured in the priests' dispute, San Bartolomé had not been officially founded as a *reducción* in the Toledan era. Rather, it came into being—or was re-created—when Andeans from another neighboring parish, officially settled fifteen miles away in the village of San Damián de Checa, took up semipermanent residence there near the end of the sixteenth century in order to cultivate the land. Only retrospectively was it granted official status by the Spanish authorities, who, unable to control the Andeans' gradual return to traditional sites of residence and cultivation, accepted that unruly realities would have to be made to fit their neat administrative models.[26] The (re)establishment of a permanent indigenous community at San Bartolomé brought significant changes to the parish—not merely in terms of material presence, but also in terms of the priest's everyday engagements with the landscape, for it added several leagues of travel to his circuit.[27] Not surprisingly, Guerrero made no mention of the existence of San Bartolomé or of the fact that he was obliged to visit it on his parish rounds, until Mojica brought it to the attention of the ecclesiastical tribunal. Given the nature of his accusations against Mojica, it is not surprising that he was anxious to conceal this aspect of his everyday experience when he first initiated the legal proceedings.

Mojica may have considered priestly morality instrumental in shaping parishioners' spatial practices, yet he also believed that they enjoyed almost unrestrained physical mobility. In contrast to the priests, whose spatial movements were heavily constrained by the geographies of their jurisdiction, parishioners could choose to move elsewhere, inhibited neither by attachment to their place of residence nor by their assignment to a particular parish, for "they possess nothing except for their own persons and there is nothing that prevents them from moving from one place to another."[28] Needless to say, this claim belied the powerful ancestral bonds that tied many parishioners to the rural landscapes that surrounded them (if not to their *reducciones*), as well as to the communities to which they belonged. What his belief reveals, however, is the anxiety that the prospect of a parish landscape "emptied" of its human inhabitants produced among rural priests—an anxiety founded on the economic value with which those inhabitants imbued the landscape, and compounded, perhaps, by the priests' awareness of the physical and legal limitations on their own mobility.[29]

It may also have been the case that Andean (and other) residents of Huarochirí actively exploited the physical and jurisdictional constraints on their priests' mobility, not only by exercising their own ability to move elsewhere but by means of their activities within their assigned parishes. If Guerrero's claims can be given any credence, the Quichas of San Juan employed a conscious strategy for avoiding making confession, which took advantage of the geography of Mojica's parish and the time he required to complete the journey from San Mateo. When don Andrés was absent from San Juan, those Quichas who were on their deathbed purposely refused to confess with any other priest. On account of "the distance and difficulty of the path from the town of San Juan to the town of San Mateo," they knew that he would be unable to reach them in time, "and so," Guerrero claimed, "they die miserably."[30]

In the context of the parishioners' daily relations with Guerrero and Mojica, the constraints imposed on the latter by the physical environment and by the limits of their jurisdiction may well have acquired significance for those parishioners as a resource in negotiating the colonial geographies that had been forged with the creation of the *reducciones*. Where the priests were concerned, that same physical environment may well have been experienced as a significant obstacle and limiting factor in their effective control of their parish populations.

Over the course of the dispute, however, the parish landscapes took on particular significance for Guerrero and Mojica. Any acknowledgment of personal experiences that involved struggling along steep and perilous pathways represented a distinct disadvantage to their individual interests, given that the legal battle focused on their respective abilities to attend to all inhabitants of their parishes. Challenging terrain and extensive routes came to be associated with a potential loss of parishioners; in consequence, each litigant sought to emphasize the difficult nature of his rival's parish landscapes while drawing attention to the manageable nature of his own. Although the representations of Huarochirí's landscapes by the two men were inevitably influenced by the demands of their profession and the laws that (in theory) regulated clerics' activities in the archbishopric, they were also shaped by repeated experiences of traveling through them and, no less significantly, by the spatial practices of their parishioners. The continuing decline of population in Guerrero's parish probably was the catalyst in his decision to initiate legal proceedings and, in doing so, to regard the landscapes of his neighbor's parish in a new light: that is, as a valuable instrument in his quest to secure control of the Quichas of San Juan de Matucana.

No doubt exasperated by the deeply contradictory portrayals with which he was presented, the ecclesiastical judge who dealt with Guerrero's lawsuit determined that inspectors should visit the parishes to measure the distances between each settlement.[31] The final outcome, which is missing from the documentation, is in any case incidental to this discussion. My interest is in exploring the two priests' portrayals of Huarochirí's landscapes within the context of the dispute. The highly contingent way in which these landscapes mattered to Guerrero and Mojica can be seen with further clarity by comparing what the same landscapes signified for other representatives of the church and colonial administration, who worked in the province some decades earlier.

Trajectories of Suffering: The Jesuits in Huarochirí

In 1570, before the Toledan reduction of Huarochirí's scattered indigenous populations had been completed, the region was briefly evangelized by members of the Jesuit order, recently arrived in Peru. The reasons for the brevity of their stay in the province—a mere two years—are various and complex. Their withdrawal was largely precipitated by the incompatibility between the guiding principles of the Company of Jesus and the structure and organization of the rural parishes they were urged to take on,[32] but it might also be explained by a sense of disillusionment, expressed by some priests, vis-à-vis their success in evangelizing the local population.[33] As Hyland suggests, the physical hardships experienced by these early Jesuits also probably played some part in their speedy retreat. Their everyday labors proved so harsh and debilitating that many of those who were sent to Huarochirí soon sacrificed their health, and in the case of two priests, their lives.[34] Rather than dwell on the reasons for the Company's retreat from Huarochirí, however, I wish to outline, albeit briefly, how subsequent Jesuit accounts of this episode made strategic use of the first missionaries' encounters with the landscape, in ways that differed profoundly from the portrayals that Guerrero and Mojica would make in the following century.

Following the Jesuits' arrival in Peru, as an anonymous history of 1600 recounts,[35] the Company was requested by the archbishop of Lima and Viceroy Toledo to take charge of one of two rural districts—Lunaguana or Huarochirí—both of which suffered from a severe shortage of clergy. Whereas Lunaguana was "the most comfortable [district] that exists in that bishopric," the Huarochirí region was "almost inaccessible . . . because at that time the Indians lived according to their old customs, not in consolidated towns, but divided into communities, with three or four families living in one place and a similar number in another, separated by one, two, or more leagues."[36]

The province contained seventy-seven communities in all, scattered across an area of over twenty leagues. These were precariously connected by pathways that were "barely passable either on foot or on mule and the weather conditions so varied, that there were some communities in the harshest parts of the high moorland and others in very hot areas."[37] Seeing that both the need for spiritual care and the difficulties of providing it were so great in Huarochirí, the Jesuits took charge of this province instead of Lunaguana, "which was much less work and more comfortable."[38] At that time, the chronicle states, there were no more than two regular priests in the whole of Huarochirí, and in consequence the parishioners attended mass only once every six months, while many died without confession or even, in some cases, without ever having known Christianity at all.[39]

Despite the positive tone of some early reports about Jesuit activity in Huarochirí, the rapid abandonment of the province not only reflected the Company's lack of faith in this venture but also ensured that the venture would be regarded as a failure—indeed, as a betrayal—by church and government in both Peru and Spain.[40] By placing dramatic emphasis on the bodily suffering endured by the missionaries as they walked the pathways of Huarochirí, however, the anonymous chronicle recast it as a showcase for the Fathers' heroic disregard for physical and earthly comforts in their determination to implant Catholicism in the most remote Andean communities. The extreme physical and physiological challenges of the landscapes of Huarochirí were employed by the chronicle's authors to celebrate their order's resilience and to portray Jesuit missionaries as those most willing and able to bring Christian knowledge and devotion to inhospitable areas shunned by the secular clergy. Vivid descriptions of missionary itineraries that involved the negotiation of harsh natural environments feature prominently in Jesuit accounts of missionary ventures throughout Peru, so in this sense, the emphasis on corporeal suffering in Huarochirí is unremarkable.[41] However, given the aura of disillusionment that surrounded the Company's abandonment of the province, and the fact that rumors circulated about how "we do not venture out to that for which we have been sent, namely to the Indians,"[42] portrayals of ceaseless journeying and of struggles in and against Huarochirí's landscapes assumed a particularly significant role in Jesuit accounts of this episode.

The pathways of the province, experienced by the Jesuits on a daily basis, were portrayed as endless trajectories of suffering, stoically borne by men who have rejected all personal comfort in order to save souls: "No one can believe the sufferings borne by those priests unless they have seen for themselves those pathways and the variety of climates, for the majority are such that they can only be traversed on foot, and even then with great danger and intolerable difficulty, due to all the mud and pools of water and swamps and other extremely difficult passes."[43] A relentless mobility that took no account of distance, terrain, or weather was, the chronicler suggested, fundamental to the lives and labors of the Jesuits in Huarochirí. On many occasions, having received reports of a patient close to death, they would set off without delay in the snow or sun and even in the dead of night, traversing "those high moors and precipices that can hardly be crossed by day," in order to attend in good time to their charges' spiritual needs.[44]

These descriptions undoubtedly are reminiscent of the accounts of the bodily sufferings endured by conquistadors in hostile physical environments. Whereas the conquistadors offered up physical sufferings as a service to their monarch, the Jesuits portrayed them above all as evidence of their absolute devotion to the service of God. Given the Jesuits' rapid retreat from the province, these portrayals clearly may be interpreted as examples of what Pastor Bodmer, with reference to accounts of sixteenth-century conquests, terms the discourse of failure.[45] Nevertheless, the detailed descriptions of Jesuit itineraries were also intended to illuminate the special qualities that set Jesuits apart from other religious orders and, most particularly, from the secular clergy. For Guerrero and Mojica, it was imperative to suppress the difficulties involved in their own personal experiences of negotiating Huarochirí's pathways; for Jesuit chroniclers and historians, the theme of constant journeying along the viceroyalty's most arduous pathways offered a valuable means of portraying Peru's Jesuits as fearless and dedicated missionaries.[46]

The prominence of such struggles in the chronicle's account of Jesuit endeavors by no means indicated that the subsequent reordering of Huarochirí's places of habitation, through the creation of the Toledan *reducciones*, would be regarded in a negative light. Far from it. The Jesuits were directly involved in the creation of these colonial towns,[47] and their foundation is described by the chronicle in superlative terms as "the work that is most heroic and of greatest service to God that has been carried out amongst those Indians."[48] The towns' construction, however, marked the moment at which the Jesuits' work in Huarochirí was done: with their foundation, the chronicle declared, "those parishes became attractive to clerics, as the difficulties had been removed and they could now be comfortably managed by them."[49]

The Company's withdrawal from Huarochirí may be understood primarily as a response to irreconcilable contradictions and difficulties in their undertaking. By explaining this retreat in the light of the *reducciones*' foundation, however, the author of the chronicle was able to portray it as a mission that had been brought to a successful conclusion by the imposition of a new and easily managed spatial order. Having removed the need for the arduous journeys that they had stoically undertaken, the Jesuits could now embark on new and more challenging itineraries, "in traveling through the whole kingdom, preaching to and confessing the Indians in every village [pueblo], and teaching them as they are accustomed to do, helping their own [the Indians'] priests in this task."[50]

Authoring the Landscape

One of the self-proclaimed instruments in the transformation of the Huarochirí landscape was the *corregidor* Diego Dávila Briceño, who by 1586 had spent at least thirteen years working in the greater Yauyos province to which Huarochirí belonged. In that year, like other *corregidores* throughout Peru, he received a copy of the Council of the Indies' geographical questionnaire and (in contrast to many of his colleagues) produced a highly detailed account accompanied by a map (see fig. 8) of his jurisdiction.[51] It is worth examining this account—familiar to historians of Peru—not only because of the idiosyncracies that set it apart from other Peruvian *RG*s,[52] but also because it provides useful insight into how Huarochirí's landscapes took on distinctive meanings for a Spanish colonial official within the context of his work as a *corregidor* and as a respondent to the geographical questionnaire.

Having spent so many years in Huarochirí, Dávila Briceño had undoubtedly accumulated extensive experience of the province and its inhabitants. He apparently took the geographical questionnaire as an ideal opportunity to showcase his extensive knowledge of the province and, at the same time, to provide evidence of his exemplary services as *corregidor*. Although he insisted that every question had been answered in his response, Dávila chose to ignore official instructions that stipulated that each question should be answered individually and in the prescribed order. Instead, he produced a description of Huarochirí that was structured by an account of his own activities in forging a new and enduring colonial geography.

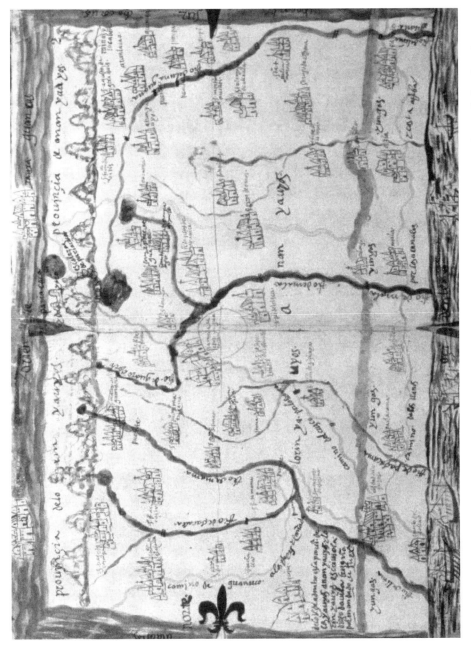

Fig. 8. Map of the Yauyos province drawn by Diego Dávila Briceño in 1586. Photo © Real Academia de la Historia, Madrid. Reprinted by permission.

His experience and knowledge of the province, Dávila proudly affirmed, was such that no one else could describe it as well as he,

> for I have measured it step by step, tearing down the old settlements, which were more than two hundred . . . and reducing it to the said thirty-nine villages, as it stands today and, God willing, will continue to stand. And in the said [text] all the questions in the instructions have been answered, because I, the said *corregidor* . . . have been in charge of the province for over fourteen years and have visited it to determine the tribute and to see if there still remained any little hamlet hidden away amidst the snowy peaks and the wilderness.[53]

Having provided a general overview of the dimensions and physical geographies of the province, Dávila went on to describe each of the five *repartimientos* of the Yauyos province,[54] repeatedly insisting that "I, the said *corregidor*" had destroyed the old places of habitation and founded the settlements that were currently inhabited. Rather like the religious who labored in Huarochirí before him, Dávila's account insisted that frequent and sustained travel was central to his everyday labors in the province. Above all, however, the purpose of his journeys to remote and scattered settlements was to remove their inhabitants from those sites and compel them to congregate in accessible locations that he had selected. In the first instance, then, his spatial practices within the province served to create a new colonial order. Oriented away from the native sacred topographies of the rural landscapes, this new order was focused on a hierarchy of settlements that began with the *reducciones* and culminated in the viceregal capital. Given that the town of Huarochirí was the site of the provincial capital at the time of the *reducciones* and hence the habitual place of residence of the *corregidor,* Dávila described his role in its foundation and that of the remaining six settlements of the *repartimiento* with particular pride: "This *repartimiento* is reduced into seven towns which I, the said *corregidor,* reduced and made into what they are today . . . building beautiful temples and hospitals and destroying all the old settlements and bringing the Indians to live in the said *reducción,* not just the ones in this town but all those in this province, and in this I have been greatly aided by the *cacique mayor* of this *repartimiento,* don Sebastian, who is fluent in our Spanish tongue and is a very intelligent man."[55]

Although acknowledging (on this one occasion) the assistance he received from an Andean leader in "reducing" the local populations, Dávila in general described the province of Huarochirí as in essence a landscape of his own creation.[56] If his account is to be believed, he intervened in virtually every sphere of life, even ensuring the provision of food supplies to the hospitals, teaching the art of blood-letting to the local people, and, during one term of office, assuming "the office of priest, preaching the Christian doctrine and baptizing and burying the dead."[57] Frequently obscured by his strident self-aggrandizement, Dávila's testimony nevertheless contains a sense of genuine attachment to and personal investment in the province—and particularly to the *repartimiento* of Huarochirí—that is strikingly absent in the geographical accounts provided by most *corregidores.*[58] Given his sustained efforts to transform the landscapes of Huarochirí, his attachment to those landscapes was almost proprietary in nature.

Dávila's desire for the permanence of the landscape he claimed to have forged almost single-handedly was clearly expressed in his observation that, at the time of writing, the thirty-nine *reducciones* he had created in the early 1570s were still in existence and, with God's assistance, would continue to exist in the future.[59] The *corregidor*'s desire for "his" landscape to be permanent may be interpreted as an early manifestation of the "universal fixity" that, Craib argues, is fundamental to all modern government.[60] In nineteenth-century Mexico, the pursuit of fixity was given particularly powerful expression in the form of state-sponsored cartographic projects with the (often elusive) promise of giving "space a stable signification, permitting it to be more effectively appropriated, transformed, and regulated."[61] In early colonial Peru, by contrast, cartography was still far from being attributed with the potent transformative and stabilizing powers that nineteenth-century statesmen believed it to hold; nevertheless, the sense of permanence and fixity that Dávila sought to attach to this landscape was emphasized, perhaps intentionally, by the map of the province that he submitted along with the text.[62] As we will see below, however, his cartographic vision of fixity was undermined by certain features of the map as well as by elements of the written account.

Identified by means of prominent ideograms, the *reducciones*—with the town of Huarochirí located at the very center—dominate the central portion of the map. A representation of Hispanic civic order, the map is simultaneously a portrayal of a newly established Christian order made visible in the crosses that mark each settlement's chapel and in the saintly prefixes of each place-name. Dávila's colonial towns, conveyed by means of a map that imitates the cartographic projections of Europe's professional geographers, become fixed in space and—with all traces of process suppressed within the image—are rendered permanent.[63]

The permanence in the spatial configurations of the landscape that Dávila so desired was not self-perpetuating. It had to be maintained by means of ongoing embodied *practice*—a situation that Dávila openly acknowledged by drawing attention to his repeated, post-reduction tours of duty of the province. The creation of the *reducciones* did not signal the end of his peregrinations to the "crags and *puna* and sierras and fortified places"[64] where the local populations once lived, for he was obliged to return to these places on a regular basis to ensure that no sites of habitation had been overlooked and, moreover, that no one had returned to their former homes.[65]

Fixity, however, implied not only preserving the landscape's material dimensions but also consolidating the particular meanings with which it had been invested. This required the redirection of the indigenous inhabitants' imaginative geographies, by directing these inhabitants both mentally and physically away from indigenous sacred spaces—the natural features of previously lived-in highland landscapes—and toward colonial urban space as the source of all spiritual and political authority.[66] In describing his repeated efforts to punish local people for continuing to make offerings to the mountain deities, Dávila provided evidence of his diligence in seeking to transform indigenous perceptions of the landscape. He portrayed the indigenous sacred topographies as features of a landscape that no longer existed. The peak of Pariacaca "*was* a famous place of devotion where the Indians made their sacrifices and worshipped, and even today they have not rid themselves of this: because it will be about four years ago, not much more, when I, the said *corregidor,* punished some *caciques* . . . and I confiscated from them four hundred heads of native livestock along with fourteen silver cups, with which they made their sacrifices."[67]

This historical past tense, however, may best be understood as an expression of desire rather than of reality, for it is followed by the author's recognition that the native inhabitants of Huarochirí continue to ascend to the peak of Pariacaca to pay tribute to the deity. Pariacaca is prominently visible at the top of the *corregidor*'s map—as a mountain peak but also as a native deity, for it bears the label *ydolo yaro* (the idol Yaro), an alternative name that, according to Dávila Briceño, was used by local people to refer to Pariacaca.[68] Dávila Briceño thus tacitly acknowledged the precarious and partial nature of his transformation of Huarochirí's landscapes by drawing attention to the unruly spatialities of the Andean inhabitants. Traveling in body as well as in spirit to the mountain-deity Pariacaca, they continuously challenged the colonial geographies he had labored so hard to cement.

❋ Dramatic reconfigurations of the region's human geographies took place long before the arrival of the Spanish. Like other areas of the Andes, Huarochirí experienced successive waves of migration for centuries before Europeans came on the scene, and, as a consequence, it was an arena of ongoing struggles that revolved around the control of water and cultivable land. Continued conflict played out between established groups and newcomers and between the respective inhabitants of distinct ecological zones.[69] Well into the colonial period, memories of these struggles were kept alive and interpreted by the native peoples of Huarochirí in the form of an evolving body of myths describing the exploits of the region's deities. At the instance of the Jesuit priest Francisco de Avila, the myths were recorded in Quechua around 1598 by an unknown Andean editor, ostensibly to assist the priest in his efforts to extirpate idolatries among his parishioners.[70] Although the myths were deeply rooted in the precolonial era, the manuscript was unavoidably and unmistakably a product of the colonial world. The traces of Spanish colonialism, perceptible in the linguistic and structural elements of the document, may also be detected in repeated references to the Toledan reduction settlements, to extirpation, and to the changing nature of indigenous religious practice in the province as a result of the Spanish presence.

At the same time, however, the myths' detailed tracing of the itineraries and exploits of Andean deities provides another eloquent illustration—this time the direct product of native testimony—of the partial and often superficial nature of Dávila Briceño's transformative efforts. The *corregidor* proudly described his dismantling of a major temple in the town of Mama, yet a decade later, for instance, the memory and significance of the deity Chaupi Ñamca was still deeply rooted in the consciousness of local people. Although the festivals and dances once performed in her honor no longer took place, she was still believed to be present in Mama, albeit beneath the surface of the earth: "Later on, when the Spaniards appeared on the scene, people hid Chaupi Ñamca, the five-armed stone, underground in Mama, near the Catholic priest's stable. She's there to this day, inside the earth."[71]

Tantalizing resonances connect the Huarochirí myths with Dávila Briceño's account and map. Most notably, these resonances may be found in the shared prominence of the mountain and deity Pariacaca in the Huarochirí document and in the *corregidor*'s text. The life and exploits of Pariacaca are absolutely central to the Andean manuscript, in terms of both the structural organization of the text and the ways in which it represents Huarochirí's past and the lives of its contemporary inhabitants. Chapter after chapter relates his origins, his conflicts with other deities, his acts of seduction, the feats of his offspring, and his interactions with the human communities that paid homage to him.[72] The towering peak that is both his dwelling place and his physical embodiment appears in the text repeatedly as a focal point of the Huarochirí people's geographical imagination as well as of their routes of pilgrimage. At the time of writing his account, Dávila Briceño indicated that Andean pilgrims continued to ascend the mountain of Pariacaca. According to the Huarochirí document, by the close of the sixteenth century this particular practice had ceased, no doubt as a result of Spanish efforts to eradicate so-called idolatries. Instead, the author of the manuscript explained, the inhabitants of the province now climbed a variety of neighboring peaks to conduct their rituals. The manuscript emphasized the disruption that was brought about by the Europeans, but it also indicated in no uncertain terms that Pariacaca continued to be a focal point of devotion and of indigenous movement, as new routes of pilgrimage were adopted: "Regarding all these places on mountains for worship of Paria Caca, it was only later on, when the Spaniards had emerged and came to look into it, that they were established."[73]

Given that the entire physical landscape of Huarochirí was—in the eyes of native inhabitants—molded and marked by the actions of Pariacaca, the legends surrounding the deity and his exploits were evoked no less by the agricultural landscapes of everyday life than by the dramatic features of high peaks and deeply-cut valleys. Making remarkably detailed reference to local topography, the Andean narrator explained that Pariacaca created the irrigation canals and fields in the vicinity of San Lorenzo de Quinti in his efforts to seduce a beautiful local woman named Chuqui Suso. In return for a canal that carried water directly from the river to her parched fields, the woman slept with him on a high mountain ledge.[74] Not long after she had done so, she turned to stone at the mouth of her canal, exclaiming: "Right in this canal of mine, that's where I'll stay!"[75] As the local people went about their everyday business in the landscapes described by the narrator, there can be little doubt that they recalled the stories about how they had been brought into being by the agency of their principal deity.

As we have already seen, Dávila Briceño described the cult of Pariacaca in the context of his efforts to eradicate and consign it to the past. In his vision of a newly ordered Christianized landscape centered on the *reducciones,* the deity had no legitimate place. Nevertheless, the towering mountain range that is associated with Pariacaca naturally occupies a position of striking prominence in the *corregidor*'s account. While the exploits of the deity are thematically central to the Andean narrative, the mountain range that bears his name is a pervasive and structuring presence in Dávila Briceño's descriptions of the region's physical geographies as well as its principal routes of communication. The province, he explains, is demarcated by "the very high snow-covered mountain range of Pariacaca"[76] that runs from north to south, and it is from this range that all the rivers that transect the province on their way to the sea descend. Describing the major rivers individually, Dávila Briceño repeatedly mentions their place of origin: "The largest river that descends from this province of Yauyos is the one that is known as Lunaguana.

It emerges at the foot of the high peak and saddle that compose the highest mountain of the said snow-covered range of Pariacaca; and on its western slopes, next to the foot of the stairway of Pariacaca, as it is known, because it is on the royal highway that goes from the city of Lima to the city of Cuzco and beyond, a big lake is formed, and from this the said river flows."[77]

Another river flows from a second lake created by meltwater from the snows of Pariacaca: although smaller than the Lunaguana, the Mala is renowned for supplying "the best water"[78] in the kingdom of Peru. Like the narrator of the Huarochirí manuscript, Dávila Briceño in his account acknowledges and conveys the vital importance of the high peaks as a source of water for the lands that lay to the west—in other words, as the origin of a scarce, life-giving, but at times also highly destructive force, which had long been at the center of human conflicts in the region. The significance of the rivers to human life in the province is also conveyed emphatically by his map, for their presence is marked by means of thick and heavy lines that dissect the map from top to bottom.

Although (as one would expect) Dávila Briceño rejected as idolatrous the web of myths and meanings that Andeans had woven around Pariacaca, the omnipresence of the mountain in his text was a tacit acknowledgment of its importance in the everyday lives and consciousness of the people. The mountain featured prominently in the *corregidor*'s own life in Huarochirí, partly in terms of the challenges that it presented to his efforts at Christianization, but also as a massive physical presence in the landscape of which he was keenly aware and that demarcated the eastern boundaries of his jurisdiction.

In the interstices of his text, as I have argued, Dávila Briceño tacitly acknowledged the impossibility of bringing about fixity in the meanings and spatial configurations of Huarochirí's landscapes. Yet he also conveyed a sincere and deeply rooted confidence in his knowledge of the landscape and in his own ability to reveal the meanings invested in it by the indigenous people. The writings of ecclesiastics who were involved in early-seventeenth-century campaigns to extirpate idolatry in Huarochirí and in neighboring provinces, in contrast, offer a glimpse of a very different relationship with landscape—a relationship in which all sense of familiarity and ease of interpretation were absent.

Landscapes Rendered Alien

In 1609 the priest Francisco de Avila dramatically declared that the native people of Huarochirí were still as idolatrous as they were on the day the Spaniards set foot in Peru. Avila's revelation, it appears, was not triggered by a sudden chance "discovery" of practices and beliefs to which he had previously been blind, but instead by a desire to assert his authority over his indigenous parishioners, who in 1607 had denounced him to the ecclesiastical tribunal for immoral behavior and economic exploitation.[79] For parish priests, the continuation of what the church deemed to be idolatrous practices was no secret: many, however, chose to turn a blind eye to the plethora of meanings that, through Andean belief, continued to animate the landscape. Nevertheless, the church authorities in Lima, along with many inspectors and missionaries who ventured into the highland provinces under the banner of the campaign, expressed what appeared to be genuine dismay at the prospect of rural landscapes still enlivened by sacred geographies that had been thought to belong to a rapidly fading past.[80]

In the 1580s, as we have seen, Dávila Briceño portrayed his repeated visits to the most remote areas of the province as necessary for the *maintenance* of an already established colonial order. As K. Mills observes, however, the journeys that were undertaken by seventeenth-century extirpators who ventured out from the *reducciones* in search of Andean sacred topographies were nothing less than an invasion "into an unconquered countryside," albeit late and imperfect, and "with the expectation of a retreat to the safety and order of their urban bases."[81] Beyond the colonial villages, which themselves harbored idolatries, lay a vast domain of mountains and *puna,* of rivers, lakes, and gullies, wherein the potential not only for sacrality but also for its concealment was apparently limitless. At times the extirpators explicitly conceptualized their journeys to such places as a second wave of conquest, but this was a conquest in which the landscape's formerly lucid text, for those who attempted to read it, was now obscure and open to doubt.

The goal of extirpation was to locate idols and sites of veneration so that they might be physically destroyed or symbolically stripped of their sacred significance through the planting of crosses. In their quest to destroy and Christianize native sites of worship, the religious—many of them Jesuits—once again ascended mountain peaks, along pathways so perilous that they risked their lives. In these places, wrote the Jesuit Fabián de Ayala in 1611, huge numbers of dead bodies were hidden, many of these probably disinterred from the Christian cemeteries below[82]—yet they were so carefully concealed that, without native assistance, they would never have been found.[83] Faced with prolific networks of deities and ancestors, who resided in the features of the natural landscape, the writings of priests and extirpators conveyed a growing sense of desperation at the need to scrutinize every detail of the terrain they traversed, as well as frustration at their own inability to reveal its secrets. In the same letter of 1611, Ayala described his experiences during an ecclesiastical inspection of Huarochirí. Initially, he said, there appeared to be little of note,

> because I could not see, nor discover, anything, but once the visit got under way, I saw so much, that I was astonished. First they took us to . . . [a] green meadow from where they all used to worship Pariacaca, Chaupiñamoca, and the other idols, and all the blood of the animals that they killed, and the *chicha* and other offerings they threw into a deep pit . . . and covered with a few tiles and with such artifice and concealment that nobody would have looked at it if they themselves had not revealed it, as happened to us, for we had it beneath our feet and did not know what it was.[84]

The extirpators' journey into the minute details of the landscape did not terminate at the surface but continued underground, as objects of sacred significance were literally unearthed. These idolatrous underground geographies were to be found not only in the countryside but also below the Andeans' very dwellings, which, Ayala reported, were all "riddled and filled with similar idols and with bones of their ancestors whom they worshipped and to whom they offered sacrifices."[85] The process of excavation brought to the attention of the extirpators perilous and previously ignored networks of meaning in the "vertical third dimension" of the subterranean.[86]

Added to the uncertainties of the underground and what it might conceal was the danger of inadvertently creating new sacred topographies by carelessly disposing of destroyed idols. The Jesuit Pablo Joseph de Arriaga warned that natives should be prevented from seeing where the remains were placed, for fear of creating new sites of worship: the Huaylas Indians, he said, worshipped at the bridge of Lima, "because there some of the *huacas* confiscated from them . . . had been thrown in the river."[87] Ironically, the proliferation of native sacred topographies that Spanish accounts appear to describe may, as Urioste suggests, have been a direct result of the very campaigns that sought to destroy them: in Huarochirí, the persecution of idolatry coincided with the multiplication of sites of worship dedicated to the regional deity Pariacaca.[88]

In 1621, Arriaga wrote a manual entitled *La extirpación de la idolatría* (The Extirpation of Idolatry), which gave practical advice to priests in their struggle against idolatry.[89] Included within this text was a questionnaire, which for many years was used by priests in their efforts to locate and destroy the landscape's sacred geographies. What is the name of the principal idol, it asks? Is it a peak, a cliff, or a small stone? Does it have children who are also stones, a father, a brother, or a wife? Which idols are worshipped for the fields, which for the maize, the potatoes, and the livestock?[90] While mummified bodies and small portable objects such as figurines, pebbles, or shells could be burned or smashed—this was standard practice during ecclesiastical inspections—the extirpators stood helpless before the physical landscape. The only solution was to plant crosses in a symbolic act of extirpation and reconsecration: although descriptions of this act were often clothed in triumphant rhetoric, such language overlay, as Mills suggests, "a sense of futility before an insurmountable problem."[91] Once again, the extirpators' act of planting crosses may be understood as the expression of an impossible desire to "fix" the landscape,[92] not only in terms of its material characteristics and spatial organization, but also with regard to the meanings that they wished it to contain.

In the anonymous history of 1600, Jesuit activities in late-sixteenth-century Huarochirí are conveyed as a struggle with landscape that was overwhelmingly physical in nature. Keenly aware that the landscape was replete with sacred significance for its native inhabitants, the early Jesuit missionaries made use of the persuasive power of bilingual *mestizos* in order to bring to light and destroy these sacred geographies.[93] The greatest challenges that the landscapes of Huarochirí presented to them, however, lay less in the uncovering and extirpating of illicit meanings than in the perils of negotiating harsh terrain and inhospitable climates. Difficult journeys into remote highland areas were just as central to the experience of the seventeenth-century extirpators of idolatry as they were to the first Jesuits who labored in Huarochirí. In the writings of these later extirpators, however, the physical dimensions of their struggles against the landscape were greatly overshadowed by their frustrated efforts to map and control its diverse and shifting networks of sacrality. Relentless travel and the physical endurance it required were highlighted but no longer portrayed as the greatest hurdle to be overcome: instead, this now consisted in revealing the properties of a landscape that seemed treacherously resistant to discovery and control.

As the extirpators' own testimonies reveal, the cause of their anxieties was the Andeans' unshakeable belief in the landscape's sacred qualities, as well as their spiritual resourcefulness in the face of material destruction.[94] Knowledge of these sacred geographies and the physical unearthing and destruction of idols were dependent on verbal disclosure by the Andean people, as priests themselves admitted. Conscious strategies were developed to achieve this: as Spalding shows with reference to investigations carried out in Huarochirí in the 1660s, officials did not hesitate to exploit personal rivalries and rifts both between and within Andean communities as a means of extracting information that could be used to make further denunciations.[95]

Once again, however, these colonial struggles over sacred geographies in Huarochirí and other rural provinces involved more than a clash between Andeans and ecclesiastics. For some parish priests, the extirpation campaigns allowed the sacred geographies that criss-crossed their parishes to be transformed into a valuable bargaining chip, which they could use, as Avila had done, in local struggles over power and resources.[96] Other clerics, however, were decidedly hostile to the activities of extirpators and on occasion appear to have colluded with Andean communities in concealing "idolatrous" geographies from inspectors' eyes. In 1626, for example, Archbishop Gonzalo de Campo informed the king of a certain priest named Francisco de Rivera, whose parish of Bombón was allegedly full of "idolatry and heresy." Rivera "attended not to this [his pastoral duties] but to money-making and other inappropriate things, and not only did he do this, he also defended don Felipe, *cacique* of the parish, who was the captain of idolatry and the greatest heretic of all, and he covered over for him, beseeching all the Indians not to denounce him when I come."[97]

While such purposeful concealment may have constituted an alternative strategy for securing power and economic benefits within the local community, it may also have reflected the angry response of individual priests to what they regarded as a shameful intrusion on their territory by outsiders and an affront to their authority and reputation. In either case, instances of collusion suggest that priests' personal interests may at times have encouraged or demanded the concealment of native sacred geographies from those who sought to destroy them. Not only the Andeans, therefore, but also on occasion their priests played what might be described as games of revealing and concealing with the extirpators: games determined, on the one hand, by each clergyman's relationship with the native community and, on the other, by his relationship with the church authorities. Granted that official anxieties had emerged about what Peru and its inhabitants ought to be like after almost one hundred years of Spanish rule, it is clear that those who obstructed the creation and perpetuation of ordered Catholic landscapes as envisaged by Toledo and the crown embraced not only the colonized but also many of the agents of colonial government.

Ironically, the very individuals who were expected to help restore Catholic order in the countryside, namely, the inspectors of idolatry, were sometimes suspected of subverting this objective. These suspicions appear with particular clarity in an interrogatory prepared in 1622, which was directed at Andean parishioners and used to investigate the actions of the extirpators who had recently inspected their communities.[98] The possibility of inspectors' collusion with the Andeans and failure to carry out their duties is a central concern of this questionnaire: the sheer number of questions that address this issue—eight out of twenty-six— eloquently conveys the depth of concern. Several questions deal with concealment: Did the inspectors fail to inventory, as they were obliged to, any idols or objects recovered from burial sites, particularly those of material value? Another question asks if they destroyed the sites of worship and planted crosses in their place, or "if they failed to do so for certain purposes or reasons."[99]

Question 25 raises the possibility that games of collusion for personal profit were more complex, for it concerns not the actions of the inspectors but rather those of their servants and assistants, who in turn are suspected of deceiving the inspectors. It asks the parishioners "if they know whether the servants of the said inspectors and other hangers-on sold idols and other things to the said Indians so that the Indians, in order to please and satisfy the said inspectors, could display them saying that they were the idols that they worshipped or were related to their cult."[100]

Such fears, of course, were not unique to the extirpation campaigns in Huarochirí, but were applied to the activities of extirpators throughout the Archbishopric of Lima and beyond. Apparently, neither the outward appearance of these rural landscapes nor the texts that claimed to map and elucidate their meanings could be trusted by the church leaders in Lima who ordered the investigation to be carried out. The uncovering of one set of illicit practices that shaped the landscape and its meanings—the Andean rituals that kept alive diverse sacred topographies—simply led to the discovery (or suspicion) of yet more, in a disconcerting process that led from the Andeans to the very ranks of church and government.

In the mid-1620s, Gonzalo de Campo arrived in Lima as the newly appointed archbishop. In view of the confused and contradictory reports that he had received about the spiritual state of Lima's rural provinces, he concluded that he could establish their veracity only by inspecting these territories himself. As if on a mission to gather information about a little-known frontier, he undertook the arduous task of traversing on muleback "great mountain ranges and precipices with a variety of climates and high plateaus and strange diseases"[101] in order, he stated, to determine the truth about native idolatries. Not content with inspecting each place once, he usually journeyed "along the same route twice . . . so that there remains no corner that I have not visited."[102] Having carried out this "very burdensome and difficult task," he confirmed that there was no shortage of idolatrous practices and beliefs wherever he went, "and in some [places] almost all the inhabitants are contaminated, and [by] idolatries and heresies of the worst kind, so that some believe absolutely nothing of the mysteries of our sacred Catholic faith, and in their heart they secretly deride and mock them."[103]

A few years later, in 1630, the specter of idolatry was conspicuous only by its absence in the documentation produced by Guerrero and Mojica, as they struggled for control over the human geographies of Huarochirí. In part, this may have reflected the aftermath of a vigorous and often violent process of extirpation, which succeeded in suppressing the more visible manifestations of Andean devotion to traditional deities. However, it may also have reflected these two priests' fundamental lack of interest in the question of native sacred geographies, perhaps even their active hostility toward extirpation or, at the very least, their conviction that it was irrelevant to their dispute. Notwithstanding their mutual accusations about inadequate spiritual provision and devious, poorly taught parishioners who sought to evade confession, the priests portrayed a landscape that was fundamentally Christian and domesticated, and strictly subject to the ecclesiastical laws and provisions of the archbishopric. Each priest's account of the arduous pathways in his rival's parish undoubtedly echoed the archbishop's descriptions of a perilous itinerary through the rural hinterland. However, whereas the prelate's journey appeared to lead through an alien landscape that still resembled a frontier nearly a century after the conquest, the quarrelling priests' itineraries were firmly located within the realms of the familiar and the mundane.

�; If any point of commonality connected the missionaries, *corregidores,* priests, and extirpators who visited and worked in Huarochirí over the years, it was their experiences of travel along the pathways of the province, either by mule or on foot. Determined, on the one hand, by professional demands and personal objectives, these experiences were variously shaped, on the other hand, by the spatial practices of local people and their shifting sacred geographies. Administrative officials and ecclesiastics alike expressed a desire to "fix" the landscapes of Huarochirí, that is, to embed within them European meanings and spatialities.

As this chapter illustrates, however, their writings reveal the conviction that the desired meaning and spatial order would—somewhat paradoxically—be achieved through mobility and embodied practice rather than through the production of textual or visual maps. Huarochirí's landscapes, and especially its sacred geographies, were mapped repeatedly and in ever greater detail in the late sixteenth and early seventeenth centuries. Such mapping may have been intended to make the landscape visible and known, yet it was the *corregidores'* tours of duty, the priestly parish rounds, and the visits of archbishops and inspectors of idolatry that, in early colonial Peru, seemed to hold the (impossible) promise of enduring fixity.

The meanings that the landscapes of the province came to hold for representatives of colonial rule, and the ways in which they portrayed these landscapes, were far from being unitary or predetermined. Thus, the challenging terrain and the everyday experiences of negotiating it were variously regarded as assets and as hindrances; native sacred geographies were at times ignored, at times pragmatically used in pursuit of power and economic gain, and at times viewed with genuine alarm as evidence of the disintegration of colonial control. Most compellingly, perhaps, accounts of Huarochirí surveyed here present a challenge to the notion of a neat and coherent progression from landscapes perceived as beyond the boundaries of colonial knowledge and control to ones that, comprehensively mapped, described, and physically transformed, lay firmly within those boundaries. For some representatives of colonial rule, the landscapes of Lima's hinterland became increasingly treacherous with the passage of time—if not in terms of their pathways, then certainly with regard to the ease with which they could be comprehended and controlled.

For others, in contrast, the landscapes of Huarochirí became deeply familiar, lived-in ones, closely interwoven with the fabric of their everyday lives and experiences. While this may appear to state the obvious, it is all too easy, for instance, to interpret Dávila Briceño's textual and cartographic representation of Huarochirí as a triumphal account of colonial desire and transformation, thus placing him discursively in the same "locus of enunciation" as the viceroy in Lima and the Council of the Indies' officials in Spain. Although clearly conveying his enthusiasm

for rigorously implementing Toledan policy, Dávila's account simultaneously reveals a genuine sense of local attachment, expressed primarily
in the guise of authorship and unrivaled knowledge, which developed
from the prolonged nature of his stay and his profound involvement
in the affairs of the province and its people.

For Guerrero and Mojica, too, Huarochirí became an intimately
known, lived-in landscape. By 1630 both men had spent at least a decade
in their neighboring parishes. Although they located their arguments
within a framework of ecclesiastical legislation constructed in Lima, the
origins of their dispute and their geographical assertions were firmly
located within the realm of local relations, negotiations, and mundane
experience. Above all, this dimension of prolonged local entanglement
united the priests' experiences and perceptions of Huarochirí—despite
their vigorous disagreements—and set them apart from the experiences
of visiting archbishops and inspectors of idolatry, who portrayed Lima's
rural hinterlands as almost indomitably alien and unruly.

By the mid-seventeenth century, Lavallé argues, Lima's *criollo* élite
for the most part had turned its back on the vast and seemingly un-
knowable rural provinces beyond the boundaries of the viceregal city.
Although these American-born Spaniards utilized New World nature
and geography as a means of expressing and celebrating their American identity, the Peru that was portrayed in their florid descriptions was
entirely confined to the urban spaces they inhabited, and above all to
Lima.[104] This narrow geographical vision contained no place for the
mountains or coastal deserts of Peru, much less for the tropical forests
that lay to the east of the Andes. For others, however, the distant Amazon lowlands still held profound promise as a space of conquest and
colonization.

FIVE

Negotiating Amazonia

The Accounts of Juan Recio de León

The first foundations of Spanish control had barely been established in the Peruvian highlands when new expeditions of conquest headed eastward toward the Amazon frontier. Propelled by the spectacular success of the Peruvian campaigns and by rumors of wealthy polities beyond the Andes, wave after wave of would-be conquistadors left Quito, Cuzco, and the embryonic *Audiencia* of Charcas to make the vertiginous descent into the jungle. Failure to find the promised wealth did not bring the Spanish explorations to a halt but resulted instead in an ongoing geographical displacement of the search for elusive Amazonian marvels. In the northern Amazon basin, the search for El Dorado migrated steadily westward toward Guiana, eventually becoming entangled with reports of the no less elusive kingdoms of Paititi and Moxos, which were anxiously pursued in the lowlands from Paraguay to Peru. Although Amazonian ventures of a military nature had largely been suspended by the end of the seventeenth century, the reports of such kingdoms lived on into the Bourbon era, as missionaries strove to penetrate the lowland regions that had defeated their secular predecessors.

The astonishing force with which tales of El Dorado, Paititi, and other marvelous locations or beings took hold among the Spanish has been a persistent theme in scholarly as well as popular discussions of the myths and their complex genealogies since the nineteenth century.[1] Even a cursory survey of the best-known accounts of exploration in South America's tropical lowlands reveals that the prominence of these mythical sites and figures in Spanish imaginative geographies of the New World cannot be questioned. However, as illustrated by a growing number of in-depth studies of exploratory and colonizing ventures in Amazonia and its western frontiers, reports of El Dorado and Paititi did not constitute the only dimension of Spanish accounts of or interest in these regions.[2]

By focusing on early-seventeenth-century endeavors to colonize the Amazon territories bordering on Upper Peru, this chapter inevitably touches on the search for Paititi; primarily, however, its purpose is to explore a much broader array of discourses about the tropical lowlands that emerged in colonial writings. Building on existing studies, I argue that colonial accounts of the Amazon were not merely the predictable products of a set of myths to which their authors had supposedly fallen victim, but instead emerged from an ongoing process of negotiation between those authors' own objectives and the interests of the royal and viceregal authorities to whom they appealed.

In particular, this chapter focuses on a series of petitions and reports produced in the early seventeenth century by Juan Recio de León, a *maestre de campo* who sought with great persistence to obtain royal backing for a colonizing venture in what is now the Bolivian Amazon. Submitted to the Council of the Indies between 1623 and 1627, these petitions bear witness to the fact that Recio continuously reworked his portrayals of Amazonia and his proposed plans for colonization within the ever-changing setting of official interests and concerns. By examining Recio's representational strategies, it is possible to apprehend the contingent and improvisatory manner in which his portrayals of the Amazon were constructed. At the same time, his case is a fascinating example of how, within the spaces of Madrid and its royal court, individual petitioners sought to harness for their own ends metropolitan interests and networks of knowledge about the New World.

Discourse and the Spaces of Opportunism

The process by which rumors of peoples and places of unlimited wealth in Amazonia were disseminated in the sixteenth century has repeatedly been likened to the rampant spread of a contagious disease, to which the Spaniards quickly succumbed. Numerous studies have viewed these myths as products of a credulity and lack of a sense of reality that were fostered by medieval tales of chivalry.[3] More nuanced analyses suggest that they emerged either from a "mythical predisposition" that was allowed to flourish, in the manner of a contagion, by conditions encountered in certain areas of the New World,[4] or else from an apprehension of reality that was propelled by desire.[5] At the same time, the important role of indigenous peoples in the dissemination of myths about the Amazon regions is clearly recognized in historical and anthropological scholarship: Europeans arrived in the Americas with ready-made expectations of finding opulent wealth, and their hopes were sustained, first by the conquest of the Aztec and Inca empires, and second, by ongoing encounters and communications with the native inhabitants of Amazonia.[6]

Contemporary scholars from various disciplinary backgrounds justifiably share the recognition that the formation and dissemination of myths about Amazonia were phenomena that cannot be understood at the level of individual actions and beliefs; as Ette would have it, the intrinsic and overwhelming power of the myths was such that they brought about "the paralysis of any form of independent action."[7] Spanish accounts and perceptions of the Amazon (and other areas of the Americas) must surely be regarded as the outcome of *collective* processes—including both the expression of a shared desire[8] and encounters with indigenous peoples.

The forces that shaped accounts of the Amazon regions (along with other regions of the New World) must also be sought, however, in the bodies of Spanish law that were intended to regulate the implementation of conquest and colonization.[9] Although legislation did little to change or determine practices on the ground, it played an increasingly prominent role, as Rabasa suggests, in molding the format and content of texts that proposed or described exploratory and colonizing ventures.[10] By the late sixteenth century, he argues, the production of knowledge had become so thoroughly systematized by means of royal legislation that all *relaciones* reflected "a common pattern and organization of topics in their evaluation and description of the land."[11] Whether produced by those who sought contracts for new ventures or by those to whom such contracts had already been granted, portrayals of the New World territories were inextricably bound up with, and created in response to, the requirements of royal laws.

Although authors were obliged to produce their accounts of the Indies within the parameters of Spanish legislation and royal interests, they were by no means bereft of the capacity for autonomous or spontaneous action. Drawing on the work of the anthropologist Dorothy Holland and her associates, I will stress the improvisatory and opportunistic ways in which prominent discourses were put to use by individuals who, like Recio, sought royal favor and support. In reflecting on the nature of the relationship between individuals' actions and the social and cultural contexts within which these are deployed, Holland and her co-authors suggest that "individually and collectively, [we] are not just products of our culture, not just respondents to the situation, but also and critically appropriators of cultural artifacts that we and others produce."[12] Consequently, discourses do not constitute "indicators of essential features or themes of the cultures in which they work," but function instead as resources, as "social tools."[13] Although individuals are obliged to make use of these preexisting tools, they select those that best serve their purposes and "piece together cultural resources *opportunistically* to address present conditions and problems."[14] Through such practical appropriation, the tools themselves are not only made to endure but are gradually reshaped.

These ideas, I suggest, provide a useful theoretical framework for thinking about the production of Spanish accounts of the New World, including those of South America's tropical lowlands. After all, the opportunistic use of dominant discourses and interests—especially those of the crown—characterized Spanish writings from the earliest moments of exploration and colonization; it is evident, for example, in Hernán Cortés's letters to Charles V. As Pastor Bodmer demonstrates, the conqueror of Mexico deftly (and successfully) put to use the concept and rhetoric of the loyal vassal in order to justify his rebellion against the governor of Cuba, who, far from authorizing a full-scale expedition of conquest and colonization, had merely instructed Cortés to carry out a brief intelligence-gathering mission to the mainland.[15] Opportunism, moreover, was not simply the preserve of narratives of exploration and conquest but was tightly woven into the fabric of everyday colonial life. As illustrated in the previous chapter, for instance, the squabbling parish priests of Huarochirí appropriated the discursive framework offered by ecclesiastical legislation in their struggle to lay claim to the parishioners of San Juan de Matucana.

If we conceptualize the myths of El Dorado and Paititi as discursive *resources* rather than as epidemics or contagions, it becomes easier to recognize that petitioners such as Recio were able to identify and draw opportunistically on a *range* of discursive tools in the pursuit of personal interests and goals. The nature of their discursive resources, however, and the ways in which they could be used to produce portrayals of the Amazon, were not uniform across space but modulated by geographical location and the social networks to which individuals had access.[16] As demonstrated by critical studies of the history of science, for example, scientific discourses are always and inevitably shaped by the geographical and social spaces in which they are produced, as well as by the networks of communication and exchange that extend outward from those spaces, connecting them with other sites of production.[17] Juan Recio's portrayals of Amazonia and his proposals for its colonization were not produced, of course, with a view to advancing scientific knowledge about the South American interior. In examining his writings, it is nevertheless important to take account of the spaces within which he produced them, for they played a crucial role in shaping his discursive strategies.

Spiritual Salvation and Material Gain—Recio's Account of Services

In 1622, Juan Recio de León arrived in Spain to present a petition that documented a highly eventful Indies career.[18] Most important, however, it described a venture on which he embarked in 1620 and which led him back to Spain in search of financial backing and reward. Arriving in

Cartagena in 1604, by 1620 he had become *justicia mayor* and deputy to the *corregidor* of the Omasuyos province, on the northern shores of Lake Titicaca.[19] Apparently having heard of Recio's numerous services to the crown, Pedro de Leáegui Urquiza, governor of the as yet unpacified province of Chunchos, Paititi, and Dorados, made his way to Omasuyos that same year to request Recio's help in reconstructing an abandoned frontier settlement. In 1615, Leáegui had led two expeditions into Upper Peru's frontier territories and there founded the towns of Nuestra Señora de Guadalupe and San Juan de Sahagún.[20] The first of these, which lay farther into unpacified territory in the Apolobamba valley, was soon evacuated because reinforcements and food supplies failed to arrive on time.

In return for Recio's assistance, Leáegui offered him the titles of *maestre de campo, teniente de gobernador* (deputy governor), *capitán general,* and *justicia mayor* of the unconquered provinces. Accepting the post, Recio spent large sums of money organizing and outfitting a new expedition, which departed in June 1620. Within less than a year, according to his account, he had successfully secured the alliance of the previously hostile Aguachiles and Lecos peoples,[21] reestablished the settlement of Guadalupe, and explored deep into unknown tropical territory along the Diabeni (now Beni) river (see fig. 9).

Leáegui's project initially had enjoyed the cautious endorsement of Viceroy Esquilache; while admitting in correspondence with the king that it appeared to promise little in the way of revenue for the royal coffers, the viceroy pointed out that gradual progress was being made in missionary work, and this, he urged, had to be regarded as "the principal concern."[22] By the time the viceroy's period of office ended in 1621, however, he had decided to withdraw his support for any further activities of a military nature, on the basis of complaints about the damage that Leáegui's first expedition had caused six years earlier.[23] In 1621, Recio returned to Peru in search of four captains who had been instructed to muster new recruits. On arriving in Cuzco, however, he discovered that they had failed in this endeavor, having been prohibited by the viceroy from publicly advertising Leáegui's venture. Undeterred, Recio traveled to Lima, where he presented his case to the Royal Audience but to no avail. All he was granted were the living expenses for five friars and permission to travel to Spain in pursuit of his cause.[24]

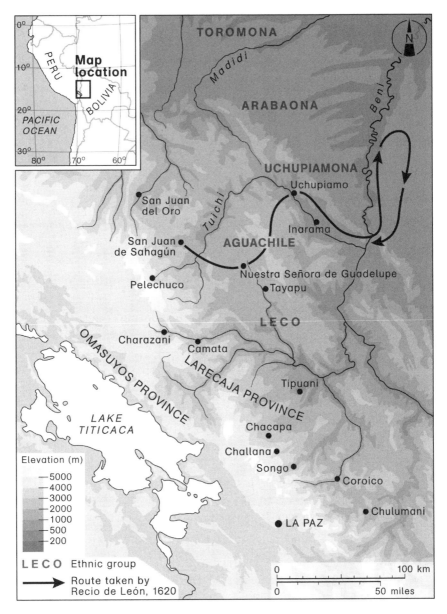

Fig. 9. The Amazon frontier regions to the north of La Paz and Juan Recio de León's route of exploration in 1620.

Following Recio's appeal to the *Audiencia* of Lima, its *oidores* informed the king that they had rejected his petitions and, moreover, advised the monarch "to order that his papers and accounts be examined with care, for those who undertake these expeditions always make them appear easier than they are, and promise a lot but achieve little."[25] Invoking royal legislation on discoveries and colonization, the *audiencia* judges insisted that, as far as possible, the pacification of unconverted peoples be carried out by means of evangelization, for—echoing the words of the viceroy—"truly this is what matters most."[26] In the language employed by colonial government and crown, the terms "conversion" and "pacification" had largely come to replace "conquest," reflecting not only moral unease but also concerns about the damage that large-scale military expeditions inevitably brought to the shrinking native populations.[27] Besides the fact that Recio's project had been preceded by countless other chimerical ventures into the Amazon, growing pressures on the colonial administration to supply the monarchy with urgently needed revenue helped to ensure that the government's appetite for supporting further expeditions was limited.[28] Recio could hardly have known about the *audiencia*'s letter, yet he was clearly aware of the immense difficulties he would face in obtaining backing for his project. Once in Madrid, however, he displayed striking tenacity and optimism in pursuing his goal.

Recio's account of services, presented to the monarch and forwarded to the Council of the Indies shortly after his arrival in Madrid in 1622, reveals the fervor with which he, like many of his contemporaries, sought to portray himself as a model colonizer who faithfully obeyed royal legislation on the discovery and settlement of new lands.[29] With complaints about the destructive behavior of expeditionaries in 1615 no doubt fresh in his mind, Recio insisted that his own foray into unpacified territory, in the company of thirty soldiers, twenty-five auxiliaries, and numerous mules and livestock, was carried out "without any Indian or Spaniard being wronged in any way."[30] Above all, he represented his role in Leáegui's venture as one that involved reconstruction and the prudent nurture of carefully laid foundations. Not only could he justly refer to himself as the *reedificador* (reconstructor) of Guadalupe, his account suggested, but thanks to his provision of supplies to the needy colonists in San Juan de Sahagún—generously paid for out of his own pocket—he ensured the continued survival and development of the precarious frontier settlement.

Banishing all references to "conquest" from his account, Recio embraced with enthusiasm the discourse of conversion and spiritual salvation that had attained prominence in official correspondence. Portraying a dramatic frontier encounter at San Juan de Sahagún with twelve *caciques* from the lowlands, he emphatically located his activities within the sphere of peaceful missionary endeavors. The twelve had apparently come to speak to Recio in the name of Zelipa, leader of the Chunchos people,[31] to request assistance in defending his people against four enemy provinces. In return, Recio claimed, they offered to become Christians and vassals of the Spanish monarch and refused to return home without missionaries. Before departing, the Augustinian friars who agreed to accompany the *caciques* to their homelands turned to Recio and beseeched him "to open up the pathways as far as the area we inhabit so that, assured of your proximity to us, we are consoled; see . . . that as a man in whom such confidence is placed in all these kingdoms, you do not fail to follow us for the love of God, and that you do not permit what has happened on so many other occasions, when others have attempted this and then given up, which has prevented God from being served in any way whatsoever."[32]

Recio contested the growing hostility of crown and viceregal government to expansionist adventures precisely by invoking the discourse of conversion, arguing that by bringing his colonization plan to a halt, God would not be served. Earlier unsuccessful expeditions were portrayed not as missed opportunities for territorial expansion but as tragically aborted attempts to bring to the natives the word of God they so strongly desired.[33] Toward the end of the document, Recio once again rejected the very notion of conquest by insisting that the native people had not attempted to impede entry into their territories but, on the contrary, had repeatedly requested missionaries and the friendship and protection of the Spaniards.[34]

Contradictions lay at the very heart of Spanish theories of empire in the fraught yet inevitable coupling of spiritual and material aims. Recio's petition was obliged to reproduce those contradictions and to speak not only to the crown's religious and humanitarian pretensions but to its economic interests and needs. It is hardly surprising, then, that the conquest's most pervasive motif—the promise of abundant gold and silver—took its place alongside the religious rhetoric, inevitably adding to the account a current of violence that flowed just below the surface. Guarding either end of the Apolobamba valley containing the settlement of Guadalupe stood two mountains, Recio explained, one full of gold and the other full of silver. He envisaged a future landscape of abundant and productive mines, "so rich and powerful that from this moment onward your Majesty may enjoy greatly augmented and copious income,"[35] and drew on and adapted to his ends contemporary theories about the formation of metals to transform the frontier provinces into areas of fabulous and as yet unexploited wealth.

Although early modern opinions differed considerably on this matter, the qualities and formation of gold were frequently associated with the sun and the effects of its rays on the earth below. In addition to possessing a natural affinity with the sun, as reflected in its splendor and excellence, gold—argued the physician Juan de Cárdenas in 1591—demonstrates a tendency to ascend toward the surface of the earth, attracted by the warmth and light of its "familiar planet," and is therefore often to be found in very hot, dry lands.[36] Recio appropriated this argument about the sun's influence on the occurrence of gold and extended it to silver and other metals.[37] Given that Peru's most important mines were situated on the eastern slopes of the Andean cordillera, he argued, even greater riches would be found in the tropical lowlands beyond, "for we are certain that the sun produces gold, silver, and the other types of metal: from this may be inferred that in the eastern regions the land will be the richest and most powerful . . . as in those parts where the sun reigns with particular vigor."[38]

Toward the end of his account, Recio composed a list of the resources that he believed necessary in order to convert his proposal into reality. These included a sum of 200,000 ducats for a period of four years to pay for the basic necessities of Spanish settlers, allowing them to cultivate the land and establish mines. Undercutting his earlier efforts to deny the venture any association with invasion and exploitation, the account quietly slipped at this point into the pragmatic language of planned conquest, specifying the need for supplies of soldiers, muskets, and crossbows. Just as the current of violence now bubbled to the surface, so too—despite Recio's emphatic declarations to the contrary—did his undeniable self-interest. On the grounds that the area would serve as an entry point for settlers on their way to the frontier, he requested the post of *corregidor* of the Larecaja province for a period of six years.[39] He also laid provisional claim to the governorship of the unconquered provinces, requesting that it be entrusted to him "if the Governor [Leáegui] should die in the time that I spend returning from these kingdoms [Spain] to those [Peru], or if he has not sustained the town of Nuestra Señora de Guadalupe in the state that I left it, or as a result of any other personal impediments."[40] On July 14, 1623, Recio's request for financial assistance, along with the *corregimiento* of Larecaja and everything else he had petitioned for, was rejected by the Council of the Indies, which decreed that he should again present his documents to the viceroy of Peru. Undeterred, he promptly resubmitted his petition along with a lengthy geographical description dated October 1623.[41]

The twin themes of spiritual salvation and material gain are strongly reiterated in Recio's geographical description, which offered a profusion of details about the peoples and natural resources of the lands that he visited, as well as an account of his journey. The abundant native populations were anxious for spiritual salvation, and their territories—extending from the forested foothills of the Andes to the lowlands of the Beni river and beyond—were rich not only in silver and gold but also in spices, amber, precious woods, fertile pastures, and forests filled with game. This was a land of plenty, inhabited, moreover, by "extremely appreciative people, gaily dressed and clean and diversely colored, some being dark and [some] white, and others so blonde that they are shortsighted."[42]

Claiming that he was welcomed by the peoples who inhabited the plains to the east of the Tuichi river, Recio availed himself of their geographical knowledge as well as of their hospitality. Beyond the confluence of the Diabeni and Manú (Madre de Dios) rivers—no more than a few days' journey distant, Recio was informed—the waters flowed into a vast lagoon called Paytite. In its center were islands inhabited by "infinite people" so wealthy that they adorned themselves with many pieces of amber and with shells and pearls harvested from the waters. Not far from the lagoon rose a snow-capped cordillera inhabited by another numerous people, who were rich in silver and llamas like the peoples of Peru. In another neighboring province, meanwhile, dwelled a tribe of warlike women who lived without men.[43] With apparent bitterness, Recio declared that he could have found out much more about the wonders of these lands, had it not been for his fear of angering the native people with his questions, and had he not felt restrained by "[t]he vice established in the world of not giving credit to things that at present cannot be seen."[44] As if to emphasize that such reports were ignored at the peril of the crown and Council of the Indies, he warned that "blonde foreigners"—either the Dutch or English—had found their way to Paititi over eighteen years ago and, to the detriment of Spain, were enjoying the rich rewards of trading their countries' manufactured goods for the gold, silver, pearls, and amber of that powerful kingdom.[45]

In seeking to persuade his readers that Amazon women and other peoples of almost inconceivable wealth were to be found just a short distance beyond the limits of his own travels, Recio contributed to a representational practice that was established in the earliest phases of European exploration in the New World.[46] Like many of his contemporaries, moreover, he presented as reliable and trustworthy the testimonies of native inhabitants of the Beni river who described to him the wonders that lay ahead. In the established colonial worlds of Spanish America, the testimony of native peoples—who were regarded as legal minors—was considered of lesser worth than that of Spaniards and hence was often treated with suspicion or disdain. The linguistic barriers that so often hindered successful communication between Spaniards and indigenous groups provided further grounds for skepticism about the veracity of information obtained from native informants. Nevertheless, indigenous eyewitness accounts of regions as yet unknown to Europeans were often accorded great value: used strategically by would-be conquistadors who made representations to the crown for new colonizing ventures, information obtained from indigenous sources also directly triggered the launching of new expeditions.[47] Recio, however, was clearly aware that the dazzling reports he had obtained from native informants possessed limited persuasive power, not only because of the growing climate of

skepticism that he so bitterly lamented, but also because the crown's enthusiasm for endorsing new (and potentially fruitless) colonizing ventures
on the fringes of the empire was dampened by more pressing geopoliti-
cal concerns.

In shifting the emphasis of the 1623 narrative toward foreign competition, Recio situated the elusive kingdom within the context of royal pre-
occupations over the growing colonial ambitions of Spain's increasingly
powerful northern rivals. Since the early years of the seventeenth century,
reports of northern European incursions into Amazonia's northeastern
territories had trickled into Madrid's royal court. In 1622, on behalf of
the crown, a captain named Arana de Vasconcelos set out for the Amazon in order to pursue and evict the Dutch who had established themselves along its lower reaches.[48] Only months before Recio's submission
of his geographical account, the Council of Portugal reported that an
assortment of one hundred and fifty soldiers from England, Ireland,
and the Low Countries had established a threatening presence on the
mouth of the river.[49]

Despite Recio's attempts to capitalize on a discourse that had clearly
attained great prominence at the royal court, his efforts to secure royal
support again resulted in failure. The determination with which he pursued his objective, however, was not destroyed by the Council of the
Indies' second rejection of the petition in October 1624.

Re-presenting Amazonia I: The Transatlantic Silver Route

Although legislation prohibited the Council of Indies from considering the same petition on more than two occasions,[50] Recio submitted his
account of services for a third time, in June 1625. A few months later, it
was followed by another document that expounded a new argument in
support of his Amazonian venture and addressed contemporary concerns regarding the hazards of transporting Peruvian silver to Spain.[51]
The prospect of losing the precious shipments of bullion on the long
voyage from the Indies, whether as a result of adverse weather conditions or of enemy attack, was a source of constant concern for the monarchy, and attained particular prominence in official discourse from the

late sixteenth century onward. These concerns were not without foundation. In 1622 and 1624, shortly before Recio presented his document,
the Tierra Firme fleet, which carried Peruvian silver from Panama to
Spain, was shipwrecked with a substantial loss of bullion.[52] Peru's viceroys, meanwhile, were perennially occupied with the defense of the Pacific, in view of repeated Dutch attempts to capture the silver fleets on
their way to Panama.[53]

Recio, expanding on a point that briefly appeared at the end of his
geographical description, declared that the interior waterways of South
America could provide a new and infinitely superior route for conveying the ore to Europe. If the silver were transported by mule to the lowlands via Pelechuco in the Larecaja province, he argued, it could then
be carried by boat all the way from the Beni river to the ports of Spain,
thereby avoiding the circuitous, costly, and dangerous trajectory via Lima
and Panama. Not only would the new route take a mere two to four
months instead of over a year, the grave problems of dangerous seas
and enemy attacks in the Pacific and Caribbean would be eliminated,
while the abundance of food and other provisions in the tropical lowlands would ensure a significant decline in the cost of transportation. In
addition to possessing the best roads and pastures in the whole of Peru,
Recio insisted, Pelechuco was optimally located on the transport route,
given that it lay "almost at the center of all the mining settlements, towns,
and cities and the best provinces of the said kingdom."[54] Seizing the opportunity to display the extent of his geographical knowledge, Recio
proceeded to cite the precise distances separating Pelechuco from Peru's
principal settlements and to describe the route from Pelechuco to the
mouth of the Amazon river.[55]

Preempting any objections that could be raised, Recio assured his
monarch that the transport of silver through these as yet unpacified
lands would present no difficulties, given that all the native inhabitants
were anxious to convert to Christianity.[56] His language of leagues and
latitudes by no means excluded references to the great kingdom and
lagoon of Paititi: conveniently located on the riverine transport route,
the kingdom was dissected by rivers flowing northeastward toward the
Atlantic that "enter the lagoon of Paytiti at eleven and a third degrees;
they flow out of it at seven and a half [degrees], in the same direction."[57]

The riches of Paititi and the urgent action required by the Dutch presence again loomed large in Recio's discourse, and he concluded with the affirmation that "Your Majesty does not enjoy any wealth in all the western and eastern Indies as long as he does not [enjoy any] . . . from the lagoons of Paytiti and the hundred and eighty leagues of territory that lie between them and Pelechuco."[58]

In Recio's new document, the aim of locating and exploiting Paititi's wealth, although undeniably central, was structurally subordinated to the aim of creating a new transport route for Peruvian silver. The exploitation of new and as yet unseen riches within unpacified Amazonian territory was now presented as a felicitous by-product of a project intended to solve the problems of safeguarding and efficiently utilizing *existing* sources of wealth within the Peruvian highlands. By arguing that Andean silver could be transported to Spain via lowland South America's major waterways, moreover, Recio was once again drawing on a discourse that predated his own representations to the crown. As early as the 1560s, the industrious crown official Juan de Matienzo proposed to Philip II that the Río de la Plata be used for transporting ore and other goods from the Andean regions, in preference to the lengthy maritime route that was both costly and dangerous.[59] Although Matienzo's proposal was never implemented, the idea of finding a viable fluvial transportation route from the Andes to the Atlantic appears to have been a persistent one.

Recio was not the only petitioner at the royal court in the 1620s to argue that the Amazon could be used as a transport route for Andean silver. In 1626 the same captain Arana de Vasconcelos who had traveled to the Amazon in pursuit of the Dutch four years earlier presented an account of his services in Madrid and offered to return to the Amazon, this time to reconnoitre the course of the river and its tributaries all the way to the mines of Potosí. Seizing upon the same argument used by Recio, he insisted that the river could be used as an alternative route for the transport of Peruvian silver, thereby avoiding the dangers and delays of the maritime trajectory.[60]

The theme of the navigability of the Amazon and its tributaries all the way from the Atlantic to the Andean foothills made a brief appearance, moreover, in an account of the Chunchos provinces that was written at the viceroy's request in 1628 by the Franciscan friar Gregorio de Bolívar.[61] Up to the point where the Diabeni river, "breaking through this last one [range of hills] to form a narrow passage . . . emerges onto the plains, where it slows down and begins to flow gently," he suggested it would be possible "to bring upstream medium-sized boats via the Marañón [Amazon] from the Atlantic."[62] The friar had already returned to Lima by the time he wrote his account in 1628, but in 1626 he was resident at the royal court in order to negotiate his proposed spiritual conquest of the Amazon lowlands that bordered on Larecaja and that he claimed to have thoroughly explored in 1621.[63] Almost certainly, Recio would have had contact with these two men in Madrid; not only did he mention Arana de Vasconcelos's venture in his report on the transportation of silver, but in another document he named Gregorio de Bolívar as one of a number of individuals resident at the court who were willing to provide information in support of his cause.[64]

Re-presenting Amazonia II: Silver Mining and the Potosí Mita

The safety of the silver fleets was a perennial worry to the crown. The problems surrounding the extraction of ore from the mines of Potosí, however, had come to be of equal and possibly greater concern by the early decades of the seventeenth century. Since the turn of the century, the royal revenues produced by these mines had gone into steady decline, attributable in part to the exhaustion of high-grade ore but also to the breakdown of the *mita,* the colonial system of draft labor that supplied Potosí and other mines with indigenous workers. The phenomenon of massive native migration to areas where the draft, along with other forms of colonial exploitation, could be evaded was fundamental to this breakdown. It was exacerbated by the *entero de plata,* a practice whereby mine proprietors accepted payments in silver in place of the draftees, or *mitayos,* who were assigned to work for them. As a consequence of this practice, less ore was extracted and the crown was defrauded of its mining revenues.[65] The urgency that was felt within Peru's viceregal administration to force native populations back to their assigned reduction villages in order to rehabilitate the Potosí *mita* is strongly reflected in the growing volume of seventeenth-century documentation that addressed this issue. In the 1620s the crown continued to receive reports that the problems relating to the reductions and the Potosí *mita*—problems already hotly debated in the 1610s—were becoming more acute by the day.[66] The outbreak of violence among Spanish factions at Potosí in 1622 and, in 1626, the collapse of the Cari Cari reservoir, which caused immense destruction in the city below,[67] further ensured that Upper Peru was high on the agenda in Madrid by the closing years of the decade.

The prominence of mining-related issues at the royal court in these years, especially in the wake of the 1626 disaster, very likely encouraged Recio to write three reports that focused primarily on the territories of Upper Peru.[68] Appearing, at least initially, to distance himself from the lowlands where his own interests were located, he now addressed and proposed solutions to urgent problems that beset the southern highlands. In producing these documents, Recio clearly drew on his own experience of the Pacajes and Omasuyos provinces, where he had spent at least two years before joining Leáegui's venture to the Amazon frontier. However, given the presence in Madrid of two former *corregidores* of Potosí—don Rafael Ortiz de Sotomayor and don Francisco Sarmiento—the royal court may also have proven to be a useful site for gathering and confirming information about the state of affairs in Upper Peru and Potosí in particular: like the friar Gregorio de Bolívar, these two were explicitly named by Recio as residents of the court who were willing to give evidence in favor of his petitions.[69]

While each of Recio's reports engaged with differing aspects of the shortage of *mitayos* for the Potosí mines, all three were united by a dominant theme: the insistence that Peru's true wealth lay not in the mines or in other material resources but rather in the native populations, who extracted these riches by means of their labor. One report, however, which discussed the reasons for and the solutions to Peru's depopulation, brought this theme to the fore with particular emphasis.[70] The kingdom of Peru, Recio declared, was known to be the world's richest in gold and silver: not only Spain but also her other New World possessions were built on the foundations of Peruvian wealth. Contributing to a chorus of voices that had raised the specter before him, he warned that if efforts were not made to protect the natives, Peru would soon be as devoid of an indigenous population as the Caribbean, thereby rendering useless its rich natural resources.[71]

The reasons for the natives' disappearance, he suggested, were threefold. First, many Indians fled their homes to escape daily abuses at the hands of *corregidores,* priests, and other Spaniards. Second, the majority of those who went to Potosí never returned home, knowing that nothing but a life of hunger and misery awaited them. Finally, Recio insisted, the cruel treatment inflicted on the native people by Peru's numerous vagrants—especially *mestizos* and *mulatos*—caused "the last ones to flee and take refuge."[72] Of those who had disappeared, he argued, the majority had not died but had instead fled to parts where they could not be found—which, he commented drily, amounted to the same thing.[73]

The notion that large numbers of tributaries and their families were concealed in remote and inaccessible places featured very prominently in seventeenth-century administrative discourse. Recio, however, availed himself of these anxieties in a manner that allowed him to guide his reader's attention back to the Amazon territories that had apparently been forgotten. Initially, he reasoned, those people who fled their homes did not go far, but settled in places that were perhaps fifteen to thirty leagues distant, where their *curacas* could easily find them. When officials were first dispatched to seek out and return these people to their reduction villages, they encountered few difficulties in doing so. In part, this was because the Andeans were still new to the game of concealing themselves from the Spanish, but also because "Peru is so devoid of forest that I am unaware of any man who knows where to conceal an Indian from anyone who endeavors to seek him out."[74] Experience, however, taught the Andeans that they should flee not to the places they had hidden in before "but to the lands of idolaters, and other lands, 100, 150 and 200 leagues distant from their own, where they practice their old rites, and have unbaptized children of 15 or 20 years, which is the greatest loss of any that may arise."[75] These idolaters' territories that concealed the greatest part of Recio's vanished natives were none other than the forests that Recio had explored: it was these areas, he exclaimed dramatically, that "hour by hour the few that remain [in Peru] are entering."[76]

Recio was by no means alone in suggesting that tributaries from highland Peru fled to the lowlands to escape their labor and tribute obligations; prominent figures such as the bishop of Huamanga, who in 1618 voiced his opposition to the viceroy's planned reductions, gave credence to this notion.[77] Contemporary research has confirmed that a significant movement of highland populations toward the subtropical valleys of the east did indeed take place. However, while individuals such as the bishop of Huamanga identified Peru's Amazon frontiers as one possible destination among many for Andeans fleeing the reductions, Recio appeared to envisage a wholesale exodus toward the jungle.[78] His portrayal of Andean territory as a space so easily surveyed and patrolled that it did not offer a single hiding place stood in striking contrast to other commentators' representations of the highlands as a vast natural labyrinth, which all too easily concealed those who wished to withdraw from colonial society. In Madrid, Recio shaped the Andean landscape to suit his own needs, smoothing over its dramatic heights and deep crevices to leave nothing but a treeless plain, and thereby endowing his discursive return to the jungle with the force of logic.

Recio's document, having identified three particular factors that had caused Peru's native populations to disappear, outlined three distinct solutions to the problem. The first involved the introduction of certain new freedoms to be granted to natives who remained in their reduction villages and denied to those who did not, in order to encourage *indios forasteros* to return to their places of origin. The second proposed that fifteen hundred Spanish settlers should be taken to Chile to engage in offensive war against the Indians, thereby securing Spanish control and simultaneously relieving pressure on the natives of Peru. The third solution, however, which involved colonizing the territories explored by Recio, was declared to be the "most important part of the retention and reduction of the Indians."[79] Nothing was more important, he insisted, than for Spaniards to occupy the areas to which Peru's Indians had fled, for in this way the Indians would become

> completely relieved of all the hardships that they flee, and enlightened to the fact that they will be unable to escape the Spaniards, and they will recognize that they will be better off serving them in their own lands than in alien ones, especially as they are to enjoy new freedom in their lands but not in any others, and

consequently, not only will those who remain refrain from entering [foreign lands]; but rather those who have entered will leave
and return to their homes, knowing than nowhere else will they
enjoy greater freedom.[80]

According to Recio, then, the outcome of his elaborate plan would be
the voluntary return of countless Andeans who had taken refuge in
the tropical lowlands. Through the implementation of his plan, he suggested, the Spanish crown would be more powerful than all other mon-
archies put together, and the king himself the world's most untroubled
and best-served monarch.[81] This was a tacit yet powerful challenge to
the belief, prominent within the viceregal administration and the Council of the Indies, that expansion beyond Peru's subtropical boundaries
was likely to imperil the prosperity and security of provinces that had
already been conquered. With great dramatic effect, Recio returned his
Amazonian venture to the center of attention—no longer as an end in
itself, but as the most effective remedy to administrative and economic
problems of highland Peru.[82]

For the last time, the appeal for backing, now repackaged as advice
on matters of government, was rejected by the Council of the Indies. It
remained firm in its decision that Recio's only option was to present his
papers to the *Audiencia* of Lima, should he wish to pursue the matter
further. While the acute financial situation of the royal treasury undoubtedly influenced this decision—bankruptcy was declared in 1627[83]—
another reason was the Council's evident distrust of Recio's credentials:
a report written for Philip IV in 1627 drew the monarch's attention to
"how bereft Juan Recio was of authentic documentation when he came
and how frivolously he insisted in his claim."[84] The exercise of caution
was always necessary, it warned, in the case of individuals who "declin-
ing the judgment of the viceroys . . . , come here, where they attempt
to negotiate with greater ease than they could over there [in the New
World]."[85] Ultimately, it seems, it was not so much the content of Recio's
proposals that underlay the Council's resolute refusal to consider his petitions, as the fact that the venture had been assigned to and implemented,
not by Recio himself, but by Pedro de Leáegui Urquiza: "while it is true
that the Council does not find his person to be lacking in merit . . . what

is certain is that the one who did it was the Captain Pedro de Leáegui Urquiza who today is Governor and General Captain and Chief Magistrate of those provinces, and who sent him [Recio] as representative to these kingdoms in order to act on his behalf."[86]

❋   Madrid and its royal and administrative institutions may be usefully conceptualized, drawing on the work of Latour, as a "center of calculation" that initiated and controlled flows of information from distant places, thus situating it in a position of power over those places and the peoples who inhabited them.[87] It should not be forgotten, however, that such imperial centers were also places of diversity, difference, conflict, and negotiation, rather than well-oiled bureaucratic machines that worked relentlessly in pursuit of a unified objective. As Elliott comments, the royal court of the early seventeenth century acted as "an irresistible magnet to petitioners, place-hunters, and *pícaros* from all over Spain"[88]—an observation that can be extended to include individuals, such as Recio, who traveled to Madrid from distant areas of the empire.

The Council of the Indies' officials were keenly aware of Madrid's magnetic pull as a place of opportunity—a site at which individuals hoped to harness metropolitan power and resources for the pursuit of their own ends. Information about the New World, transported to the capital by countless individuals and presented in texts, maps, and oral testimonies, could not be unproblematically appropriated by the monarchy and its council in the consolidation of imperial power. This was partly because the bureaucratic system was overwhelmed by the sheer volume of paper, but also because the reliability of these offerings, frequently regarded with profound suspicion, was often impossible to verify.[89] Precisely for this reason, petitions such as Recio's were judged to be the remit of the viceroys, who, being physically present in the Indies, should be better able to make informed judgments about their worth.

Madrid's royal court, a space of rivalry and intrigue where individuals vied for favors and advancement by seeking the patronage of influential favorites,[90] also constituted a space in which information about the New World was circulated and where discourses could be appropriated, shaped, and deployed with a view to diverse interests. During his period of residence at the court, Recio came into contact with numerous contemporaries who had experience of, and interests in, South America; as indicated above, his petitions explicitly named individuals who were contemporaneously present in Madrid and many of whom, he claimed, were willing to give evidence in support of his cause.[91] While the nature of these contacts and exchanges can only be reconstructed in fragmentary and tentative ways, it is nevertheless possible to glimpse how such interactions may have influenced the production of discourses about the Amazon within the spaces of the imperial city and its court.

Petitions such as those presented by Recio inevitably emerged from collective processes rather than the personal experiences and knowledge of a single individual. The portrayals of the Amazon in Recio's petitions, however, were by no means the result of "contagious" discourses to which the Spaniards helplessly fell victim, nor were they straightforwardly produced in accordance with a prior plan or ready-made set of ideas that Recio brought with him to Madrid. Instead, as I have tried to illustrate, they emerged out of an improvisatory and opportunistic use of diverse discourses that sought to establish persuasive connections between proposed ventures in the region and the dominant concerns and interests of the Spanish crown.

Despite his failure to secure royal backing, Recio's writings are a striking example of how certain discourses were appropriated by individuals within colonial society to pursue personal ends. When the invocation of certain discourses failed to produce results, he brought others to the fore: thus, the emphasis shifted from a discourse of "anti-conquest" and Christian conversion toward a strategy for solving the economic and social problems that afflicted Upper Peru. This shift was also spatial, for Recio moved away from his initial, predominant focus on the Amazon regions, reframing his proposals for colonization of the lowlands in terms of the benefits that such a move would bring to areas already under Spanish control.

Recio's later petitions and reports inextricably bound the destiny of the highlands to that of the lowlands, by portraying the latter as a territory harboring and concealing great numbers of people, including refugees from the *altiplano*. If the former was devoid of hiding places and population, the latter, by contrast, was replete with both. In the numerous colonial accounts, Recio's included, of Amazonia's southwestern frontiers, however, a dualistic vision of the Andes and the Amazon as opposed yet neatly juxtaposed entities is complicated by representations of the geographical zones of transition that connected or separated the two. As the next chapter argues, colonial experiences and portrayals of these in-between landscapes of the frontier in the sixteenth and seventeenth centuries played a highly significant role in the struggle over geographical knowledge of the Amazon and its relationship to the Andean heartlands of empire.

SIX

Contested Frontiers and
the Amazon/Andes Divide

A curious paradox marks Inca and Spanish relations with the tropical lowlands. The Spaniards—unlike the rulers of Tawantinsuyu, for whom a concept of opposition between Andes and Amazon was fundamental to their sense of identity—did not generally articulate such a binary at the time of their arrival in Peru, nor, like the Incas, did they regard the tropical forests in predominantly negative terms.[1] Only with the repeated failure of military forays beyond the Andes did the tropical lowlands emerge in Spanish discourse as a coherent entity that stood in opposition (whether positive or negative) to the highland regions.

Once established, however, the colonial rupture between Andes and Amazon was considerably more profound than that which had existed under the Incas, who regarded the forest as a realm complementary to that of the highlands. The dualism that emerged in Spanish geographical portrayals was an asymmetric one, for the Amazon regions had come to represent an alien space that lay *outside* the boundary of dominant colonial identities. It was relevant only as a repository for disruptive elements that threatened the order and security of the consolidated colonial territories.[2] The dream of expansion into the Amazon nevertheless endured throughout the colonial period and emerged as a prominent force in the construction of national self-images and identities in the Republican era.[3] In the writings that promoted such expansion, such as the petitions of Juan Recio de León, the solutions to problems that beset colonial (and later also Republican) society in the Andes were to be found in the unexploited territories of the eastern lowlands. Whether as a space of barbarism or as one of natural exuberance and plenty, the Amazon provided discursive counterpoints to the highlands that dramatically revealed the "need" for its conquest and colonization.

Despite the prominence of binary oppositions between Andes and Amazon in colonial imaginings, however, these dualisms were also inflected and modified by portrayals of the eastern piedmont regions that, depending on the commentators' point of view, either connected or separated the highlands and the tropical lowlands. Just as the histories and geographies of these regions have received relatively scant scholarly attention, so too, the place that the piedmont held in colonial representational practices is often subordinated to an interest in the broad binary oppositions between Andes and Amazon, which structured so many imaginative geographies of the colonial era.[4]

This chapter, which attempts to go beyond the identification of this fundamental binary, examines diverse portrayals of the colonial frontiers of Charcas and Cuzco (see fig. 10) produced by soldiers, missionaries, and colonial officials in the sixteenth and seventeenth centuries. In focusing initially on accounts of sixteenth-century military expeditions, I trace the emergence of profoundly negative portrayals of the piedmont regions, in stark contrast with idealized visions of the Amazon lowlands, and illustrate how the idea of the piedmont as a hostile barrier was reinforced by the writings of missionaries and colonial officials. In the second half of the chapter I discuss the fact that in numerous seventeenth-century writings, the piedmont appears instead as a promising gateway to the Amazon regions and, indeed, as a territory that connected rather than divided the highlands and lowlands. Drawing once again on the work of Rabasa, I establish a connection between these discursive reformulations of the piedmont as a welcoming gateway and the stipulations of the royal ordinances on new explorations and settlements that were issued in 1573.[5] The metropolitan production of legislative texts was not, however, the only factor that shaped colonial portrayals of the piedmont. Embodied experiences of these tran-

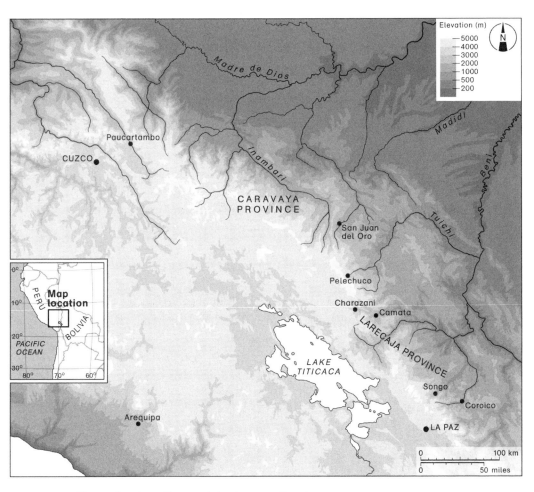

Fig. 10. Southern Peru and the Amazon frontier.

sitional landscapes, the agency and representational practices of indigenous groups, and the enactment of locally and regionally focused rivalries over the colonization of the Amazon all played important roles in the negotiation of these colonial frontiers.

Before considering in detail the eastward-bound expeditions that were launched from the southern Andes, it is worth reflecting briefly on Francisco de Orellana's famous navigation of the Amazon river in

1541–42. The portrayals of Amazonia that emerged from his expedition reveal some striking parallels and continuities with those of later expeditions.

The Orellana Voyage and the Northwestern Amazon Frontier

In the wake of the conquest of Peru, the equatorial regions that form the watershed of the Amazon were the principal center for Spanish expansionist adventures into the tropical lowlands. Compared to the piedmont regions farther south, especially those beyond Cuzco, many parts of the equatorial Amazon fringe were relatively accessible to Spanish incursion, due to the lower altitude of the northern Andes and the gentler descent into the lowlands. Equally important, the extensive nature of contact with the inhabitants of the piedmont and eastern lowlands, who were linked by precolonial trade networks to the Andean regions, facilitated Spanish settlement on the tropical frontier and provided a source of information about Amazonia that fueled interest in the search for El Dorado and the Land of Cinnamon.[6] As a consequence, parts of the piedmont to the southeast of Quito and to the northeast of Cajamarca experienced rapid Spanish settlement, together with early and sustained efforts to push deeper into the Amazon basin.[7]

Among the early ventures that departed from Quito, Orellana's voyage was especially significant in its contributions to Spanish geographical notions of the tropical interior and to the gradual emergence of the idea of "Amazonia" as a coherent region. Orellana and his companions, bearing tales of the wealth of the Omaguas, who inhabited the central stretches of the river, as well as of other populous chiefdoms farther downstream (including the domains of the Amazon women), undoubtedly contributed on their return to Spanish-controlled territories to the ongoing development of the El Dorado legend; they thereby played a crucial role in keeping alive Spanish hopes of finding wealthy civilizations in the Amazon basin that would rival or even outdo those found in Mexico and the Andes.[8]

The events of Orellana's voyage and the geographical knowledge that it generated were documented in detail by the friar and expedition member Gaspar de Carvajal. Although his account remained unpublished until the nineteenth century,[9] it provides valuable insights into the ideas and images that were produced by the expedition. In addition to extensive riverside settlements, evidence of gold and silver, and highly organized societies that cultivated skilled artisans as well as fierce warriors, the Spaniards encountered, according to his account, wonderfully fertile and temperate lands that were well-stocked with game and in which European crops, fruits, and livestock would thrive, "because there are many plants like those found in our Spain, such as oregano and spotted and striped thistles and many other very useful herbs."[10]

As the expedition journeyed toward the Atlantic, hunger was a frequent companion—not because the indigenous peoples who inhabited the banks of the Amazon lacked food, but rather because the hostile reception that the Spaniards received on many occasions made it impossible for them to go ashore and obtain the supplies that they needed. Hunger also marked the early stages of the expedition, as the Spaniards, under the initial leadership of Gonzalo Pizarro, made their way downstream along the Napo on the western fringes of the Amazon basin. In the frontier regions of the piedmont, however, the situation was dramatically different. Here the Spaniards reached the point of starvation because of the absence of food and, perhaps more important, the absence of indigenous populations who—unlike the Europeans—would know how to obtain it.

Pizarro's decision to send Orellana farther downstream with a small group of men was motivated not by the initial aims of the expedition—namely, to go in search of the Land of Cinnamon and El Dorado—but instead by the urgent need to find sustenance.[11] Similarly, Orellana's decision to continue traveling downriver rather than attempting to return to Pizarro's camp was determined by the search for food and the impossibility of returning upstream against the strong river currents. The extreme situation in which the Spaniards found themselves was vividly related by Carvajal:

> lacking other sustenance, our necessity was such that we ate only leather, belts and shoe soles boiled with a few herbs, as a result of which we were so weak that we could not stand up, and there were some who, either crawling on all fours or using walking sticks, entered into the forests in search of some roots that they could eat,

and there were some who ate unfamiliar plants and were on the brink of death, for they behaved like madmen and lost their minds, but as it was the will of Our Lord that we should continue our journey, none of them died.[12]

When at last the starving men came across signs of human habitation, "the joy that everyone felt was such that all the past troubles were forgotten because now we were in inhabited country and could no longer die of hunger."[13]

In Carvajal's account, the western frontier regions through which he passed thus took shape as a barren and unpopulated wilderness — as an area not only lacking in any source of wealth that might make it worth colonizing, but in which it was virtually impossible even to satisfy the basic necessities that would ensure human survival. Crucially, however, the perseverance of the starving expeditionaries in continuing their journey downstream was rewarded, first with the food that they so desperately needed, but second, with glimpses of populous societies and — so it seemed to the Europeans — abundantly fertile lands. Given that Orellana was denounced as a rebel and traitor by Pizarro for failing to return to the camp, it was politically expedient for Carvajal, who sought to portray Orellana in the best possible light, to emphasize the men's suffering on the Napo and the fact that any attempt to turn back would have spelled their death.[14] The friar's account thus constructed a markedly negative vision of the western extremities of the Amazon. Nevertheless, placed within the broader context of the tantalizing reports with which the expedition members returned to Peru, his portrayals of the western frontier regions as a hostile barrier were not intended to discourage future expeditions to Amazonia. Rather, his account clearly indicated that this was a barrier worth crossing, because rich rewards awaited those who reached the territories beyond.

In-between Landscapes of Suffering

Cieza de León, pausing in his account of Pedro de Candia's and Perançures's expeditions to the Amazon to reflect on the sufferings borne by Spanish explorers of the New World, predicted that in the future these men would be remembered and celebrated for laboring so tenaciously in the face of unspeakable hardship. What he pondered on most, he wrote, "are not the conquests nor battles with the Indians, but rather the work of discovery, and in no part of the world have those who have gained this kingdom been outdone in this respect: and this expedition to the Chunchos has been the most harmful and distressing of all that have been carried out in the entire Indies, for more than a third of the Spaniards were lost, all of whom died of hunger as they had no food."[15]

In 1538, Candia had set out from Cuzco with an army of about two hundred Spaniards and thousands of Andean auxiliaries in search of the wealth that was rumored to lie to the east of the Andes. Instead of riches, his men encountered only impenetrable forests, through which they struggled for three months before emerging, defeated and near starvation, to the east of the *altiplano* of Collao. In view of Candia's failure and the hostility with which he had come to be regarded by his companions, the venture, or *entrada,* was entrusted instead to the captain Perançures, who, later in 1538, led three hundred men back into the forests from the valley of Caravaya. Although he succeeded in reaching the open savannah of the lowlands, the anticipated wealth, great populations, and abundant food remained elusive; lacking the necessary supplies for the difficult return journey to Peru, about one hundred and forty Spaniards and over four thousand auxiliaries lost their lives to hunger, exhaustion, and disease.[16]

Cieza de León's descriptions of these disastrous expeditions to the piedmont regions call forth a landscape that was unrivaled in terms of the sufferings and perils that it presented to the explorers. Echoing his accounts of the equatorial jungles of the Pacific coast, he vividly conveyed the incessant downpours, the impenetrable tangles of vegetation, the treacherous terrain, furious rivers, and, above all, the sufferings of the Spaniards and their auxiliaries, whose dead and dying bodies marked the route that the expeditions had taken. Shunned even by wild beasts, these forests not only harbored "Indian archers who habitually eat human flesh," but also converted the starving expedition members into cannibals: "The pathway was covered with the dead, and the living were eating the dead. . . . At that time, brotherhood was of no worth, and everyone spoke only of their hunger and of when it might be satisfied."[17]

Cieza de León did not participate personally in these events, but numerous survivors of the fateful expeditions provided equally harrowing accounts of their sufferings and those of their companions, in accounts of services presented to the crown. In these accounts the forest appears as a vast labyrinth of nearly insuperable difficulty and danger—a formidable barrier of such magnitude that the expeditions tried in vain to reach the much-desired "good lands" beyond it. Indeed, the possible existence of wealthy territories in the lowlands is wholly obscured by the "discourse of failure,"[18] which focuses on and illuminates the sufferings of the expeditionaries.[19] Spanish belief in the existence of opulent lands beyond the Andes persisted, however, and was reflected not only in the continuation of attempts to conquer the eastern regions, but also in the writings of Cieza de León. Despite the horrors of a seemingly impassable jungle, described in such detail in his own chronicle, he insisted that more promising lands lay beyond: "Many are the people who live beyond these forests of the Andes, and large are the provinces endowed with livestock and other food, according to what we have heard from those who came from the River Plate and arrived in the Charcas region in this year of one thousand five hundred and forty eight."[20]

The tripartite geography of rich and pleasant lowland domains that were separated from the Peruvian highlands by a vast and fearsome jungle barrier was sustained and reinforced in the account produced by Juan Alvarez Maldonado, who in 1567 led another major expedition into the high jungles to the east of Cuzco.[21] Unlike his predecessors, Maldonado succeeded in reaching the Amazon lowlands by navigating a tributary of the Madre de Dios and founded two settlements along the way. The interference of a rival expedition from Peru, however, together with native resistance, caused the venture to be abandoned within two years. Maldonado's description of the venture, sent to Madrid along with his accounts of merits and services with a view to securing royal support, achieved a delicate balance between highlighting the suffering of expedition members, on the one hand, and the prospect of material reward, on the other. His file of documents included a geographical description of the territories that he had set out to explore, which foregrounded their abundant wealth and fertility.[22] By contrast, his account of the expedition emphasized the rigors of the descent to the lowlands.

The governor and his men, resolving to explore and settle a territory that in Peru was "considered almost bewitched,"[23] opened a route through the high-altitude forest, or *montaña,* "although it seemed impossible for human forces."[24] Once a settlement had been founded, the expeditionaries set to work constructing canoes that would carry them to the Amazon basin below. Given that the forest was "extremely dense and terrible,"[25] Maldonado suggested, this was a task that would have overwhelmed his men, had his encouragement not ensured that they cast aside all thoughts of defeat. At this juncture, the success of the expedition, first in establishing a settlement and then in negotiating a fluvial route to the lowlands, allowed Maldonado to portray the *montaña* as a barrier that, although terrible, could be heroically overcome by means of stoic endurance, courage, and determination.[26]

The governor's second encounter with the Amazon frontier, however, was less fortunate. Having returned to Cuzco to gather reinforcements and fresh supplies for the men who remained on the frontier, he learned of the activities of a certain Gómez de Tordoya. In the company of assorted adventurers and fugitives, Tordoya had entered the jungle via Camata with a view to contesting Maldonado's claim to the venture. Feeling compelled to go immediately to the aid of his captain, Descobar, who had been left in charge of the new settlements, the governor led his recruits into the forest, "although it was winter and river floods and storms were feared."[27] These fears were fully realized, for the swollen rivers claimed the lives of many and swept away their precious supplies. Those who survived the torrential rivers were ambushed by warriors who "assaulted them in such a manner that, although the Spaniards were more numerous and better armed, they were unable to resist and even less to attack."[28] After discovering that Descobar, Tordoya, and nearly all of their respective followers had died at the hands of the native people, the governor humbly accepted the offer of Tarano, leader of the Araona[29] and former ally of the Spaniards, to provide his men with shelter and food and with guides who would lead them back to Peru. Following a sixteen-day journey, Maldonado's much-diminished group arrived at the frontier town of San Juan del Oro, "so tired and worn from the journey and the wounds and sores that many developed there, that it was the most pitiful thing in the world."[30]

If Maldonado was able to recount with drama and pathos the crushing defeat sustained by his men on being confronted with the perils of the *montaña* in the wet season and the unanticipated hostility of its native peoples, it was because human folly—namely, that of Tordoya—could be made to bear the blame. Not only did Tordoya's actions transform indigenous allies into enemies, but they also obliged the governor to undertake the Amazon-bound river journey in the fury of the winter rains, "although . . . it appears reckless."[31] Providing a dramatic contrast to the modest success of the venture's initial phase, the calamitous events resulting from Tordoya's intervention demonstrated that the colonization of the lowlands could only be achieved under the control and guidance of a leader of absolute rectitude, discipline, and good faith.

On the one hand, the governor's attribution of his venture's failure to human malice may have been intended to dispute visions of the piedmont as an insuperable barrier separating Peru from the riches of the Amazon, by implying the possibility of success under wise and diligent leadership. On the other hand, however, Maldonado's retreat from the Amazon, together with the vivid account of that failure, surely worked in unison to reinforce and perpetuate Spanish perceptions of the piedmont region as a "bewitched land."

The Piedmont as Barrier

In colonial as well as republican times, as Taussig illustrates, descent into the Colombian Amazon from the highland plateau was experienced and imagined as a descent into a hell, in contrast to the "terrestrial paradise" of the highlands. For the Capuchin monks who championed the construction of a road from Pasto into the jungles of the Putumayo in the early twentieth century, it was by means of their downward journey that light and redemption would at last be brought to the dark places that they penetrated: physical descent into the jungle was inextricably tied to the spiritual ascent and salvation of its peoples.[32] Like these twentieth-century Capuchin monks who established a base on the edge of the Colombian Andes, the Spanish Jesuit Andrés López yearned to descend into the jungles below. Following a visit to the Amazon fringes of the

Cuzco province in the late sixteenth century, he wrote of his desire to submerge himself in the seemingly endless forests that stretched out beneath the vantage point where he had stood: "I, to be sure, gazed upon that land from a high peak, from where it seemed to me that I could see almost as far as the Atlantic and the end of the great cordillera . . . and it would not have taken much, had my obedience allowed me, to go downstream among the heathens; imagining myself among them, with only the aid of God and a companion, it seemed to me the most fortunate life and destiny that could ever fall to me."[33]

The process of descent, of course, was replete with hazards, and these were often made to feature prominently in ecclesiastical reports and chronicles of missionary activities. Like the stoically borne sufferings of the Jesuits on the mountain paths of Huarochirí, the travails of the missionaries who descended to the Amazon frontiers of Cuzco and La Paz were brought to the fore and celebrated as illustrations of their piety and dedication. Describing repeated efforts to bring Christianity to the piedmont regions beyond Larecaja, the friar and chronicler Bernardino de Torres referred to the hardships gladly endured by his fellow Augustinians as they made their way into the forests in 1623; they journeyed "on foot and at times also barefoot through impenetrable forests so difficult that it seemed like a conspiracy among all the inconveniences of bad paths, slopes, rivers, undergrowth, heat, troublesome and harmful insects, but they passed through all of them as gladly as if they were walking over roses through a level and delightful wood."[34]

Ecclesiastical writings, however, by no means portrayed the tropical regions as an undifferentiated inferno. Some of the regions beyond the Andes, wrote Bernardino de Torres, were inhospitable places of impenetrable jungle and swamp, while others, by contrast, were delightful and salubrious.[35] As in the writings produced by soldiers and explorers, the plains beyond the easternmost outliers of the Andes were overwhelmingly identified as rich and pleasant lands: those missionaries who braved the dangers and discomforts of the jungle-clad slopes would find their efforts rewarded with vast and welcoming populations, eager to embrace the Christian message. On reaching the piedmont settlement of Tayapu, de Torres mused, the Augustinians imagined they were gazing down from the Mount onto a Promised Land that awaited their discovery, "that new world, those extensive provinces of the Chunchos."[36]

The promised land, however, remained elusive. While some of the many attempts to establish missions in the frontier regions of Charcas in the early seventeenth century produced modest achievements, these were invariably short-lived. The frequent souring of relations with indigenous groups and lack of adequate support from the viceregal and ecclesiastical authorities compelled many friars to abandon their efforts in frustration and return to Peru.[37] Others, caught in the crossfire of interethnic conflicts and negotiations, did not return at all but died at the hands of those they hoped to convert.[38]

In 1638 missionary activities in the piedmont came to a definitive end (lasting for a period of almost thirty years) when a fragile alliance, established in 1634 between the Spanish and the Aguachile people of the frontier regions, was once again broken.[39] In the earlier parts of Bernardino de Torres's account of the eastern missions, the forested frontier was positively imagined as a gateway—albeit a hazardous one—that led to a populous "new world." The dominant vision that emerged toward the end was of an insurmountable barrier that had established itself between the missionaries and the Amazon plains below. While the region acted as a "receptacle and refuge for all the idolaters and criminals who flee Peru via Larecaja,"[40] the machinations of its inhabitants had allegedly triggered the collapse of the alliance. The Lecos—described by Torres as treacherous idolaters—were inspired by the devil, he insisted, to enter the lands of the Aguachiles and there "spread their poison everywhere, discrediting the Fathers and advising the Indians to drive them from their lands or kill them."[41]

The vision of the Franciscan Diego de Mendoza nearly thirty years later, conveyed in his 1665 chronicle of the Charcas province, was equally negative. Like his Augustinian counterpart, Mendoza regarded the frontier territories as dangerous spaces that magnetically attracted idolaters and rebels, while simultaneously providing their native inhabitants with the weapons—in the form of dense forests, abundant rivers, and arduous terrain—to evade the Spaniards' control and block their route to the lowlands.[42] The scant success of his order's repeated attempts to convert the peoples of the piedmont, Mendoza insisted, was not so much due to the challenges of the terrain and climate as it was to the obstinacy and hostility of the natives. The conquest of this region by the Spaniards was not impossible, but it could be achieved only "with the force of defensive weapons, and by subjugation,"[43] and only if carried out "slowly and in an orderly manner, and with persistence, spending the winter in comfortable locations, creating places or settlements from which . . . they can proceed; and to which they can return when they encounter difficulties and there fortify themselves, being in their own refuge; exploring them [the territories], and gaining ground, until they reach the [lowland] populations and fully discover the new world, and the places of significance within it."[44]

For Mendoza, then, the conversion of the lowland populations depended on the slow and pragmatic business of transforming a hostile landscape into a familiar one by establishing frontier settlements—a landscape that would provide a refuge, not for rebels or idolaters, but instead for the advancing Spaniards. While Torres regarded the corporeal sufferings of descent through a hostile frontier landscape as a necessary and pious sacrifice for achieving conversions, Mendoza, by contrast, could envisage missionary success only through that landscape's domination.

❊   The continuous setbacks experienced by seventeenth-century missionaries were mirrored by sporadic attacks carried out by piedmont groups on the precarious colonial settlements of the frontier.[45] Together, these events no doubt encouraged the creation and reinforcement of negative perceptions and portrayals of the piedmont and the adjacent *yungas,* regions on the lower eastern Andes slopes. In the discourse of local administrators, emphasis was persistently placed on the defense of a hostile frontier that posed a threat to colonial order. In presenting his account of services to the viceregal authorities in 1631, the former *corregidor* of Larecaja, Rodrigo de Herrera Hurtado, emphasized his conscientious efforts to defend the province against hostile attacks and incursions: "I proceeded with the vigilance, care, and diligence that are required on a frontier like this one which is so commonly infested with unpacified Chunchos and Lecos Indians who are proud and rebellious by nature, sending assistance to the frontiers in the form of soldiers, weapons, and munitions, at my own cost . . . for had I not attended to this with great promptness, they would have destroyed and killed the Spaniards and Indians of the province."[46]

As was overwhelmingly the case in Spanish America, however, the colonial frontiers, in this instance of Larecaja, in no way resembled a clearly demarcated line of defense.[47] They consisted of a scattering of tiny settlements and sites of fortification, which, although precariously interconnected, were surrounded by territory in which colonial control was extremely weak and at times nonexistent. Here, where pockets of unsubjugated native populations were interspersed with Christianized Amerindians, campaigns of military defense appeared to alternate with tactics of appeasement.

Having returned from an inspection tour of his jurisdiction in 1635, the bishop of La Paz described his experiences of visiting the eastern *yungas*—"which no Prelate has ever reached . . . as the pathways are rough and dangerous, and have many slopes and precipices."[48] The indigenous inhabitants of these regions, he suggested, had to be treated with as much caution as the precarious pathways. Given that the three parishes that he visited were coterminous with the territories of "unsubjugated Indian infidels," who frequently launched attacks on converted natives, those "infidels" who lived peacefully within the parishes were "exempted from *mitas* and personal services because they may be prepared to take up arms whenever the opportunity presents itself."[49]

The bishop's report distinguished clearly between volatile "infidels" and "our Indians," who lived side-by-side on the frontier. It is evident from other documents that the latter group played an active role in the defense of Spanish frontier posts and fortifications. In Camata, for example, don Pascual Sucucayo served for at least a decade as *alferez* and captain of other native residents, governing them "in things relating to the art of warfare" and supervising their sentry duties at the fortress.[50] Not only was he commended by local Spanish officials for his diligent services in defending the frontier, but he complained on several occasions that he was unable to attend to his duties as thoroughly as he should, given that *caciques* and other individuals constantly sought to occupy him in personal services.[51]

The boundaries between indigenous "friends" and "enemies" of the Spaniards, however, were often as blurred and changeable as the geographical frontiers of colonial rule. The "pacified" inhabitants of the *yungas,* it seems, actively exploited Spanish fears of the Chunchos' belligerence in order to resist colonial demands; in doing so, they encouraged the portrayal of the frontier regions as treacherous spaces that were not only perilous to enter but that also exercised a dangerous and insidious influence on the colonial domains of Upper Peru. According to an anonymous sixteenth-century account, a group of Spaniards who attempted to settle in the *yungas* beyond Tipuani to exploit gold mines were driven out, not by the attacks of unpacified groups from the piedmont, but by the carefully calculated moves of the local Amerindian population. After carrying out an ambush in which two Spaniards and a number of black and Andean auxiliaries died, the Amerindians reported to the Spanish colonists that the Chunchos were attacking and had already killed fifty of their own people: "that same night they [the Spaniards] fled, leaving behind everything that they had brought with them, understanding them to be Chunchos warriors, as the very same Indians who were the culprits of this betrayal had made them believe."[52] Although, since that time, a number of other individuals who possessed information about the mines had attempted to discover them, "those said Indians fill them with such fear of the Chunchos, that no one dares to enter into them [their territories]."[53]

Those areas of the frontier that lay, at least nominally, under Spanish control were frequently portrayed with as much fear and suspicion as the unpacified territories beyond, a perception no doubt encouraged by their physical and climatic attributes. In an account of an uprising orchestrated by the Christianized natives of Songo, Challana, Chacapa, and Simaco, a soldier who helped to suppress the rebellion emphasized the difficulty with which this was achieved, given the "great advantages" that the rebels enjoyed over the Spaniards in this environment: "it is their natural environment, and they can take refuge among the mountain peaks, and in the forests where it rains continuously, and thus by nature it is easily defended territory, and at the same time impregnable."[54]

The overwhelming sense of threat to the Spaniards, however, came not only from the broken, jungle-clad terrain that surrounded the four settlements but also from their close proximity to the "lands of Chunchos infidels."[55] Just as the invasion of the *yungas* by unconquered piedmont groups was feared by many Spaniards who resided there, so too, their writings often expressed anxiety over the possibility of alliances between these groups and the indigenous people already under colonial rule. The rebels, wrote the anonymous soldier, were determined to take refuge in the territories beyond Spanish control, and had to be hunted down like rabbits to prevent them from doing so.[56] His words found resonance in the account of services presented by don Luis de Ulloa, who claimed to have played a leading role in the punitive campaign: his achievement consisted not only in having hindered the rebellion from spreading to neighboring colonial settlements, but also in having prevented the perpetrators from communicating with the Chunchos.[57] News of the rebellion, however, reached the inhabitants of the high Andean plateau, who threatened to evade the Potosí *mita* and flee to Songo: "And whenever they requested a *mitayo* in the Indian towns, they were told that they should go to Songo to look for him, and in Guaycho, a town in the *corregimiento* of Omasuyo, the Indians behaved insolently toward their priest, and had the *corregidor* . . . not arrived quickly and punished them, the inhabitants of all the provinces would have gone there."[58]

The rapid growth of the *yungas* population in the early seventeenth century as a result of Andean immigration from highland provinces provides compelling evidence that the frontier regions were perceived and used, in very real and physical ways, as spaces of refuge from colonial demands, most notably from the mining *mita*.[59] For some Andeans who remained on the *altiplano,* however, the frontier territories may also have provided a discursive tool that was deployed in the form of continuous threats to flee there, and that was fed by and accentuated Spanish fears of a region in which control was precarious at best. For Spanish administrators, the frontier was doubly threatening, for its geography was perceived as a dangerous facilitator of indigenous mobility, just as it hindered that of the Spanish and, in consequence, their ability to maintain colonial control.

The Spaniards, however, were by no means united in their struggle against what was perceived to be a difficult and dangerous landscape.

It is clear from the writings of Diego de Mendoza that the Spanish and *mestizo* populations residing in the frontier regions were often perceived by members of the church and government as responsible for *intensifying* the threat that these marginal landscapes posed to the security, prosperity, and integrity of the viceroyalty. Driven by greed and forgetful of their "Christian obligations,"[60] the local Spanish and *mestizo* residents of Larecaja provoked the Songo rebellion, Mendoza insisted, by harshly exploiting the labor of the native people in the lucrative production of coca.[61] Not only could the actions of unscrupulous locals lead to violence, however: living in such close proximity to the territories of the Lecos and Chunchos, the recently converted Indians could "easily cross the cordillera, and join the infidels in order to flee the abuses; and if the land were not so devoid of supplies, and so full of noxious creatures, many would cross over to the infidels."[62]

Those Spaniards and *mestizos* who lacked moral integrity, the Franciscan implied, should be kept distant from the frontier to safeguard colonial order and control. Here, in view of the immoral behavior of the supposed guardians of royal justice, the territories of the piedmont are portrayed by Mendoza not as obstacles to Spanish mobility, but instead as welcome barriers that helped prevent the steady trickle of indigenous migration turning into an unstoppable flood.

From Barrier to Gateway

The royal ordinances of 1573, issued to regulate new explorations and settlements throughout the Indies, did not merely emphasize the need for expedition leaders to fulfill missionary obligations and to establish control over new territories in as peaceful and orderly a manner as possible. In copious detail, they stipulated how every aspect of such ventures was to be conducted, from the organization and funding to the process of exploration and the establishment and maintenance of colonial settlements. Marking the decline of an era of unregulated expansionist adventures, the ordinances required that colonizing ventures be implemented in a systematic manner.[63] Before new territories could be explored and possessed, colonial control and settlement in adjacent, recently pacified regions had to be consolidated. At the same time, the document specified the required characteristics and resources of lands that were to be settled:

> Select the province, region, and land that is to be settled, taking into consideration that they should be salubrious, which may be deduced from the number of old people, and youths of good complexion, temperament, and color, and without diseases, and from the number of healthy animals of good size, and of good fruits and [other] foodstuffs: they should not be breeding-grounds for poisonous and harmful things; they should possess a good and fortunate constellation, clear and benign skies; pure and soft air . . . and a good temperature, without excessive heat or cold, and if this is not possible, it is better that it be cold.[64]

Regions chosen for settlement, moreover, were to be fertile and well-populated, possessing abundant pasture, woods, and water, as well as "good maritime and terrestrial entries and exits along good roads and routes of navigation, so that it is possible to enter and leave, trade and govern, and to provide aid and defense with ease."[65]

These requirements were in striking contrast to the visions of the southern Amazon frontier that had been constructed by various soldiers, missionaries, and colonial officials since the time of Candia's disastrous expedition into the forests. While the Amazon lowlands were often portrayed as benign, even idyllic regions, wealthy in natural and human resources, they were separated from the highlands by what was both experienced and portrayed as a hostile and insalubrious territory. This territory was not only virtually impregnable but threatened the security and stability of areas under Spanish control—it was wholly unsuited for settlement and incorporation into the colonial order. Even if the enthusiastic reports of the lowlands proper were to be believed, these lowlands were rendered distant and barely accessible from the Andean highlands by the perils of the intervening frontier.

As Rabasa argues, it is difficult to overestimate the importance of the 1573 ordinances: in practice, their requirements and stipulations may have been largely disregarded, yet they played a central role in shaping the writing of contracts issued to expedition leaders as well as of individual accounts and petitions.[66] So, while the dangers and difficulties of the frontier regions were dramatized by individuals engaged in the defense of the frontier or by missionaries intent on publicizing their voluntary corporal sufferings, petitioners anxious to obtain official authorization and funding for the colonization of the lowlands instead tended to *minimize* both the perils of the piedmont regions that they intended to cross and the challenges involved in opening an effective route of communication between highlands and Amazon.

Such tactics may be clearly perceived by turning, once again, to the writings of Juan Recio de León. His writings, and especially his earliest documents, register the presence of a frontier region that had to be traversed in order to reach the Amazon lowlands: in the *relación* of 1623, he drew attention to his efforts in opening up a route from San Juan de Sahagún to Apolobamba, without which, he insisted, it would have been impossible to transport all the tools, livestock, and food supplies required for reestablishing a settlement there.[67] In similar fashion, Recio's geographical description mentioned his labor in opening up a pathway to the lowlands, enumerating the leagues in the process. Having seen to the foundation of Guadalupe, "from this town, walking in the said direction, I cleared eight leagues of pathway, where I found a forest and a small mountain chain, and from there to the two settlements that are named Uchupiamo and Inarama, the capitals of fifteen Chunchos provinces, it is twelve leagues, and this path was also cleared."[68] These dry and matter-of-fact descriptions of route and distance are a far cry from the dramatic accounts of missionaries and explorers and, indeed, from many military and administrative reports of the frontier regions and their inhabitants.[69]

In place of the hostile physical environment and stealthy human enemies that abounded in such accounts, Recio's texts portrayed a frontier landscape that served as an ideal entry point to a wealthy and unclaimed region and that offered a profusion of natural resources of its own, including incense, gold, cedar wood, cacao, and, in many parts, wonderfully fertile soils.[70] As for the native people of these regions, they gladly granted him passage into their lands. In the report of 1625, which proposed that Peru's silver be transported to Spain via Pelechuco and the

Beni river (see chapter 5), Recio's vision of the Larecaja frontier as an accessible and welcoming gateway to the Amazon was articulated with still greater clarity. Indeed, his insistence on the ease of passage from Andes to Amazon via Pelechuco worked to minimize the existence of a barrier between the two, allowing the highlands and lowlands to be imagined as *connected* rather than separated by the territories of the piedmont.

As in the writings of missionaries who entered the jungle, Recio's documents held out the promise of salvation—not only for the souls of the original inhabitants of the lowlands but equally for the souls from the highland realms of colonial Peru: the descent of Spanish colonists into the Amazon would secure the return of countless Andean fugitives to their homes, thus ensuring, by means of their physical ascent to the Christianized highlands, the subsequent ascent of their souls to heaven and the simultaneous salvation of Peru's labor-starved mines.[71] Here, however, the Spanish descent that brings about salvation is no longer associated with the ritual of passage through an infernal jungle, but instead involves the unification of two complementary parts. By portraying the eastern frontier as a natural gateway to the lowlands that, rather than being a formidable obstacle, was itself fit for settlement, Recio's texts conveyed that his undertaking amply fulfilled the requirements of the royal ordinances. As I have argued, Recio urged that the salvation of highlands and lowlands depended on their interconnection.

❊   The reports and accounts of service of the *corregidores* and soldiers who were posted to Larecaja did not always portray the frontier regions as dangerous spaces requiring constant defense against incursion. There were exceptions. Moreover, given the appropriate circumstances, visions of a hostile territory could rapidly be transformed into perceived spaces of opportunity or vice versa.

The *yungas* uprisings of 1624 had prompted representations of the frontier as a space to be sealed off from the lowlands beyond and defended. The 1621 account of services of don Diego de Lodeña, who led the repression of the rebellion three years later,[72] painted a very different picture. The conquest of the Amazon lowlands via Larecaja clearly seemed a genuine possibility in 1621, for, as Recio related in his petitions, in 1620 Pedro de Leáegui had renewed his efforts to colonize the piedmont and reestablished the settlement of Nuestra Señora de Guadalupe.

In contrast to later accounts of service by outgoing *corregidores* of Larecaja, Lodeña mainly presented himself not as the defender of a hostile frontier but instead as a potential competitor in the penetration and consolidation of new spaces of exploration and conquest.[73] In 1618, his account of services explained, a peaceful embassy of Aguachile warriors made a brief appearance on the Pelechuco frontier and communicated the desire of their leader Abiomarani to embrace Christianity and swear allegiance to the Spanish king. Three months later, the Aguachiles returned to Larecaja, this time to Charazani, where they apparently gave their promises of vassalage in a formal ceremony presided over by Lodeña. Asked why they had not made their offers of peace to the governor Pedro de Leáegui but had asked to do so before Lodeña, they replied that:

> they have not wished to give, nor have they given it [their obedience] to the said Pedro de Legui [*sic*], because it appears to them that it would not be received with the same authority as in giving it to the *corregidor* of this province, and because they have always understood that this province of Larecaja has been governed in the name of His Majesty, and justice administered, whereas that [authority] which Pedro de Legui possesses is very recent . . . and because of the good name that the said *corregidor* enjoys among them due to his good treatment of the Indians.[74]

On the following day, the Spanish inhabitants of Charazani confirmed before the local notary that peace had been established with the Aguachiles. Urging that such a valuable opportunity should not be wasted, they declared their willingness to serve God and king in the pacification and settlement of the Chunchos territories. However, they insisted, they would do so only under the leadership of Lodeña, "as the said Indians came to seek him out of their own free and spontaneous will." They exhorted him to "carry out the said *entrada,* given that this province is such a close neighbor of that one [the Chunchos], such that no one enjoys greater convenience in terms of aid, manpower, food supplies, and everything else that is necessary for the said expedition . . . and because your honor possesses all the parts and qualities that a leader requires."[75]

All difficulties and dangers that the frontier regions may have presented were set aside by the document's authors, who gave their assurances that the piedmont territories inhabited by the Aguachiles and those that lay beyond were extremely rich in silver and gold and abundant in all types of food.[76] Although this challenge to Leáegui's authority came to nothing—he remained in possession of his governorship until his death in 1638[77]—it eloquently reveals the contingency and opportunism that perpetually underlay the discursive construction of Larecaja's eastern frontiers.

Negotiations on the Cochabamba Frontier

By the time of Leáegui's death, the viceregal government's skepticism vis-à-vis armed expansionist adventures had not diminished. It was preoccupied with the defense of the Pacific and with continued pressure from Spain to protect the royal treasury. A letter written by the viceroy Conde de Chinchón in 1639, expressing his lack of inclination to encourage expeditions of discovery, presented the Spanish monarch with a long list of reasons for his stance on this matter. Besides the inevitable exaggerations, the heavy financial and human costs, the uncertain outcome, and the fact that participants always disregard the instructions and ordinances with which they are issued, the document warned that "discoveries of this kind provide new opportunities for . . . obedient Indians to go to other provinces, in order to flee the payment of their tribute and fulfillment of their *mita* quotas and from the efforts of their priests and *corregidores* to compel them into religious instruction and civility and extirpation of their concupiscent ways."[78]

Indeed, the viceroy added, those who possessed even a moderate understanding of geography realized that the great expanses of unexplored territory that lay between Peru and Brazil's western limits "are lacking in population and in any minerals equal to or richer than those found here."[79] Chinchón's vision of the tropical lowlands was that of an alien and sterile space rather than a reservoir of untapped resources, which, when connected to Peru by means of armed *entradas,* merely drew toward it and consumed the dwindling Andean labor force.

In Upper Peru's frontier regions, however, ambitions to take possession of the Amazon lowlands persisted. Perhaps encouraged by the arrival of a new viceroy in 1639 and by the growing prominence of official concerns over Portuguese incursions from the east,[80] a group of prominent Spanish residents of the *Audiencia* of Charcas mounted a campaign in 1644 to garner support for a new proposal to colonize the lowlands, this time via the tropical frontiers of Cochabamba. In January of that year, large numbers of witnesses, who included Andeans as well as Spaniards, were called upon to give evidence about the attributes of the Raches[81] and Moxos territories and the ease with which they could be accessed and colonized.[82] Elaborating on reports of the Moxos that had circulated in Peru and far beyond it since the late sixteenth century, the majority of the testimonies asserted that the lowlands were blessed with an exuberant and almost infinite wealth in both human populations and natural resources, including precious metals.[83]

The key to this campaign of persuasion, however, did not lie in the tantalizing descriptions of the Moxos, but rather in the portrayals of the piedmont regions that separated Cochabamba from the tropical plains and, most particularly, of the ease with which they could be crossed. In the hills behind Cochabamba, declared the principal witness, General Francisco Rodrigues Peinado, he stumbled across "many Inca pathways that descend to the said plains,"[84] along a short and easy route that would take no more than a week to clear, allowing the passage of horses and loads. By means of these pathways, access to large lowland populations, who lived "in the very heart of Peru and at the door of the mining settlements of Oruro and Potosí and of the city of La Plata,"[85] was assured. The significance of these precolonial pathways, newly "discovered" by Rodrigues Peinado, was reiterated in further testimonies. The lowland territories of the Raches, insisted Captain Sancho Abarca, were actually very close at hand; only the lack of an adequate pathway had prevented their conquest and colonization. Consequently, he said, the general's discovery of a pathway to the lowlands "is the most important thing that could happen today in this kingdom, because, this inconvenience having been removed, in his judgment there will be none in the pacification of the said province and the venture will be the most useful of all that have been carried out in the vicinity of this kingdom and said *corregimientos*."[86]

In fact, the captain insisted, the proposed venture should be regarded not as a conquest of new lands but instead as an extension of Peru itself, which would become richer and more powerful as a result of the material wealth and human populations that the lowlands undoubtedly would yield.[87] A third witness, describing a vantage point at which he had once stood in the mountains beyond Cochabamba, recalled the tears of frustration and desire that his companion shed on seeing smoke rising from indigenous settlements in the plains below, still unconquered yet so close at hand.[88]

By emphasizing the Amazon's proximity to the highlands and the ease with which it could be reached, these witnesses challenged—as Recio had done—the notion of the piedmont as an insurmountable barrier. They conceptualized it instead as a *gateway* or point of entry to "a new world of many Indians and much wealth in gold"[89] that was destined to be incorporated into Peru. Again, like Recio, they insisted that the opening of this gateway would not only allow the unification of the lowlands with the highlands but would also facilitate the return of thousands of Andeans who had fled eastward in the wake of the Spanish conquest. The projection of the piedmont as a gateway, however, was highly selective; the testimonies of 1644 placed repeated emphasis on the notion that Rodrigues Peinado had discovered the *only* viable route of entry to the lands of the Moxos. Maldonado's efforts to conquer the lowlands in the previous century had been doomed to failure, some of the testimonies suggested, by the physical geographies of the frontier: due to the great breadth of the cordillera that lay to the east of Cuzco, "he got lost on two occasions along with four hundred men without being able to cross . . . the said cordillera and its rivers and difficult passes without reaching the plains."[90] A similar fate, according to the testimonies, awaited Pedro de Leáegui and his men, who by attempting the conquest via Larecaja were forced to concede defeat, "because in all those parts the plains are very distant and it rains a lot and there are very fast-flowing rivers."[91] Those, meanwhile, who attempted the *entrada* by advancing northward across the savannah from Santa Cruz found their chosen route blocked by vast and impassable swamps.

Whereas Maldonado blamed the failure of his venture primarily on the malicious intervention of Tordoya, the testimonials of 1644 attributed it to the physical geographies of the frontier regions beyond Cuzco. The two sets of accounts coincided, however, in their mutual recognition of the great difficulties that these geographies presented to Amazon-bound expeditions. The challenges of crossing the cordillera in the Cuzco region *were* significantly greater than in the vicinity of Cochabamba, where the cordillera was narrower, the terrain less abrupt, and the conditions drier.[92] By contrast, Recio's proposals wholly contradicted the assertions of the midcentury testimonies, in that they portrayed the province of Larecaja and its frontiers as by far the best gateway to the Amazon in the whole of Peru. Far from representing the piedmont region as a difficult barrier that lay between the highlands and the Amazon, Recio presented it as an accessible portal to the lowlands that was endowed with valuable natural resources of its own.

✳   In bringing these contradictions to the fore, my purpose is not to demonstrate that one party or another was guilty of lies or exaggerations, but instead to illustrate that those who solicited colonizing commissions to the Amazon after 1573 were anxious to show that their proposals complied with the requirements of the *Ordenanzas*. This task involved challenging, wholly or highly selectively, the profoundly negative perceptions of the piedmont regions found in early reports as well as in the discourse of colonial administrators, officials, and ecclesiastics. Perhaps most strikingly, petitioners sought to achieve this by claiming experience or knowledge of particular *pathways* that would bring the lowlands into easy communication with the established colonial territories and facilitate their incorporation into the kingdom of Peru. Indeed, the *Audiencia* of Charcas, which enthusiastically endorsed the *entrada* via Cochabamba, went as far as to suggest that, in view of the monarchy's urgent need of assistance, the Inca pathways had been revealed to Rodrigues Peinado by the will and grace of God.[93] The pathways described by aspiring seventeenth-century colonizers removed, almost miraculously,

the many obstacles that had sealed the fate of earlier expeditions—
fulfilling, as they did so, the conditions of easy accessibility laid down by
the *Ordenanzas*.

The requirements of the *Ordenanzas* were undoubtedly central in
molding portrayals of the Amazon frontiers, but they were by no means
the only factor. Embodied experience of the landscape played a significant role, as did the activities of indigenous groups and the nature of
their relations with the Spaniards. The appearance of a peaceful Aguachile embassy in Charazani, for example, was fundamental in prompt-
ing local Spaniards to call for an expedition led by their *corregidor* Diego
de Lodeña. Similarly, indigenous agency was largely responsible for
shifting missionaries' portrayals of the frontiers from spaces of willingly
borne physical suffering that would lead to salvation of souls, to sterile
spaces of absolute hostility. Proposals for the conquest of the lowlands,
meanwhile, possessed their own ambiguities. Their rejection of negative discourses about the piedmont regions was partial and selective, and
was intended to emphasize the petitioners' exclusive advantages in terms
of geographical knowledge and location.

The discursive negotiation of the Amazon frontiers was shaped
but not simply driven by legislative texts created in Spain and circulated
throughout the Indies. As I have argued on many occasions in this book,
a variety of conflicts, negotiations, and interests of a local and regional
nature, together with embodied experiences of the piedmont environments, played a no less significant role in this process. Combining and
intersecting, they continuously made and remade the landscapes of the
Amazon frontier in diverse and sometimes unpredictable ways.

CONCLUSION

Mapping Peru in the Sixteenth and Seventeenth Centuries

Between the 1520s, when the first Spaniards tentatively set foot in the northern extremities of the Inca empire, and the final third of the seventeenth century, the human and physical landscapes of what was administered as the Viceroyalty of Peru underwent significant and in some respects dramatic and irreversible changes. In a very material sense, Peru's landscapes underwent a joint process of destruction and colonial reconstruction made manifest in the creation of Spanish towns and places of worship, the planting of European crops, and the gradual imposition of European notions of land ownership. In this respect, the predictions of early chroniclers such as Cieza de León, who envisioned the emergence of prosperous agricultural, urban, and religious landscapes reminiscent of those of distant Europe, were at least partially realized and are described, for example, in some of the *Relaciones Geográficas* of the late sixteenth century. In terms of sheer volume, the geographical information about the viceroyalty and its inhabitants that the viceregal authorities and crown had at their disposal increased dramatically over the course of the sixteenth and seventeenth centuries as a result of the diverse censuses, reports, and geographical descriptions that accumulated in colonial and metropolitan archives.

Despite this cumulative process of knowledge-gathering, however, colonial texts convey little sense of a coherent progression from Spanish experiences or perceptions of Peruvian landscapes as hostile and alien to perceptions of the same landscapes as intimately known, possessed, and controlled. Indeed, while early accounts of successful conquest in Peru frequently portrayed its landscapes as comprehensible and easily controlled, many later administrative texts clearly lacked such optimism. Although some of the Spanish-authored *Relaciones Geográficas* conveyed visions of an ordered and thoroughly known colonial landscape, others portrayed landscapes that seemed deeply alien or, at least, only vaguely known to those who produced the reports. In similar fashion, ecclesiastical anxieties over the persistence and apparent resurgence of indigenous sacred geographies in the central Andes, which emerged with particular vigor in the early seventeenth century, stood in stark contrast to earlier, optimistic predictions regarding the rapid Christianization of the landscape. Like the landscape itself, the Spaniards' perceptions and portrayals were never static, fixed, or homogeneous, but instead underwent constant modification.

The ongoing discursive negotiation of particular landscapes—such as those of Huarochirí—may be detected by tracing the ways in which they were portrayed by members of colonial society over the course of many decades. As the petitions and reports of Juan Recio de León illustrate, however, change and negotiation can also be found in the writings of single individuals. Only by considering Recio's writings *collectively* and chronologically is it possible to appreciate how his representational practices were subject to continued, improvisatory change. What these changes reveal is evidence of an ongoing, imaginative reconstruction of Amazonia and the landscapes of Upper Peru. This reconstruction was not rigidly determined or fixed in place, but drew creatively on the social networks to which Recio had access at the royal court. Recio's contact with the landscapes and territories about which he wrote during his years in Madrid was of course mediated by personal memories but also, no less significantly, by the textual and verbal information about events in the New World that he was able to secure within the spaces of the city and its royal court.

Recio's representations of Amazonia, examined individually, were by no means unique: in variously portraying the Amazon territories as an alternative route for silver transportation, as a hiding place for countless Andean refugees, and as a region that held the key to resolving the problems of the Andean highlands in the early seventeenth century, he put forward ideas that were to be found in the writings and reports of a great many contemporaries. Such correspondences exemplify the uniformities in Spanish accounts of the New World to which Altuna refers.[1] Although these uniformities bear eloquent witness to the collective shaping of Spanish geographical ideas, they were also products of opportunism: as I have demonstrated with reference to Recio de León's petitions, it is precisely by tracing the ways in which particular discourses were subject to ongoing and sometimes unexpected change that this opportunism may best be brought to light.

Just as Recio de León's writings were shaped by his presence at the royal court in Madrid, so too, the representational practices of other Spaniards situated in Peru were shaped by their local contexts. On the one hand, the demands of ecclesiastical legislation strongly influenced the manner in which the neighboring parish priests of Huarochirí portrayed the landscapes of their respective jurisdictions. Earlier Jesuit missionaries had strategically highlighted the physical challenges and privations they encountered in negotiating the pathways of this mountainous region; the priests Guerrero and Mojica were instead concerned to prevent such difficulties from coming to light when describing their own experiences. In this respect, their testimonies were obliged to engage with discourses that originated far beyond the local contexts of their lives. On the other hand, however, the priests' everyday experiences, together with the arguments that supported their respective claims, were also locally determined by changes in the human landscapes of the parishes, brought about by the mobility of their resident populations within and beyond the parish limits. In similar fashion, the vacillation between positive and negative portrayals of the piedmont regions—as either enticing gateways to the east or as formidable barriers—had as much to do with shifting colonial relations in localities along the frontier as with the requirements of royal legislation on discovery and settlement.

Despite the frequent tailoring of the landscape to suit personal objectives and official expectations, extant accounts of services, geographical descriptions, and other related texts should be regarded as authentic. By this I do not mean that they convey the truth about what Peru's landscapes were "really" like, but rather that they bear within them traces of lived experience and of sincerity. Although this authenticity was manifested in a variety of ways—an attachment to place, or a sense of genuine conviction based on locally garnered knowledge and insight—it was expressed most forcefully in the intensity and immediacy with which landscape was experienced and negotiated through the body.

Although accounts of services unquestionably served as vehicles of self-aggrandization and promotion, even these display authenticity, including the *relaciones* presented by survivors of the first Peru-bound expedition from Panama. In documents such as these, recollections of a struggle for survival in hostile environments cannot be reduced to a mere discursive strategy, despite possible exaggerations and the formulaic manner in which they were expressed. The intensity with which landscape was experienced in such situations as a relentless assault on the body is impossible to dismiss or to overlook.

Elsewhere, however—for instance, in the geographical description produced by Diego Dávila Briceño, the long-serving *corregidor* of the Huarochirí province—it is easier to overlook the physicality of Spanish experiences of landscape in Peru, and to dwell instead on the shared geographical images and cultural values that connect such writings to the metropolitan "center." Dávila, a dedicated (albeit self-promoting) servant of the colonial government and crown, offered the Council of the Indies an account of colonial order that was projected through the linguistic and numerical categorization of people, resources, and geographical distances, as well as through the disembodied vision of his map. At the same time, however, his account reveals and is structured by a direct, corporeal experience of the landscapes that he described and categorized—experience that was gained by repeated journeying along the pathways of his jurisdiction.

Colonial texts such as these do not simply contain within them eclectic snapshots of a static landscape viewed from afar: they record a diversity of nonrepresentational *practices* that shed light on the embodied and spatial ways in which the Spanish colonizers experienced, used, and negotiated the landscape. By attending carefully to these practices, it is possible to restore to Peru's landscapes a materiality that is all too easily lost by confining colonial writings to a rarefied textual world.

Moreover, a concern for praxis opens up possibilities for acknowledging the prominent role of indigenous people and other non-Europeans in shaping Spanish experiences of landscape. While Spanish-authored texts can offer little more than unreliable, mediated insights into the meanings that Peru's native peoples attributed to the landscapes they inhabited, these texts clearly reveal that the ways in which those landscapes were experienced and made to matter by the Spanish were intimately linked to indigenous practices and agency.

In the initial period of exploration and conquest, the Spaniards' mobility was variously hindered or facilitated by characteristics of physical landscape and climate. It was also affected, no less significantly, by the nature of the relations that were established with indigenous peoples. The dramatic shift from stasis to mobility that marked the Spaniards' arrival in the Andean regions—a shift conveyed in accounts of service and histories alike—cannot be attributed solely to transformations in the natural environment, dramatic though these were. Without the provision of food, porterage, and shelter, and in the absence of long-term indigenous labor that shaped agriculture, roads, and places of habitation, embodied Spanish experiences of landscape certainly would have featured much more prominently in their testimonies and accounts of Peru. As we have seen, the corporeal experience of landscape, and above all of the landscape's nonhuman elements and forces, often resurfaced in Spanish writings in the absence of an indigenous presence.

The diverse body of texts produced in early colonial Peru bear eloquent testimony to how the Spanish presence altered the ways in which many indigenous communities and their members inhabited and experienced landscape on a daily basis. The creation of the reductions, the establishment of the mining draft of Potosí, and the suppression of "idolatrous" religious practices are just a few of the dramatic colonial phenomena that changed Andean peoples' spatial, embodied, and imaginative relationships with their lived-in landscapes. In turn, however, indigenous communities continued to shape their colonizers' encounters with landscape in colonial times. The returns to sites of habitation outside the reductions, the longer-distance migrations to other provinces, the strategic suppression of particular local knowledge, and the continuation of prohibited spiritual practices all played a part in modifying the everyday spatial trajectories of *corregidores,* priests, and missionaries, and in strengthening the conviction, expressed most persistently in administrative correspondence, that Peru's rural landscapes were stubbornly resistant to being thoroughly known and controlled.

In many instances, it is arguably appropriate to regard the indigenous practices and beliefs that contributed to such administrative anxieties over Peru's provincial landscapes as clear expressions of resistance to the imposition of colonial control. The intentional withholding of knowledge about the landscape's sacred geographies and material resources, or the physical concealment of illicit objects of spiritual significance beneath its Catholicized surface, certainly appear to provide two compelling illustrations of the colonial landscape as a focus for indigenous resistance to Spanish domination. However, if, as Rose argues, the category of resistance inescapably and persistently accords primacy to the act of domination,[2] then it cannot provide an adequate means for conceptualizing the struggles over landscape that unfolded in colonial Peru.

As a close scrutiny of the *Relaciones Geográficas* and the circumstances of their production indicates, the Huancas' "resistant" strategies in representing the Jauja landscape were by no means simply reactive, nor did they involve inevitable or unambiguous opposition to Spanish worldviews and practices. Although the documentary evidence is fragmentary, enough of it exists to trace the unfolding of Huanca-Spanish relations at different times and in different circumstances. Interpreted in the light of these shifting relations, the Jauja *RG* and the representations of the province contained within it appear less as products of a predictable opposition than as the outcome of ongoing, improvisatory negotiations, which exceed the boundaries of domination and resistance. The activities of individual Spaniards, moreover, were on occasions strikingly comparable to "resistant" indigenous practices—if not because they were motivated by shared beliefs or interests, then because they *both* helped to fuel official perceptions that Peru's provincial landscapes continuously evaded thorough knowledge and control.

At the outset of this study, I suggested that notions of unpredictability, contingency, and compromise are usefully conveyed by speaking of "negotiations" over landscape. As the preceding chapters have

shown, the ways in which Peru's landscapes were experienced, portrayed, and put to use by its colonizers were shaped, in part, by such
conditions. The meanings that could be attributed to landscape were
not infinite, for inevitably they were molded by past experience and
shared cultural practices, norms, and beliefs. Within these constraints,
however, there is evidence not only of diversity but of encounters with
landscape—imaginative, discursive, and embodied—that were subject
to continuous modification. There is another reason, however, why the
complex interweaving of colonial practices and landscape might be conceptualized as "negotiation," provided that the realities of unequal power
relations are not obscured by the use of this concept. More effectively
than the binary concepts of domination and resistance, it allows us to
recognize that *all* members of colonial society—and not just those who
occupied positions of dominance—were proactive agents in the material and discursive shaping of Peru's colonial landscapes.

Dramatic encounters and events were not absent from these processes. At the very least, drama made a frequent appearance in the Spanish reports, chronicles, and accounts of service that described terrible
suffering endured by missionaries en route to the Amazon, bewilder-
ing networks of native sacred geographies "discovered" in the Andes, or
the swiftness with which the first conquistadors swept across the land.
However, the everyday experiences of colonial officials and the petty intrigues of parish life are every bit as important as dramatic accounts of
conquest and exploration. They demonstrate that Peru's landscapes were
largely shaped and negotiated within the realms of the ordinary and the
mundane. My emphasis on the mundane does not seek a "normaliza-
tion" of colonial landscapes, nor is it a denial of the violence that is so
often central to their creation: violence, as Stern observes, was integral
and endemic to everyday life in colonial Peru.[3] Rather, unless we attend
to the everyday, it is difficult to comprehend colonial landscapes as sustained *processes* that unfolded through the activities of all those who inhabited them, or to obtain rich, multidimensional insights into Spanish
experiences and perceptions of those landscapes.

The descriptions of the New World flowing from the pens of
colonial chroniclers, historians, and geographers are, of course, inesti-
mably valuable in revealing how its landscapes were both imagined and

experienced by Europeans. As this study has demonstrated, careful readings of many of these published texts effectively bring to light some of the mundane practices that were the context for Spanish encounters with landscape—even within the tumultuous circumstances of the conquest and early colonial era. As such, they offer a valuable means of demystifying conquest and providing evidence, albeit in partial and fragmentary ways, of the indigenous agencies that played a prominent role in shaping those encounters. However, voluminous writings are still confined to the archives—writings describing in detail the intricate affairs of everyday colonial life—and in these lie the greatest potential for reanimating Peru's colonial landscapes.

GLOSSARY

alferez: second lieutenant.

altiplano: the high plateau of the southern Andes.

audiencia: judicial and administrative council, and the territory under that council's administration.

ayllu: ostensibly kin-based Andean segmentary unit of social organization.

cacique: a Caribbean word introduced to Peru by the Spanish that was used to refer to an indigenous lord.

cacique mayor: a high-ranking *cacique* or lord.

cacique principal: a paramount *cacique* or lord.

capitán general: captain general. Spanish military rank above that of *maestre de campo.*

chicha: in the Andes, a fermented beverage made of maize.

corregidor: crown official with administrative and judicial authority over a district.

corregimiento: the administrative district to which a *corregidor* was assigned.

criollo: a term used in Spanish America to refer to Spaniards who were born in the Indies.

curaca: Quechua term for an Andean lord. In colonial times it was often replaced by *cacique.*

encomendero: an individual who possessed an *encomienda.*

encomienda: a grant of Indians made to a Spaniard by the crown. In return for labor services and tribute, *encomenderos* were expected to provide protection and religious instruction.

entrada: an exploratory or colonizing venture of either a military or a religious nature.

fanega: A measure of volume that was generally equivalent to approximately 1.6 bushels (British measure). One bushel is equivalent to about 36.4 liters.

forastero: an Andean living in a community from which he or she did not originate.

huaca: a place or object imbued with sacred or extraordinary qualities.

indio ladino: a Hispanicized indigenous person who was familiar with Spanish language and customs.

justicia mayor: chief magistrate.

maestre de campo: campmaster; a Spanish military rank immediately below that of captain general.

mestizo: an individual of mixed (Spanish and indigenous) descent.

mezquita: the Spanish word for "mosque."

mita: a rotational system of forced labor that was introduced in colonial times, especially for the mines. The word derives from the Quechua term *mit'a,* meaning a turn of labor.

mitayo: a person assigned to the colonial labor draft or *mita.*

montaña: in Spanish America, a term used to refer to areas of forest, and in particular to the dense cloud forests on the eastern slopes of the Andes.

mulato: an individual of mixed European and African parentage.

oidor: crown official, usually a judge or professional with legal training, who served as a member of an *audiencia.*

parcialidad: lineage group.

policía: a complex term that may be translated as "civilized life."

puna: dry, high-altitude grasslands, at an elevation of 4,000 meters or more.

quinoa: a protein-rich grain cultivated in the Andes.

quipu: Quechua term that refers to a device made of knotted, twisted, and variously colored cords used for storing information in Inca and early colonial times.

reducción: a colonial settlement to which indigenous populations were forcibly relocated.

relación: an account or report.

relación de servicios: account or testimony of services presented to the monarch or his representatives with the aim of obtaining rewards or favors. Also known as *probanza* or *información.*

repartimiento: area of jurisdiction pertaining to an *encomendero*. Although the word's territorial connotations came to dominate following the conquest, it was also used as a synonym of *encomienda* until the late seventeenth century.

tambo: a Quechua word referring to a type of inn or resthouse that had its origins in Inca times.

teniente de gobernador: deputy governor.

yanacona: in precolonial times, a personal retainer of the Inca ruler or other ethnic lord. In colonial times, an indigenous person who, having severed links with his or her community of origin, was attached to and served a Spaniard. The Spanish adopted the plural form (*yanacona*) of the original Quechua word *yana* for use in the singular.

yungas: warm, low-altitude regions on the eastern and western fringes of the Andes.

NOTES

ONE. Landscape and the Spanish Conquest of Peru

1. *Relación Samano-Xerez,* 68.

2. Pagden comments, "Attachment led to possession. But most things possessed, if they are to be of any value to the possessor, have to be capable of mobility." Pagden, *European Encounters with the New World,* 27.

3. With reference to this text, Fraser comments, "These are all signs of a prosperous and civilized people, a people well worth conquering." Fraser, *The Architecture of Conquest,* 23.

4. Mignolo, *The Darker Side,* 16.

5. This draws on the work of Jane Jacobs, who insists on the importance of attending not only to the metaphorical but also to the "real" geographies and spaces of imperialism. See Jacobs, *Edge of Empire,* 1.

6. See, e.g., the following edited collection of geographical accounts published in the nineteenth century by a Spanish geographer: Jiménez de la Espada, ed., *Relaciones Geográficas de Indias: Perú.*

7. Significant examples include Butzer's special issue of the *Annals of the Association of American Geographers* entitled "The Americas before and after 1492: Current Geographical Research"; Greenblatt, *Marvelous Possessions*; Pastor Bodmer, *The Armature of Conquest*; Zamora, *Reading Columbus.*

8. For examples, see Mundy, *The Mapping of New Spain*; Arias and Meléndez, eds., *Mapping Colonial Spanish America*; Kinsbruner, *The Colonial Spanish-American City*; Millones Figueroa and Ledezma, eds., *El saber de los jesuitas.*

9. See, e.g., Salomon, "Vertical Politics on the Inka Frontier"; Molinié Fioravanti, "El simbolismo de frontera en los Andes"; Bauer, *The Sacred Landscape of the Inca.*

10. Cañedo-Argüelles Fabrega, "La tenencia de la tierra en el sur andino"; Gade, "Landscape, System and Identity in the Post-Conquest Andes."

11. See, e.g., Sempat Assadourian, "Los derechos a las tierras del Ynga"; Stavig, "Ambiguous Visions."

12. Examples include Gade and Escobar, "Village Settlement and the Colonial Legacy in Southern Peru"; Fraser, *The Architecture of Conquest*; Cummins, "Forms of Andean Colonial Towns"; H. Scott, "A Mirage of Colonial Consensus."

13. Lavallé, *Las promesas ambiguas*; Pease G.Y., *Las crónicas y los Andes*; Someda, *El imperio de los Incas*.

14. Graubart, "Indecent Living," 215.

15. A narrow approach to what constitutes geography in early colonial Spanish texts is a feature of much scholarly work. In 1992, Butzer took historians such as J. H. Elliott to task for suggesting that sixteenth-century southern Europeans had scant interest in geography, and drew attention to the ample contributions made by the Spanish in the New World to the development of European geographical inquiry. Butzer's own exploration of Spanish geographical perceptions of the Americas, however, remains firmly within the boundaries of texts that deal explicitly with geography or natural history. See Butzer, "From Columbus to Acosta," 558.

16. Elliott, "Final Reflections," 399.

17. As Pagden writes, the Spanish empire was "an empire based upon people, defeated subjects who could be transformed into a physical labour force." Pagden, *Lords of All the World*, 65.

18. Sluyter, "Colonialism and Landscape in the Americas," 414. See also Sluyter, *Colonialism and Landscape*.

19. Sluyter, "Colonialism and Landscape in the Americas," 415–20.

20. Elliott, "Final Reflections," 406. Although I agree with Elliott's suggestions that the diversity of European voices and experiences has been neglected in much recent scholarship on early Spanish America, I part ways with him over his apparent assumption that indigenous populations played little or no part in shaping the New World's colonial landscapes and European perceptions and experiences of them.

21. See Cosgrove, "Landscape and the European Sense of Sight"; Cosgrove and Daniels, eds., *The Iconography of Landscape*.

22. Bender, "Introduction," 3. See also Cresswell, who argues that the concept of landscape is "too burdened with its own history—too fixated on origins." Cresswell, "Landscape and the Obliteration of Practice," 269.

23. Matless, "Introduction: The Properties of Landscape," 231.

24. Influenced by phenomenology as well as by broader concerns for engaging with theories of practice, cultural geographers and anthropologists

alike have increasingly embraced approaches to landscape that explore the material and symbolic practices that shape it and give it meaning, and that acknowledge the corporeality of landscape experience. Recent work includes Bender, *Landscape*; Dubow, "From a View on the World"; Ingold, *The Perception of the Environment*; Rose, "Landscapes and Labyrinths."

25. Rose, "Landscapes and Labyrinths," 457.

26. Pastor Bodmer, *The Armature of Conquest*; Piqueras Céspedes, *Entre el hambre y El Dorado.*

27. See, e.g., Ahern, "'Llevando el norte sobre el ojo izquierdo'"; Elliott, "Final Reflections"; Elliott, *The Old World and the New*; Mignolo, *The Darker Side*; Rivera-Ayala, "Riding High, the Horseman's View."

28. Bolaños, "On the Issues of Academic Colonization."

29. On the need for scholars of landscape to look beyond the confines of the local, see D. Mitchell, "The Lure of the Local."

30. See Craib, "Cartography and Power"; Harley, *The New Nature of Maps*; Mignolo, *The Darker Side*; Rabasa, *Inventing America.*

31. See Butzer, "From Columbus to Acosta." This view is also detectable in Ashcroft, who cites Seed's suggestion that "'Spanish colonialism produced the census, British colonialism the map.'" Ashcroft, *Post-colonial Transformation,* 124.

32. I borrow this expression from Jacobs, who, with reference to British imperialism in Australia, argues that "[t]he map has . . . become the over-determined signifier of the spatiality of the imperial imagination." Jacobs, *Edge of Empire,* 20.

33. This view is expressed in Mundy, *The Mapping of New Spain,* as well as in Padrón, *The Spacious Word.*

34. For discussions of "popular" forms of mapping in Spanish America and Iberia, see Mundy, *The Mapping of New Spain*; Padrón, *The Spacious Word*; Kagan, *Urban Images.*

35. It must be emphasized, however, that written text and cartographic images were complementary rather than mutually exclusive in the production of geographical knowledge of the New World. Conveying this interconnection, Padrón unites both within the term "cartographic literature." Padrón, *The Spacious Word,* 12. See also Mundy, *The Mapping of New Spain,* on the function of written text on the maps of the sixteenth-century *Relaciones Geográficas* from New Spain.

36. Blunt and Rose, eds., *Writing Women and Space.*

37. In colonial Latin American contexts, see, e.g., Myers, "Writing of the Frontier"; Pratt, *Imperial Eyes.*

38. For a discussion of this segregation and of the need to overcome it, see Barclay Rey de Castro, "Olvido de una historia." Important examples of historical work challenging the Amazon-Andes divide in the precolonial

and colonial eras include Renard-Casevitz, Saignes, and Taylor, *L'Inca, l'espagnol et les sauvages*; Saignes, *Los Andes orientales*.

39. Viola Recasens, "La cara oculta de los Andes," 12–13. See also Saignes, *Los Andes orientales*.

TWO.   Beyond Textuality: Landscape, Embodiment, and Native Agency

1. The civil war was not a dynastic struggle in European terms, but rather a conflict framed within a complex of rituals. Atahualpa, who was captured by the Spaniards at Cajamarca and eventually executed, was identified as the bastard son and Huascar as the legitimate successor, thus enabling the conquistadors to justify their actions. See Pease G.Y., *Las crónicas*, 139 and 287–88.

2. Restall, *Seven Myths*.

3. See Wachtel, *The Vision of the Vanquished*.

4. See, e.g., Harris, "'The Coming of the White People'"; Restall, *Seven Myths*.

5. Pastor Bodmer, *The Armature of Conquest*.

6. Examples include Espinoza Soriano, "Los señoríos étnicos"; Piqueras Céspedes, *Entre el hambre y El Dorado*; Restall, *Seven Myths*.

7. For examples, see Burnett, *Masters of All They Surveyed*; Dubow, "From a View on the World"; Martins, "A Naturalist's Vision"; Myers, "Colonial Geography and Masculinity"; Naylor, "Discovering Nature."

8. Pizarro and Almagro were by no means the only individuals with an interest in exploring the Pacific coast: by 1524, many others were planning to explore the same route. Competition intensified further in 1527, perhaps due to exaggerated reports brought back by members of Pizarro's second expedition. See Varón Gabai, *Francisco Pizarro*, 17–18, for a detailed discussion of the characteristics and development of the type of conquest company set up by Pizarro and Almagro. See also Lockhart, *The Men of Cajamarca*.

9. For a detailed account and chronology of the Pacific explorations, see Murphy, "The Earliest Spanish Advances," and for the years of conquest, see Hemming, *The Conquest of the Incas*.

10. One participant of the first two expeditions, who wrote in 1527 to a royal official in Panama, estimated that the venture had already cost 180 Spanish lives. Published in Porras Barrenechea, *Cartas*, 7.

11. Cieza de León, *Crónica del Perú. Tercera parte*, 10–11.

12. The men who stayed behind with Pizarro are frequently referred to as the "thirteen men of fame." Lockhart, *The Men of Cajamarca*, is noncommittal about their precise number.

13. Pastor Bodmer, *The Armature of Conquest*, 120.

14. See also Molloy, "Alteridad y reconocimiento." Examining Cabeza de Vaca's account, Molloy illustrates how the early narrative, describing the conquistadors' wanderings in the swamps of Florida, is framed by the search and desire for maize.

15. Pastor Bodmer, *The Armature of Conquest,* 116.

16. See, e.g., Pastor Bodmer, *The Armature of Conquest,* on the letters written by Hernán Cortés to Charles V.

17. In the presence of a royal official, the petitioners' statements, presented in the form of a questionnaire, were verified by selected witnesses. Because these documents were produced with the aim of turning "*honra* (honor and status) into something more tangible," they must be interpreted with caution. Exaggerations or intentional distortions were not uncommon, although, MacLeod argues, as the sixteenth century progressed, outright lies became rarer, given that "people watched each other carefully and were ever ready to set the record straight and correct or denounce errors of fact." See MacLeod, "The *Relaciones de Méritos,*" 26 and 29.

18. The decision of the "thirteen men of fame" to continue with Pizarro was not, however, purely the result of personal endurance and determination. Such expeditions were financial ventures and not "egalitarian" bands of adventurers who treated each other as equals or distributed resources equally. As Lockhart indicates, participants often included men who were retainers or even slaves of captains or backers; free agents, meanwhile, borrowed money to outfit themselves, or borrowed money on credit. Expedition leaders often carried supplies that they would later sell to their men at inflated prices. "Those coming back to Panama must have been mainly undersupplied debtors, while the heroic Thirteen staying were probably investors and creditors for the most part." Lockhart, *The Men of Cajamarca,* 67–68.

19. AGI, Patronato 150, N. 3, R. 2, fols. 65v–66.

20. AGI, Patronato 150, N. 3, R. 2, fol. 75.

21. In discussing the discourse of failure, Pastor Bodmer, *The Armature of Conquest,* 124, similarly identifies a drawing together of human subject and physical surroundings. She comments that "*landscape* disappears altogether as an aesthetic concept or category of perception to be replaced by *environment.*" In contrast to Pastor Bodmer, however, whose understanding of "landscape" appears to be predominantly associated with a detached mode of vision, my own use of the term advances the notion that landscape is experienced corporeally. Like Dubow, "From a View on the World," I suggest that vision should also be recognized as an embodied faculty.

22. Emphasis added. AGI, Patronato 150, N. 3, R. 2, fol. 75v.

23. AGI, Patronato 150, N. 3, R. 2, fol. 66.

24. Emphasis added. Pizarro's soldiers to the Governor of Panama, 05.VIII.1527. Porras Barrenechea, *Cartas,* 9–10. Another individual repeats this sentiment in a letter to his brother, lamenting that "at present we are on an island where with great difficulty we go to the mainland to the huts [of the natives] and search for maize in the hills and carry it on our backs, because neither I nor anyone else has people to carry it for them, and so we live dying, not being able to fill ourselves with maize alone . . . enough is enough, for I have already spent two years like a beggar with no one to serve me." Maestre Baltasar to his brother, 15.VIII.1527. See *Cartas,* 17.

25. In a fascinating study that addresses alimentary aspects of the conquest expeditions in northern South America, Piqueras Céspedes emphasizes the crucial auxiliary role played by indigenous and other servants or slaves forced to accompany the conquistadors. In addition to their primary function as porters and providers of food, native servants were utilized as guides, interpreters, and informers. Native women, who played all these roles, performed the additional tasks of satisfying sexual needs, preparing food, and nursing the sick or wounded, thereby helping to bring the Spaniards closer to something resembling "a situation of lived normality." The utter decimation of indigenous auxiliaries was not unusual in these expeditions, "for if the army encountered difficulties, they [the natives] were the first to suffer the consequences." See Piqueras Céspedes, *Entre el hambre y El Dorado.* Quotes at 196 and 172.

26. Ribera was among those who remained with Pizarro on the Isla del Gallo. Ribera's petition claims that the continuation of the voyage to Peru was largely thanks to his efforts; "knowing the service that was being made to your Highness in the discovery of these kingdoms, I persuaded many to stay with the said don Francisco Pizarro until we received reinforcements and could continue the said discovery." "Don Juan Dáualos de Riuera. Información de servicios de su padre, Niculás de Ribera," 1582. AGI, Lima 126, fol. 9.

27. AGI, Lima 126, fol. 10.

28. AGI, Lima 126, fol. 10v.

29. AGI, Lima 126, fol. 10v.

30. Pastor Bodmer, *The Armature of Conquest,* 130.

31. This phenomenon is described by Carter with reference to the colonization of Australia and its invention in the histories that were constructed of that process. With specific reference to Blainey's *Our Side of the Country,* he comments, "The uniquely spatial experience is replaced by a ritual of repetitions. Putative journeys are effaced by a cult of places." Carter, *The Road to Botany Bay,* xxi.

32. Interestingly, those who were unable to be present at these sites, either through duty or misfortune, offered this up as a form of service that deserved recognition. Alvaro Muñoz, a surgeon and barber, stated in his petition that he stayed behind in San Miguel "curing many people of their illnesses and wounds on the order of the governor, for which reason I did not accompany the people who went ahead, nor obtain a part of what was seized in Cajamarca where Atabalipa [Atahualpa] was captured." AGI, Lima 118, "Probanza de Alvaro Muñoz, vezino de Granadilla."

33. AGI, Patronato 150, N. 6, R. 2, fol. 186v.

34. AGI, Patronato 150, N. 6, R. 2, fol. 189. Many further examples of accounts of confrontation with great numbers of extremely hostile human adversaries may be found in the *relaciones de servicios*. See, for instance, AGI, Lima 118, "Probanza de Martín Salas," fol. 1.

35. Cieza de León, *Crónica del Perú. Tercera parte*, 119.

36. In Cieza de León's view, of course, the ultimate force resided not with the physical environment but with God: "I have represented Peru as three deserted and uninhabited cordilleras: from these, by will of God, the valleys and rivers I have mentioned emerge, [and] outside of these it would be impossible for humans to live." *Crónica del Perú. Tercera parte*, 119.

37. Raffles, *In Amazonia*, 108.

38. See Espinoza Soriano, "La guaranga" and "Los huancas." Recent research suggests that, prior to the Inca conquest, "Wanka society comprised a series of hierarchical polities in chronic conflict with one another." Despite this political fragmentation, they were "sophisticated and populous enough to pose a substantial military threat" to the Incas. Equally, the fertility of Huanca lands and their location at a crossroads between the north-south highland route and east-west routes connecting jungle and coast made it imperative for the Incas to secure control of this region. As well as constructing a highway, they built over three thousand storage buildings, resettled the Huancas from their fortified hilltops to the valleys, and introduced *mitmaqkuna* (settlers of other ethnicity and regions). They also divided the region into three *saya*, or divisions—Hatun Xauxa, Lurin Huanca, and Hanan Huanca—which apparently corresponded to pre-Inca ethnic and political divisions. See D'Altroy, "Transitions in Power." Quotes at 81 and 94.

39. D'Altroy, "Transitions in Power," 93. The Huancas were not the only group to side with the Spaniards—the majority of local lords did so, suggests Rostworowski de Diez Canseco, *History of the Inca Realm*, 133–34. In central Peru, however, the Huancas assumed particular importance as allies because of their abundant resources. The alliance between the Spaniards and the northern Chacha group is examined in Espinoza Soriano, "Los señoríos étnicos."

40. AGI, Lima 205, N. 7, fol. 3. I have chosen to use the original archival documents, but full transcriptions may be found in Espinoza Soriano, "Los huancas."

41. For strategic reasons, Lima was chosen instead in 1534 as the site of the capital.

42. AGI, Lima 118, "Información de méritos y servicios de Sebastián de Torres," fol. 3. Interestingly, Nicolás de Ribera—of Isla del Gallo fame—acted as one of Torres's witnesses. In responding to this question, he recalled that when Quizquiz attacked Jauja, the Spaniards went to resist him accompanied by Indian allies. In his own *relación,* however, he is completely silent with regard to the Huancas' role as allies.

43. For the meaning and history of usage of *repartimiento,* see Lockhart, *Of Things of the Indies,* 5–6.

44. AGI, Lima 205, N. 16, fol. 2v.

45. AGI, Lima 205, N. 7, fol. 3.

46. On the *fanega* as a measure of volume generally equivalent to approximately 1.6 bushels (British measure), see Larson, *Cochabamba, 1550–1900,* 403. One bushel is equivalent to about 36.4 liters, so 75,000 *fanegas* is equal to about 4,368,000 liters.

47. AGI, Lima 205, N. 7, fols. 9–26. The quantity of goods supplied early on in the conquest was particularly vast, and much was undoubtedly taken from Inca storehouses located around Jauja. Nevertheless, the storehouses were soon emptied, and the resources that the Huancas continued to provide over the next two decades were genuinely drawn from their own communities, with serious consequences for their subsistence. See Sempat Assadourian, *Transiciones,* 56–59.

48. On Andean systems of reciprocity, see Rostworowski de Diez Canseco, *History of the Inca Realm,* and Pease G.Y., *Curacas, reciprocidad y riqueza.*

49. Added emphasis. AGI, Lima 205, N. 7, fol. 3. Although Pedro de Alconchel, one of Cusichaca's witnesses, admitted that Pizarro's men stole considerable quantities of goods from the inhabitants of Jauja, Nicolás de Ribera, who also testified, attempted to exonerate his companions by shifting the blame onto the *yanaconas* whom the Spaniards had brought with them to Jauja.

50. Lima 205, N. 7, fols. 9v–10v. Again, it must be reiterated that these vast quantities were probably taken from Inca storehouses.

51. This practice is also recorded by Cristóbal de Molina (el Almagrista). See Molina, *Cosas acaescidas en el Perú,* 62.

52. In the context of expeditions of conquest in what is now Venezuela and Colombia, Piqueras Céspedes, *Entre el hambre y El Dorado,* 169, similarly speaks of an "indigenous security buffer" that allowed the Spanish

invaders "to operate with greater confidence and perseverance . . . frequently attenuating their problems or tensions and fortifying a clear psychological feeling of superiority, unity and dominion over the indigenous world."

53. AGI, Lima 205, N. 16, fol. 20.

54. Road networks existed before the rise of the Incas, but during their rule they greatly increased in number and extent, reaching from thirty to fifty thousand kilometers in total. Two principal roads existed, one traversing the highlands from north to south and one running along the coast. These were connected by lesser roads that ran from east to west, leading from coast to jungle. The nature of the roads depended on the local terrain: parts of the highland road were paved; coastal roads were unpaved but, where they passed through populated valleys, were lined by high walls and shaded by trees. Various types of *tambos* or "inns" stood at intervals along the roads. These provided lodging for the Inca and his retinue and for state officials and messengers. Rostworowski de Diez Canseco, *History of the Inca Realm,* 59–65. For a detailed study, see Hyslop, *The Inka Road System.*

55. Cieza de León, *Crónica del Perú. Tercera parte,* 174.

56. Molina, *Cosas acaescidas en el Perú,* 84.

57. Taussig, *Shamanism,* 293.

58. Xerez, *Verdadera relación,* 158.

59. Detailed discussions of the various forms of narrative prose that were used by the Spanish in the era of conquest and colonization, as well as of their particular characteristics, may be found in Mignolo, "Cartas, crónicas y relaciones," and in Someda, *El imperio de los Incas.*

60. See the study of three Spanish chronicles of Peru by Fossa, "The Discourse of History."

61. Such interest emerged with particular clarity in the 1540s, as Spanish residents in Peru, with the help of indigenous informants, began to carry out detailed investigations into the Andean world and the pre-Hispanic past. See MacCormack, *Religion in the Andes.*

62. Greenblatt, *Marvelous Possessions,* 56. Original emphasis.

63. "The destinatary (enunciatary) is present in the text . . . [and] is part of the constitutive efforts to configure it. These aspects inform the use of a particular language, help devise specific strategies, model a specific type of communication, of certain meanings and senses, of allusions to a specific referent; most important of all, they contribute to the construction of the intrinsic logic, coherence and pertinence of the text." See Fossa, "The Discourse of History," 17.

64. Raffles, *In Amazonia,* 108.

65. The Council of Jauja to the Emperor, 20.VII.1534. In Porras Barrenechea, *Cartas,* 127.

66. Xerez, *Verdadera relación,* 98.

67. Xerez, *Verdadera relación,* 130–31.

68. Those who lacked portable wealth were most likely to remain: "Everyone who returned at all went rich; otherwise there was no point." See Lockhart, *The Men of Cajamarca,* 44–64, for a discussion of the factors that influenced conquistadors' decisions to return or stay in Peru.

69. Graubart, "Indecent Living," 218.

70. D'Altroy, *The Incas,* 3.

71. MacCormack, "Ethnography in South America."

72. The impact of indigenous populations, and of their dramatic decline in the wake of conquest, on the landscapes of Central America is discussed by Sauer, *The Early Spanish Main,* 283–89. The post-conquest encroachment of forest cover in many parts of the humid New World tropics is fundamental, Denevan argues, to the widespread modern belief that these areas constituted a pristine wilderness prior to the arrival of Europeans. Denevan, "The Pristine Myth."

73. Andagoya, *Relación de los sucesos,* 410–11.

74. Andagoya, *Relación de los sucesos,* 410.

75. See, e.g., Cieza de León, *Crónica del Perú. Primera parte,* 143: "in many parts where [the Devil] was once esteemed and venerated he is now abhorred, and detested as evil: and the temples of the damned gods ruined and demolished, in such a manner that there is no longer any sign of a statue or idol."

76. Fray Vicente Valverde to the Emperor, 20.III.1539. In Porras Barrenechea, *Cartas,* 312–13.

77. Rosenzvaig, "La ostra abierta."

78. Cieza de León, *Crónica del Perú. Primera parte,* 210.

79. Lizárraga, *Descripción breve,* 17.

80. Lizárraga, *Descripción breve,* 17.

81. Rabasa, *Inventing America,* 130.

82. Cieza de León, *Crónica del Perú. Primera parte,* 297–98.

83. Gade, "Landscape, System and Identity."

84. Cieza de León, *Crónica del Perú: Primera parte,* 298.

85. *Ordenanzas sobre descubrimiento nuevo y población,* 530.

86. Compare Fraser, *The Architecture of Conquest,* 49.

87. See Fraser, *The Architecture of Conquest,* chapter 3 (82–107), in which she discusses the labor of construction that was carried out by Amerindians in both Spanish towns and indigenous settlements in colonial Peru.

88. In placing emphasis on these "everyday" dimensions, I draw in particular on the work of Cresswell, who insists on the need to explore not only the "grand and distinguished" but also the "everyday and unexceptional" in the study of landscape. See Cresswell, "Landscape and the Obliteration of Practice," 280. See also Rose, "Landscapes and Labyrinths," 457.

89. Fossa, "The Discourse of History," 9.
90. Bunn, "'Our wattled cot,'" 135–36.
91. Stern, *Peru's Indian Peoples.*

THREE.   Landscapes of Resistance? Peru's *Relaciones Geográficas* ·

1. Mignolo, *The Darker Side,* 283.
2. The use of questionnaires in sixteenth-century Europe as a means of gathering information about other territories was not restricted to Spain, but only in Spain did they become a prominent tool of government. See Alvarez Peláez, "El cuestionario de 1577," c.
3. See the "Cédula, instrucción y memoria para la formación de las relaciones y descripciones de los pueblos de Indias," published in Solano, ed., *Cuestionarios,* 79.
4. Bustamante points out, however, that Philip II's initiatives were the culmination of a long-term process rather than innovation, and that greater attention should be paid to the efforts of his father, Charles V, to obtain knowledge about the New World. See Bustamante, "El conocimiento como necesidad de estado."
5. For detailed discussions of some of these maps, see, e.g., Leibsohn, "Colony and Cartography"; Mundy, *The Mapping of New Spain.*
6. Altuna, *El discurso colonialista de los caminantes,* 30.
7. See Mignolo, "El mandato y la ofrenda."
8. See chapter 2, "Memories to Order," in Gruzinski, *The Conquest of Mexico.*
9. Rabasa, *Inventing America,* 183.
10. Gruzinski, *The Conquest of Mexico,* 73 and 78.
11. See Mignolo, "El mandato y la ofrenda."
12. The difficulties involved in compelling *corregidores* to provide adequate responses or to respond at all emerge in viceregal correspondence. Referring to a later questionnaire produced in 1604, the viceroy of Peru exclaimed: "It is hardly to be believed that since your Majesty sent it [the mandate] to me, for two years I have wished to collect the work that has resulted from the questionnaires and descriptions of the territory, and have not been able to finish putting them together because not all the *corregidores . . .* have even taken the trouble to begin them and also because those that they have produced are so muddled that I have sent them back so that they correct the errors." AGI, Lima 36, N. 1, lib. IV, fols. 150–50v.
13. See Cline, "The *Relaciones Geográficas.*" The geographical accounts that were returned from the *Audiencia* of Quito are not analyzed here.

14. Recent studies, apart from Gruzinski's work, include Leibsohn, "Colony and Cartography"; Mundy, *The Mapping of New Spain*; Mignolo, "El mandato y la ofrenda." The Peruvian *RG*s have received scholarly attention but have principally been regarded as sources of ethnographic or historical data, used to reconstruct (pre)colonial histories rather than being deconstructed, like their Mexican counterparts, as complex cultural products of the contact zone.

15. Gruzinski, *The Conquest of Mexico*, 70–97.

16. *Relación de la ciudad de Guamanga y sus términos*, 195.

17. Cabeza de Vaca, *Descripción y relación*, 344.

18. Cabeza de Vaca, *Descripción y relación*, 342.

19. Mundy, *The Mapping of New Spain*, 33–34.

20. Ulloa Mogollón, *Relación de la provincia*, 328.

21. Ulloa Mogollón, *Relación de la provincia*, 331.

22. Ulloa Mogollón, *Relación de la provincia*, 331.

23. Ulloa Mogollón, *Relación de la provincia*, 331.

24. Altuna, *El discurso colonialista de los caminantes*, 32. With reference to the Mexican *RG*s, Gruzinski, *The Conquest of Mexico*, 75, observes that by the late sixteenth century, indigenous memory had been impoverished due to "the combined assaults of widespread death and deculturation." In the high Andes, demographic decline and exposure to Spanish society probably affected indigenous communities less severely than in most parts of Mexico's generally more accessible territories.

25. References to the possible concealment of such knowledge may be found, e.g., in Monzón, *Descripción de . . . los Rucanas Antamarcas*, 26; Monzón, *Descripción de . . . Atunrucana y Laramati*, 26; Dávila Briceño, *Descripción y relación*, 159.

26. Despite their embrace of Christianity, Andean communities continued to be spiritually bound to the natural landscapes that surrounded them and from which their ancestors were believed to have emerged. As Gruzinski, *The Conquest of Mexico*, 91, observes with reference to the Mexican responses, "The indigenous perception of landscape was not at all innocent, even though it escaped the vigilance of the Spaniards."

27. Monzón, *Descripción de . . . Atunsora*, 222.

28. Monzón, *Descripción de . . . Atunrucana y Laramati*, 230.

29. Jiménez de la Espada comments that the stone of Songonchi was undoubtedly a sacred site, and that it was probably of the kind known as *coillusayana*, or "resting-place of the star," at which it was believed that certain significant stars came to rest. Jiménez de la Espada, *Relaciones Geográficas de Indias: Perú*, 231 (footnote 2).

30. Vega, *La descripción*, 169.

31. Vega, *La descripción,* 169.

32. For a detailed discussion of this term and the varied ways in which it was used in the colonial era, see Ramírez, *The World Upside Down,* 138–46. As Ramírez (143) observes, the term *huaca* was used by the Spanish to refer to tombs and burials as well as other sacred sites and objects, "despite what may have been an original indigenous distinction between temples and shrines and other sacred precincts, such as tombs."

33. As Gruzinski has implied, the fact that the question was formulated in the imperfect tense — on the assumption that all non-Christian geographies did indeed belong to the past — in itself contributed to encouraging native informants to relegate their autochtonous beliefs to history. "Some [natives] grasped the pole that was offered them out of simple convenience. It was in fact convenient to consign to an already distant past, more than fifty years old, all which had to do with idolatry . . . which made it possible at the same time to dismiss the somewhat thorny question of the retention of paganism." Gruzinski, *The Conquest of Mexico,* 78–79. Only one Peruvian *RG* — that from La Paz — breaks with the pattern of framing descriptions of native religious practices in the imperfect tense, perhaps because it was compiled on the basis of Spanish testimonies. See Cabeza de Vaca, *Descriptión y relación,* 346.

34. Duviols suggests that this text summarizes far more detailed investigations already completed by Albornoz. The details of the *Instrucción* would have been contained in parish records in the provinces that the priest inspected; none of these, however, have come to light. See Duviols's introduction to "Un inédit de Cristóbal de Albornoz."

35. Duviols, "Un inédit de Cristóbal de Albornoz," 29.

36. Duviols, "Un inédit de Cristóbal de Albornoz," 29.

37. Vega, *La descripción,* 166.

38. The text explains that the Quechua words *guanca* and *guamaní* mean, respectively, a large stone (or boulder), and a valley or province.

39. Gruzinski, *The Conquest of Mexico,* 78–79.

40. To assume without reflection that colonial representations of the New World, even those which suppressed all traces of indigenous difference, were the "pure" products of European imaginations is to act as an unwitting accomplice to those very processes of erasure. See Pratt, *Imperial Eyes,* 6–7, who insists that the agency of the colonized in the production of colonial representations of themselves and their territories should be heeded more carefully. "How," she asks, "have Europe's constructions of subordinated others been shaped by those others, by the constructions of themselves and their habitats that they presented to the Europeans? Borders and all, the entity called Europe was constructed from the outside as much as from the inside out. Can this be said of its modes of representation?"

41. Altuna, *El discurso colonialista de los caminantes,* 33.

42. See Mignolo, "El mandato y la ofrenda."

43. Ortner, "Resistance."

44. Two prominent examples include Spalding, *Huarochirí,* and Stern, *Peru's Indian Peoples.*

45. See, e.g., Abercrombie, *Pathways of Memory*; Griffiths, *The Cross and the Serpent*; K. Mills, *Idolatry and Its Enemies.*

46. Sharp, Routledge, Philo, and Paddison, "Entanglements of Power," 1.

47. Rose, "The Seductions of Resistance," 387–89. Drawing on the work of Nietzsche, Rose outlines these ideas under the heading of "slave theory."

48. Rose, "The Seductions of Resistance," 395.

49. Ortner, "Resistance," 175.

50. Ortner, "Resistance," 175.

51. Sempat Assadourian, *Transiciones,* 85.

52. It is clear that the presentation of *probanzas* or accounts of services by indigenous leaders was perceived as a threat by some, if not all, members of the colonial administration. In 1575 the viceroy Toledo issued a provision prohibiting native people of all social ranks from presenting accounts of services. See AGI, Lima 127. "Para que no se rreçiban ynformaçiones de seruiçios de ningún yndio." This appears, however, to have been a dead letter, for accounts of services were presented by Andeans well after this date.

53. Solano, ed., *Cuestionarios,* 84.

54. Vega, *La descripicón,* 170.

55. Vega, *La descripción,* 167.

56. See *Gobernantes del Perú,* ed. Levillier, vol. 3, 59–60. The *curacas* denied the accusations, claiming that the weapons were made to assist in the conquest of Chile. A powerful voice spoke out in their defense, for the Archbishop of Lima dismissed the accusations as nonsense. However, historians such as Espinoza Soriano and Pease G.Y. are confident that a rebellion was being planned. For discussions of this episode, see Espinoza Soriano, *Enciclopedia departamental de Junín,* 175–78, and Pease G.Y., *Curacas, reciprocidad y riqueza,* 156–58.

57. AGI, Lima 121. "Los caciques e yndios del Perú." See letter dated 03.I.1566 and signed by the native *cabildo* (council) of the Hanan Huanca *repartimiento* in the Jauja valley, fol. 45. Letters expressing similar sentiments and requesting the retention of the *corregidores* were also written by the native leaders of the Chongos valley (fols. 57–58) and by the *repartimiento* of Lurin Huanca (fols. 59–60v), whose communities likewise belonged to the *corregimiento* of Jauja.

58. AGI, Lima 121. "Los caciques e yndios del Perú," fol. 45.

59. AGI, Lima 121. "Los caciques e yndios del Perú," fol. 45.

60. AGI, Lima 205, N. 16, fols. 18–18v.

61. AGI, Lima 121. "Los caciques e yndios del Perú," fol. 59v.

62. In 1566 the Dominican friar Balthasar de Vargas wrote a letter to President Castro in which he condemned the *curacas* of Jauja as tyrants who exploited their own people. Along with other Dominicans in Jauja, Vargas also added his signature to the letter written by the native leaders of the Chongos valley in support of the *corregidor* system, which raises the issue of possible coercion on the part of the clergy. However, given the apparently favorable nature of the Huanca leaders' relationship with Larrinaga, this seems unlikely. Moreover, given the alleged Franciscan involvement in freeing the *cacique principal* of Lurin Huanca, arrested in connection with the rumored native uprising, such vocal condemnations by a Dominican may also have been a political move intended to distance his own order from such complicities. See AGI, Lima 313. "Frai Baltasar de Vargas al licenciado Lope García de Castro."

63. Lima 570, lib. 14, fol. 173v.

64. Lima 570, lib. 14, fol. 174.

65. See chapter 5 in Ramírez, *The World Upside Down,* for a detailed discussion of *huaca* looting on the northern coast of Peru in the 1550s.

66. *Gobernantes del Perú,* vol. 4, 111–14. Written in Cuzco, Toledo's letter is dated 01.III.1572.

67. For Toledo's raising of this issue with the monarch in 1572, see *Gobernantes del Perú,* vol. 4, 429–30. See monarch's responses, dated 21.II.1575 and 27.II.1575, in AGI, Lima 570, lib. 14, fols. 109–109v and 129v–30. Private individuals who "discovered" indigenous sites of burial or veneration were entitled to keep half of any goods they contained. See royal instructions regarding legislation on this point, originally issued on 21.III.1544, in Toledo, *Disposiciones gubernativas,* 285–87.

68. See correspondence with viceroy of Peru, 21.IX.1603. AGI, Lima 570, lib. 16, fols. 108–108v.

69. The questionnaire did, however, ask about the existence of mineral deposits and mines; here again, the crown and viceregal authorities expressed anxiety over indigenous acts of concealment. The native people, they argued, concealed knowledge of such deposits for fear of being forced into mining labor or being disenfranchised. See, e.g., royal instructions to the viceroy of Peru dated 06.III.1575, in AGI, Lima 570, lib. 14, fol. 132, and 05.VI.1607, in AGI, Lima 570, lib. 16, fols. 190v–91.

70. See chapter 2 on these accounts of services.

71. See Espinoza Soriano, "Los huancas." As he points out, however, don Felipe appears to have neglected the interests of the paramount *caciques*

of Hatun Xauxa and especially those of Hanan Huanca. The account of services that was produced by the leader of Hanan Huanca is now lost: Espinoza Soriano (180) suggests that the services rendered to the Spanish by the people of Hanan Huanca were the most significant and that, in consequence, don Felipe failed to submit it to the Council of the Indies.

72. Espinoza Soriano, "Los huancas," 180–82.

73. AGI, Lima 569, lib. 11, fols. 111v–12.

74. AGI, Lima 569, lib. 11, fol. 111v.

75. AGI, Lima 569, lib. 11, fol. 111v.

76. See Espinoza Soriano, "Los huancas," 27. Nevertheless, Espinoza Soriano argues (28), the sentence never appears to have been implemented. In response to don Felipe's appeal against it, Toledo banished him to Panama, but he never appears to have left Lima. By 1582, as the *RG* indicates, he was back in the Jauja valley. Don Felipe was clearly not the only target of Toledo's displeasure, for the viceroy stated that all native peoples in Peru, "and especially those of the Jauja province, were involved in many legal disputes and disagreements without any justification or reason." BNE Manuscritos de América, Tomo de varios, N. 294, 3044, fol. 44v. On arrival in Jauja during his viceregal tour of inspection, Toledo decided to make a public example of the native communities, and especially their leaders, "by burning all those papers that were of no importance, and instructing them not to get involved in the said legal disputes." Toledo, *Disposiciones gubernativas,* 491.

77. Vega, *La descripción,* 166.

78. For incisive and detailed studies of *indios ladinos* and the difficulties and ambivalences of their relations with other groups in colonial society, see, e.g., Adorno, "Images of Indios Ladinos"; Adorno, *Guaman Poma.*

79. Ramírez, *The World Upside Down,* 121–51, describes just such a situation in her discussion of *huaca* looting in the vicinity of Trujillo. When Spanish prospectors sought to lay claim to a burial structure that contained offerings of silver and gold, the *curaca* (or *cacique*) *principal* of the community to which the site belonged petitioned the viceroy (unsuccessfully) for a license to excavate the tomb, and then formed a partnership with one group of Spanish prospectors. Drawing on documents that indicate how the *curaca* used his share of the "treasure," Ramírez shows convincingly that he formed the partnership not out of self-interest but in order to salvage at least part of the community's patrimony and redistribute it among his subjects.

80. By contrast, the *curaca principal* discussed by Ramírez was not an *indio ladino;* like the vast majority of his subjects, he was only superficially Hispanicized and spoke little Spanish. See Ramírez, *The World Upside Down,* 134.

81. AGI, Lima 31, lib. 17, fols. 140–41.

82. AGI, Lima 317. "Memorial de fray Joan Saborido."

83. AGI, Lima 317. "Memorial de fray Joan Saborido." Lima, 10. XII.1587. According to Saborido and another friar named Miguel de Monsalue, Francisco del Castillo was in prison at the time he informed the monarchy about the existence of buried treasure in Jauja. In 1598 Monsalue explained in a letter to Philip II that he was present as a witness when Francisco del Castillo "declared that he had wished to deceive your Majesty, or rather, free himself in this way from the captivity in which he found himself at the time when he wrote to your Majesty and [that] he was obliged to do it in order to gain his liberty." Interestingly, Monsalue's letter to the king declared that he had come across an "infallible" way of discovering "all the rich mines of Peru, both of gold and silver, together with all the treasures of the Inca, *huacas,* and sites of worship," which would bring the monarchy immense riches. Monsalue mentioned the affair over the elusive Jauja treasure in order to reassure the king that, unlike Francisco del Castillo, he was a trustworthy and law-abiding individual, interested only in serving the monarchy. AGI, Lima 321. "Fray Miguel de Monsalue a S. M."

84. AGI, Lima 317. "Memorial de fray Joan Saborido."

85. See Rose, "The Seductions of Resistance," 395.

86. Following Kagan, *policía* is most straightforwardly translated as "civilized life." See Kagan, *Urban Images,* 26, for a detailed discussion of *policía,* which referred to both public and private forms of government and was inextricably bound up with an urban existence.

87. See, e.g., Saignes, *Caciques, Tribute and Migration,* and Wightman, *Indigenous Migration.*

88. Such assumptions may be found, e.g., in Cummins, "Forms of Andean Colonial Towns," and Fraser, *The Architecture of Conquest.* See also Castillero Calvo, "'La ciudad imaginada,'" who regards the absence of colonial documents that explicate the merits of the grid layout as evidence that these were understood by the Spanish at a profound, almost subconscious level.

89. Solano, ed., *Cuestionarios,* 82.

90. Monzón, *Descripción de . . . los Rucanas Antamarcas,* 238. Added emphasis.

91. Monzón, *Descripción de . . . Atunsora,* 221. Added emphasis.

92. *Relación de la ciudad de Guamanga y sus términos,* 184–85. Added emphasis.

93. Similar denunciations appear in the *RG* of Abancay, which was largely based on the testimonies of Spaniards. One of the four accounts that make up this composite *RG* states that, in the past, the indigenous people

were healthier "because each one lived wherever he chose"; now, however, they inhabit "places and reductions that are insalubrious rather than healthy, as they are very humid." This particular account was based on the testimonies of two Spaniards and one Andean leader. Fornee, *Descripción de . . . Abancay*, 22.

94. Viceregal determination to re-implement the *reducciones* was particularly pronounced concerning those regions that contributed to draft laborers for the silver mines of Potosí and the mercury mines of Huancavelica, both of which were important to the colonial economy. See, e.g., Cole, *The Potosí Mita*.

95. AGI, Lima 37, lib. IV, fols. 29–42v. "El virrey a todos los corregidores," fol. 38.

96. AGI, Lima 39, N. 10, lib. V, fols. 377–84v; fol. 378v.

97. See, e.g., AGI, Charcas 36, "Joseph Saez de Elorduy a S. M."; AGI, Charcas 54, "Don Raphael Ortiz de Sotomayor."

98. This is implied by Gruzinski, *The Conquest of Mexico*, 86.

99. AGI, Charcas 54, "Don Raphael Ortiz de Sotomayor," fol. 18.

100. AGI, Charcas 54, "Don Raphael Ortiz de Sotomayor," fol. 18; AGI, Lima 37, N. 34, lib. IV, fols. 27–28v.

101. AGI, Lima 44, N. 4, lib. IV, fol. 81v.

102. Sharp, Routledge, Philo, and Paddison, "Entanglements of Power."

103. Cresswell, "Falling Down," 256–68.

104. Ortner, "Resistance," 190. Ortner contends that "resistance studies are thin because they are ethnographically thin: thin on the internal politics of dominated groups, thin on the cultural richness of those groups, thin on the subjectivity—the intentions, desires, fears, projects—of the actors engaged in these dramas." It is equally appropriate, however, to direct such criticisms at the treatment of "dominant groups"—namely, European colonizers—in many studies of colonial resistance.

105. Rose, "The Seductions of Resistance," 388–89.

106. Because the study of colonialism brings with it a particular moral duty to keep in view the very real violence that pervaded it, this may appear to be a controversial move. I would suggest, however, that the suppression of the categories of domination and resistance does not entail the concealment or trivialization of colonial violence. Rather, it allows that violence to be detached from a coherent and reified system of domination and acknowledged instead in the diverse and contingent everyday practices that continuously shaped colonial societies and provided the varied contexts for the creation of Peru's *RGs*.

107. Mundy, The Mapping of New Spain, 23–27.

F O U R .   The Mobile Landscapes of Huarochirí

1. On the latter, see Wightman, *Indigenous Migration.*

2. On the communications system in colonial Peru and, in particular, the role of indigenous populations in maintaining it, see Glave Testino, *Trajinantes.*

3. Gerbi, *Caminos del Perú,* 9. Quotation appears in Glave Testino, *Trajinantes,* 119.

4. See, e.g., Altuna, *El discurso colonialista de los caminantes*; Mundy, *The Mapping of New Spain*; Padrón, *The Spacious Word.*

5. See Mundy, *The Mapping of New Spain*; Padrón, *The Spacious Word.*

6. This notion is adapted from Ashcroft, *Post-colonial Transformation,* 50, who argues that there is "no 'master-plan' of imperialism" and proposes that the concept of the rhizome, as developed by Deleuze and Guattari, most effectively captures its workings: "The rhizome describes a root system which spreads out laterally rather than vertically, as in bamboo, which has no central root but which propagates itself in a fragmented, discontinuous, multidirectional way." Imperialism, Ashcroft argues, operates in a comparable manner, "producing its effects by a complex, diffracted, discontinuous layering rather than necessarily by acts of brute force."

7. The details of the dispute are recorded in AAL, Curatos (Huarochirí), XXX:2.

8. In the early stages of the legal proceedings, Mojica declared under oath that he had seen Guerrero working in the neighboring parish for ten years. AAL, Curatos (Huarochirí), XXX:2, fol. 9v.

9. AAL, Curatos (Huarochirí), XXX:2, fol. 1v.

10. AAL, Curatos (Huarochirí), XXX:2, fol. 1v.

11. AAL, Curatos (Huarochirí), XXX:2, fol. 2. Legislation regarding the number of parishioners that should be assigned to each priest in the Archbishopric of Lima was established in the meetings of the second and third Lima Councils in 1567 and 1583, respectively. In 1567 it was decreed that priests should be assigned no more than four hundred tribute-paying Indians (along with their families). At the third Council it was agreed that the maximum number should be lowered to three hundred, except in circumstances where it proved impossible to find another suitable priest. Guerrero's assertions, therefore, do not wholly coincide with the legislation. See *Concilios Limenses,* ed. Vargas Ugarte, vol. 1, 348.

12. AAL, Curatos (Huarochirí), XXX:2, fol. 14.

13. AAL, Curatos (Huarochirí), XXX:2, fol. 13v.

14. By 1648 the parish of San Mateo de Huanchor had an annex called San Miguel de Viso. See Carcelén Reluz, "Las doctrinas de Chaclla-

Huarochirí," 143. It seems unlikely, however, that this settlement was attached to Mojica's parish at the time of the dispute, as Guerrero—provided that he was aware of its existence—would almost certainly have brought it to the attention of the tribunal.

15. AAL, Curatos (Huarochirí) XXX:2, fols. 17–17v. With reference to the early seventeenth century, the Jesuit historian Jacinto Barrasa observed that many parish priests had to attend to seven or eight or as many as twelve settlements over a distance of eight, twelve, or even sixteen leagues, a situation that the archbishop Gonzalo de Campo was anxious to remedy. If this was indeed the case, then the size and geography of Guerrero's and Mojica's parishes appear modest by comparison. BNP, A620, Barrasa, *Historia eclesiástica,* 58.

16. AAL, Curatos (Huarochirí), XXX:2, fol. 83.

17. AAL, Curatos (Huarochirí), XXX:2, fol. 166v.

18. AAL, Curatos (Huarochirí), XXX:2, fol. 164.

19. Padrón, *The Spacious Word,* 78–84. Medieval conceptions of space were founded not on a two-dimensional expanse but instead on the unidimensional experience of travel between points. Space "only came into existence as the distance separating two places, two significant points of reference. . . . It was, in effect, the unidimensional distance that one would have to travel to get 'there,' to go to a distant place, or to return from one. Thus, 'space,' when it was used to speak of spatial extension rather than of time, did not refer to an area but to distance." Padrón, *The Spacious Word,* 58–59.

20. Padrón makes this argument with specific, critical reference to Mundy's assertion that the production of itinerary maps by colonial officials in New Spain reflected the prominence of travel in their everyday lives. This explanation is founded, he argues, on "the hegemony that the cosmographer's maps enjoys in our own historiography. . . . One assumes that if they had been allowed to stay put . . . they would have imagined and figured space and territory in some other kind of way." *The Spacious Word,* 79.

21. This was the case in theory if not always in practice. Mojica pointed out that his stipend was lower than Guerrero's, despite the fact that he had more parishioners. Demographic fluctuation in rural parishes, caused by a combination of migration and disease, meant that there was considerable uncertainty about the size of many parish populations. I am indebted to Gabriela Ramos for making this point clear to me.

22. Many priests, moreover, obtained further income in a host of illicit ways, whether by forcing parishioners to work for a scant wage and selling the fruits of their labor, by demanding goods without payment, or by coercing native people to pay extra for confessions and other religious services. See Carcelén Reluz, "Las doctrinas de Chaclla-Huarochirí." It is

not clear to what extent Guerrero and Mojica engaged in such practices; however, records of a parish inspection carried out in 1631 by the newly appointed Archbishop Arias de Ugarte reveal that Guerrero supplemented his income by cultivating a piece of land that he had purchased from a *mestizo* in the neighboring parish of San Pedro de Mama. Although he paid members of his own parish to work the land for him, two parishioners, both from San Bartolomé, testified that he paid significantly less than the usual rate (two *reales* instead of three or four) and forced them to work from dawn until dusk without any food. Interestingly, the records include a letter written by don Diego Llacxa Quispi, governor of San Gerónimo, in which he denounced the accusations brought against Guerrero by the inhabitants of San Bartolomé, an action that suggests that tensions existed between these two communities. See AAL, Visitas (Huarochirí), IX:10. In theory, it was illegal for priests to engage in commercial activities and to employ their parishioners in pursuing them, regardless of how they were treated. See *Concilios limenses,* vol. 1, 344–45.

23. Mojica, however, clearly had similar concerns. Were he to lose control of the Quichas *parcialidad,* he insisted, he would be unable to support himself adequately.

24. AAL, Curatos (Huarochirí), XXX:2, fol. 14v.

25. AAL, Curatos (Huarochirí), XXX:2, fol. 171v.

26. Spalding, *Huarochirí,* 180. Increasingly faced with this phenomenon, writes Spalding, "the Spanish authorities eventually gave up and tried to make reality fit their administrative models by officially founding a new village in an area occupied by a sufficient number of people."

27. Such spatial practices were often contested by priests, as illustrated by a complaint made to the Archbishop of Lima by residents of the pre-reduction community of Callaguaya in the Huarochirí province. In 1594 official permission had been granted for the construction of a chapel in Callaguaya, where members of the Chacacancha *ayllu* resided each year when preparing their fields and harvesting their crops. In 1617, however, they complained that their priests refused to use the chapel and forced them instead to attend church three times a week in their reduction towns of Huarochirí and Chorrillo, both five leagues distant from Callaguaya. See AAL, Papeles Importantes, III:13.

28. AAL, Curatos (Huarochirí), XXX:2, fol. 14v.

29. It is also likely that ecclesiastical legislation contributed to priests' anxieties about their parish demographics. The third Lima Council stipulated that if the numbers of tributaries in any one settlement were less than two hundred, then those tributaries should be "reduced" elsewhere: the decline of population, therefore, could potentially lead to the dissolution of a parish. See *Concilios limenses,* vol. 1, 348. As has been well documented,

furthermore, parish priests were often active agents in the concealment of *forasteros*—tributaries who had fled their assigned *reducciones* and parishes and taken up residence in other provinces. Here again it may be seen that spatial practices in colonial Peru cannot be adequately captured by a binary notion of resistance: although priests sought to prevent the out-migration of their assigned parishioners, they (along with other Spaniards) were also complicit in facilitating the mobility and concealment of Andeans from other areas.

30. AAL, Curatos (Huarochirí), XXX:2, 17v.

31. AAL, Curatos (Huarochirí), XXX:2, fols. 181–81v.

32. According to Carcelén Reluz, the primary reasons for the Jesuits' abandonment of Huarochirí were twofold: first, the incommensurability between the Company's commitment to a principle of "santa pobreza" (saintly poverty) and the fact that the rural parishes provided salaries and other emoluments; second, the contradiction between the parishes' subordination to the authority of bishops and royal officials, on the one hand, and the Jesuits' desire for autonomy, on the other. See Carcelén Reluz, "Las doctrinas de Chaclla-Huarochirí," 176–82.

33. This disillusionment followed initial Jesuit optimism that the Andeans would be converted easily. See Hyland, *The Jesuit and the Incas,* 38–47. As Hyland points out, however, the sense of disillusionment was not shared by the Jesuit *mestizo* Blas Valera, who was convinced of the sincerity with which Andeans embraced Catholicism.

34. Hyland, *The Jesuit and the Incas,* 46.

35. See *Historia general de la Compañía.* As the editor, Francisco Mateos, indicates (92–93), the chronicle was not authored by one person alone but consists of a compilation of many Jesuit sources. It draws heavily on first-hand accounts of missions and other undertakings, as well as on the annual letters written by Provincials of the order.

36. *Historia general de la Compañía,* 220.

37. *Historia general de la Compañía,* 220.

38. *Historia general de la Compañía,* 220–21. The chronicle suppresses the fact that there was considerable resistance within the order to accepting the Huarochirí parishes in the first place. See Vargas Ugarte, *Historia de la Compañía,* 62.

39. Vargas Ugarte, *Historia de la Compañía,* 220.

40. Vargas Ugarte, *Historia de la Compañía,* 46.

41. Good examples of such descriptions may be found in accounts of late-sixteenth- and early-seventeenth-century Jesuit missions to the Upper Amazon regions to the east of Peru's central highlands. See, e.g., *Historia general de la Compañía,* 413–19; BNP, A620, Barrasa, *Historia eclesiástica,* 64–67.

42. See letter by P. Luís López to Francisco de Borja, Lima 21.I.1570, in Egaña, ed., *Monumenta peruana,* 364.

43. Egaña, ed., *Monumenta peruana,* 224.

44. Egaña, ed., *Monumenta peruana,* 224.

45. Pastor Bodmer, *The Armature of Conquest.* See chapter 2 here for a discussion of Pastor Bodmer's "discourse of failure" and of conquistadors' accounts of physical suffering in the early stages of the conquest of Peru.

46. The theme of physical suffering through exposure to inhospitable and perilous environments is prominent in religious writings in post-independence as well as colonial Latin America. It was used by members of many orders, not just the Jesuits, and surfaced with particular insistence in accounts of missionary ventures to the Amazon. See, e.g., Santos-Granero, "Boundaries Are Made to Be Crossed"; Taussig, *Shamanism,* 305–21.

47. Carcelén Reluz, "Las doctrinas de Chaclla-Huarochirí," 165.

48. *Historia general de la Compañía,* 225.

49. *Historia general de la Compañía,* 225.

50. *Historia general de la Compañía,* 225. The vision of Jesuit priests traversing the entire viceroyalty on their spiritual missions is also clearly projected in BNP, A620, Barrasa, *Historia eclesiástica,* 58. At the request of Archbishop Gonzalo de Campo, "the Fathers set out and traversed the whole of the archbishopric, which is 140 leagues in length and over 80 leagues wide, until they reached the boundaries of the lands of the infidels."

51. The questionnaire was first drafted and sent out to crown officials by the Council of the Indies in 1577. A slightly amended version, which is almost certainly the version that Dávila Briceño received, was circulated in 1584. The Jauja *RG* of 1582 (discussed in chapter 3) was produced in response to the first version. See Cline, "The *Relaciones Geográficas,*" 347.

52. Unusually, Dávila Briceño's response is a first-person account. Although many of the details were undoubtedly obtained from indigenous inhabitants, the *corregidor* did not acknowledge their contributions. It appears that he did not summon members of the local Andean communities to provide answers to the questionnaire, but instead wrote the account himself on the basis of knowledge previously obtained during his years of service in the province. See Dávila Briceño, *Descripción y relación,* 155–65.

53. Dávila Briceño, *Descripción y relación,* 164–65.

54. These *repartimientos* were: Mancos and Laraos, Yauyos, Guadocheri [Huarochirí], Mama, and Chacalla [Chaclla]. When Dávila Briceño's term of office ended, the huge jurisdiction was divided into two *corregimientos,* Yauyos and Huarochirí. The two *repartimientos* of Mancos and Laraos, and Yauyos, were incorporated into the new *corregimiento* of Yauyos and the remaining three into the *corregimiento* of Huarochirí. The old Inca jurisdictions of Lurin Yauyos and Anan Yauyos provided the basis for these colonial administra-

tive divisions, which are clearly marked on Dávila Briceño's map. Before the divisions, the *repartimiento* and reduction town of Huarochirí was the capital of the greater Yauyos province and the seat of the *corregidor*. See Carcelén Reluz, "Las doctrinas de Chaclla-Huarochirí," 83–85.

55. Dávila Briceño, *Descripción y relación,* 160.

56. Those who carried out the physical labor of constructing the *reducciones* were not, of course, the colonial officials but the indigenous populations who were being resettled.

57. Dávila Briceño, *Descripción y relación,* 160.

58. See chapter 3 of this book for other accounts in response to the questionnaire.

59. In November 1586 (a few months after Dávila wrote his geographical account), the incumbent *corregidor* of Huarochirí initiated a standard audit (*residencia*) of Dávila Briceño's activities at the end of his term of office. In response to a question about his diligence in enforcing the *reducciones,* the vast majority of witnesses declared that he had carried them out very thoroughly and ensured that nobody was allowed to return to their old settlements. A few witnesses from San Pedro de Casta alleged, however, that he had permitted the members of several *ayllus* to remain in their original places of residence. In response, Dávila Briceño pointed out that these were merely temporary shelters, which those Indians whose lands were distant from the *reducción* were allowed to inhabit when sowing and harvesting their crops. Echoing the words of his *RG,* he insisted that "in this whole province of Yauyos I did not leave out a single settlement, nor was there one that I did not witness being torn to the ground." BNP, A332, fols. 308v–309 and 313–13v.

60. Craib, *Cartographic Mexico,* 8.

61. Craib, *Cartographic Mexico,* 8.

62. As Mundy notes with reference to the Mexican *RGs,* the inclusion of maps portraying indigenous settlements was not actually requested by the crown: the instructions only asked for plans showing towns and cities inhabited by Spanish populations.

63. As Padrón, *The Spacious Word,* 48, observes, these modern cartographies reveal a shift from an understanding of *espacio* as "an interval of time" to *espacio* as an "abstract, two-dimensional (or sometimes three-dimensional) expanse."

64. Dávila Briceño, *Descripción y relación,* 155.

65. To each of the three *repartimientos* of Lurin Yauyos, Dávila also appointed an official whose duty it was to inspect the old settlements every month to ensure that they remained empty. It is not clear whether he also appointed officials for this purpose to the *repartimientos* of Anan Yauyos. See BNP, A332, fol. 313v.

66. As illustrated by the sermons contained within the *Tercero catecismo y exposición de la doctrina christiana por sermones* (Third Catechism and Exposition of the Christian Doctrine in Sermons), religious discourse was intended to play a key role in this process. Published in 1585 for the instruction of native parishioners, this book of sermons not only attacked Andean nature worship but also portrayed the Hispanicized natives of the colonial cities as "good Indians" who enjoyed the privilege of communion and, therefore, the prospect of salvation. See *Tercero catecismo,* 51–55 and 169–70.

67. Dávila Briceño, *Descripción y relación,* 161. Emphasis added.

68. Dávila Briceño, *Descripción y relación,* 161.

69. See Salomon, "Introductory Essay." For a detailed discussion of the social and administrative structures in Huarochirí in Inca and colonial times, see chapter 2 in Spalding, *Huarochirí.*

70. See Salomon, "Introductory Essay," 1–4, for a discussion of the possible authorship and mode of composition of the document. While the person who assembled the manuscript was unquestionably Andean, his identity is unknown, and the precise extent and nature of Avila's involvement in its creation is also unclear. An in-depth article on the question of the document's authorship by Durston proposes that the creator may have been the scribe Cristóbal Choquecasa, a close collaborator and assistant of Avila. See Durston, "Notes on the Authorship."

71. *The Huarochirí Manuscript,* 77. Chaupi Ñamca was the most important female deity of the valleys around the lower reaches of the Rímac and the wife of Pachacamac, whose temple was located in the vicinity of Lurín. In the manuscript, the female deity appears as a sibling of the highland deity Pariacaca who was worshipped by highland groups. While this fraternal relationship symbolized harmony between the lowland Yunca peoples and invaders from the highlands, the conjugal relationships between the deities' male and female offspring indicated that, in Andean eyes, the highlanders' invasion of the lowlands had made them "indebted wife-takers to Yunca groups and their *huacas.*" See Salomon, "Introductory Essay," 9.

72. As Salomon observes, the myths of Pariacaca have been interpreted by scholars as allegorical renderings of the pre-Inca migrations of the Yauyo people, who expanded from their high-altitude homelands into the warm valleys of what became, in colonial times, the Huarochirí province. However, while the manuscript may be considered "substantially an artifact of Yauyo culture," the principal narrators of the myths belonged to the Checa and Concha ethnic groups. These considered themselves "sons of Pariacaca" but viewed the Yauyo as recent incomers and as objects of disdain. See Salomon, "Introductory Essay," 6–7.

73. *The Huarochirí Manuscript,* 75.

74. Salomon and Urioste observe that in associating the irrigation canals with Pariacaca's endeavors, the teller of the story is seeking to convey his "group's claims to water rights. In this myth a non-Yunca group (Checa?) seems to be holding that the neighboring Cupara (seemingly of Yunca origin) owe their water to the invaders and not to the ancient Yunca builders." See *The Huarochirí Manuscript,* 62, footnote 147.

75. *The Huarochirí Manuscript,* 63.

76. Dávila Briceño, *Descripción y relación,* 156.

77. Dávila Briceño, *Descripción y relación,* 156. The "stairway of Pariacaca" is clearly marked on Dávila Briceño's map. Both the geographical description and the map, therefore, indicate that the journeys of those who pass through the province on their way to Lima or Cuzco are marked by the presence of Pariacaca, given that the highway leads them over a high mountain pass directly below the snow-covered peak named after the deity.

78. Dávila Briceño, *Descripción y relación,* 157.

79. See Acosta Rodríguez, "El pleito de los indios," and Hampe Martínez, "El trasfondo personal."

80. This genuine astonishment may be detected, for example, in a letter sent by the archbishop of Lima to the king, in which he informed him that "the news that I have to offer your Majesty is that all these Indians of my archbishopric, just like those of the other bishoprics, are today just as much unbelievers and idolaters as they were when they were conquered, a situation which troubles me and breaks my heart." Published in Duviols, "Un inédit de Cristóbal de Albornoz," 253–54.

81. K. Mills, *Idolatry and Its Enemies,* 272.

82. This practice is mentioned, for example, in Romero, "Idolatrías de los Indios," 184 and 190.

83. Fabián de Ayala to the Archbishop of Lima, 12.IV.1611. Published in Duviols, "Un inédit de Cristóbal de Albornoz," 251.

84. Duviols, "Un inédit de Cristóbal de Albornoz," 250–51.

85. Duviols, "Un inédit de Cristóbal de Albornoz," 251.

86. The term "vertical third dimension" is borrowed from Carter, who argues that this concept is relatively modern. Between the mid-fifteenth and late nineteenth centuries, "a scenographic conception dominated Western thinking," allowing the world to be "imagined as a continuous planar surface on which, at intervals, objects . . . were located." See *The Lie of the Land,* 116 and 124. In contrast to Carter, I use the term to evoke a particular mode of physical engagement with the landscape rather than a form of spatial imagination: no longer confined to the surface, the extirpators' struggles with the landscape were also enacted below ground, by means of excavation. As the work of Padrón, *The Spacious Word,* shows, moreover, the process of

transition to a modern spatial imagination was gradual and very much incomplete in early colonial America.

87. Arriaga, *La extirpación,* 23.

88. See *Hijos de Pariya Qaqa,* 130 n. 10. It is interesting to note that Ortiz Rescanière also associates the present-day growth of cults connected to particular mountains with the religious and political fragmentation that has taken place since colonial times. See Ortiz Rescanière, *Huarochirí,* 117.

89. The first edition of his book drew on a fourteenth-century Inquisitors' manual, the *Directorium inquisitorium,* written by the Catalan inquisitor Nicolás Eymerich. See Griffiths, *The Cross and the Serpent,* 34–38. García Cabrera describes it as a type of manifesto that expressed the official position of those in favor of extirpation, and perhaps also of the Jesuit order in the early seventeenth century. See García Cabrera, *Ofensas a Dios,* 34.

90. Arriaga, *La extirpación,* 138–41.

91. K. Mills, *Idolatry and Its Enemies,* 278.

92. See Craib, *Cartographic Mexico.*

93. *Historia general de la Compañía,* 221.

94. Griffiths, *The Cross and the Serpent,* 81–90 and 247, suggests that the Spanish religious did not generally believe that Andean religious geographies possessed genuine spiritual (to them, diabolical) powers. In doing so, he counters Taussig's suggestion that the Spaniards feared Indian deities. Arguing that the extirpators' belief in a real demonic presence was the exception rather than the rule, he traces their skepticism back to the Inquisition's perception of those accused of witchcraft or sorcery in Spain. Nevertheless, accounts such as Barrasa's compiled history of the Jesuits in Peru contain vivid descriptions of priests' encounters with demonic beings—encounters in whose reality those priests undoubtedly believed.

95. Spalding, *Huarochirí,* 257–58.

96. As Griffiths, *The Cross and the Serpent,* 147–48, suggests, "the idolatry trial should be understood less as the automatic response of a zealous parish priest in the face of stubborn pagan traditions than as a chosen strategy employed to gain the advantage in the game of local power relations."

97. AGI, Lima 302. "Arzobispo de Lima a S. M." Lima, 06. X.1626.

98. The investigation was opened following the death of Archbishop Lobo Guerrero in 1622 and the immediate suspension of all extirpating commissions. This effectively constituted a reaction against the archbishop's policies by the ecclesiastical council and also by some of the religious orders, which had suspected a conspiracy between the ecclesiastics and the Jesuits in the extirpation campaigns. See García Cabrera, ed., *Ofensas a Dios,* 39.

99. See question 8 in AAL, Hechicerías e Idolatrías I:8.

100. AAL, Hechicerías e Idolatrías I:8, question no. 25.

101. AGI, Lima 302. "Arzobispo de Lima a S. M." Lima, 08. X.1626.

102. AGI, Lima 302. "Arzobispo de Lima a S. M." Lima, 08. X.1626.

103. AGI, Lima 302. "Arzobispo de Lima a S. M." Lima, 08. X.1626. In a letter written one year previously, the archbishop declared that the physical infrastructure of Catholicism was in a pitiful state of neglect. Throughout his jurisdiction, he lamented, he encountered Christian churches in an extreme state of disrepair, open to the elements, with their altars and ornaments broken and dirty—a situation that, he insisted, underlay the Indians' continued ignorance of the mysteries of Catholicism and facilitated their return to the "hands of the devil and to idolatry." His comments clearly reflect the significance attached to physical infrastructure and religious imagery as tools of conversion. With equal clarity, they convey—like Dávila's account of Huarochirí—the notion that Christian landscapes, once implanted, did not simply persist but instead had to be maintained and defended by means of continuous labor, physical as well as didactic.

104. Lavallé, *Las promesas ambiguas,* 118–20. The *criollos* of the seventeenth century, Lavallé writes, emerge as men of the city: "Without a doubt, we witness in the seventeenth century a reduction of *criollo* space. In fact, advances toward the unknown regions are not resumed until the eighteenth century."

FIVE. Negotiating Amazonia: The Accounts of Juan Recio de León

1. Early Spanish accounts of the Amazon have recently been the subject of revised interpretations suggesting that colonial-era reports of wealthy and populous polities were not mere figments of overactive European imaginations but possessed a factual basis. Persistent modern notions of the Amazon basin as a wilderness largely devoid of and untouched by human histories and cultures are now dismissed by many scholars as a myth of relatively recent pedigree, which can be traced back to the writings emerging from explorations of the early nineteenth century. See, e.g., Denevan, *The Aboriginal Cultural Geography*; Raffles, *In Amazonia*; Roosevelt, ed., *Amazonian Indians*; Whitehead's introduction to Ralegh, *The Discoverie.*

2. See, in particular, Saignes, *Los Andes orientales,* and Renard-Casevitz, Saignes, and Taylor, *L'Inca, l'espagnol et les sauvages.*

3. See, e.g., Arias Coello, "La imagen mítica de América en la España"; Leonard, *The Books of the Brave*; Levillier, *El Paititi.*

4. See Ramos Pérez, *El mito del Dorado,* who speaks of a "mechanism of contagion" that caused ideas and images to be transferred from one person to the next. See also Gil, *Mitos y utopías.*

5. Pastor Bodmer, *El jardín y el peregrino.*

6. See, e.g., MacCormack, "Ethnography in South America"; Taylor, "The Western Margins of Amazonia"; chapter 4 in Pastor Bodmer, *The Armature of Conquest.*

7. Ette, "Funciones de mitos," 136.

8. Pastor Bodmer, *El jardín y el peregrino.*

9. Rabasa, *Writing Violence,* chapter 2.

10. Rabasa, *Writing Violence,* 107.

11. Rabasa, *Writing Violence,* 112.

12. Holland, Lachicotte Jr., Skinner, and Cain, *Identity and Agency,* 17.

13. Holland, Lachicotte Jr., Skinner, and Cain, *Identity and Agency,* 31–32 and 62.

14. Holland, Lachicotte Jr., Skinner, and Cain, *Identity and Agency,* 276–77. Emphasis added.

15. Pastor, *The Armature of Conquest,* chapter 2.

16. As Livingstone observes, "Social spaces facilitate and condition discursive space. . . . That is to say that ideas are produced in, and shaped by, settings. They must resonate with their environments or they could not find expression, secure agreement, or mobilize followers. But ideas must also be sufficiently 'disarticulated' from their social environments to permit them to reshape the very settings they emerged from. Spaces both enable and constrain discourse." See Livingstone, *Putting Science in Its Place,* 7.

17. See, e.g., Livingstone, *Putting Science in Its Place*; Lux and Cook, "Closed Circles or Open Networks?"; Withers, "Writing in Geography's History."

18. AGI, Lima 159, "Relaciones de méritos y servicios." These *relaciones* comprise five printed documents and one handwritten, bound together in a booklet, and several loose, printed documents. These documents, along with others now held in the British Library, are published in vol. 6 of Maúrtua, *Juicio de límites.* I use the manuscript versions of Recio's documents held in the AGI but use Maúrtua's edition for those held in the British Library. Where the document is untitled, I refer to the first line of text.

19. AGI, Lima 159. "Relación que Iuan Recio de León," fol. 1v. After eight years in Nueva Granada, participating in various conquests, Recio traveled to the *Audiencia* of Quito and helped defend the port of Guayaquil against the Dutch. By 1616 he was on his way to Chile, apparently carrying secret viceregal instructions to report on the state of the territory. From Chile he ascended to the city of La Paz, initially to convalesce from an illness.

20. The area explored by Leáegui now belongs to Bolivia's northwesterly department of La Paz, which shares its western border with the Peru-

vian department of Puno. Leáegui entered the tropical lowlands via the cordillera of Apolobamba, which straddles the modern-day border of Bolivia and Peru.

21. Both groups inhabited the piedmont regions of the Andes' eastern slopes in what is now Bolivia. Doubt exists about whether these groups consisted primarily of "Andeanized" forest peoples or of the descendants of "naturalized" Andeans; in either case, Saignes argues, the piedmont regions acted as an important space of cultural synthesis between Andes and Amazon. See Saignes, *Los Andes orientales,* 75–76. See also Métraux, "Tribes of the Eastern Slopes," 505–6.

22. AGI, Lima 38, lib. III, fol. 293. See also AGI, Lima 37, lib. IV, fols. 200–201.

23. Leáegui's venture was one of several that took place in Upper Peru's southeastern borderlands during the early seventeenth century. When these were evaluated in 1618 by Viceroy Esquilache, only one, an unpromising venture in search of the Moxos kingdom led by Gonzalo de Solís Holguín, received explicit approval. According to Gil, *Mitos y utopías,* 324–25, Esquilache's support was a clear case of favoritism toward Holguín. See also 331–35 for a brief discussion of Leáegui's commission and the accounts by Recio de León.

24. AGI, Lima 159. "Relación que Iuan Recio de León," fols. 1–7v.

25. AGI, Lima 97. "La Audiencia de Lima a S. M." The *oidores* got Recio's first name wrong in their letter, calling him Pedro Recio de León instead of Juan. There can be no doubt, however, that they were referring to the same individual.

26. AGI, Lima 97. "La Audiencia de Lima a S. M."

27. In 1573, Philip II issued ordinances intended to regulate exploration and settlement in all parts of the Indies. However, these were by no means the first instructions of this type to be issued; contracts granted to expeditionary leaders routinely included instructions to which, in theory, they and their followers were expected to adhere. The Conde de Nieva, for example, viceroy of Peru from 1560 to 1564, issued a code of conduct for exploratory ventures. Like the ordinances of 1573, it avoided all reference to conquest and placed heavy emphasis on evangelization and "pacification" by means of peaceful persuasion. See AGI, Patronato 29, R. 15, 1. As Rabasa suggests, the ordinances of 1573 emerged from, and contained elements of, diverse laws and texts relating to the Indies that dated back to the earliest years of Spanish exploration. See Rabasa, *Writing Violence,* 89–90.

28. Exploratory adventures in the Amazon did not come to a standstill. During the early decades of the seventeenth century, comments Gil, *Mitos y utopías,* 228, "there was great activity surrounding the exploration of

the Amazon river and the adjoining regions, with a view to encountering there the nebulous city of Manoa that Berrío and Ralegh were searching for in the Orinoco; this was not the case only in the Iberian peninsula, but also in the rest of Europe."

29. For a discussion of this in the context of Antonio de Berrío's late-sixteenth-century expeditions to the Amazon regions, see Piqueras Céspedes, "Antonio de Berrío." See also Rabasa, *Writing Violence,* chapter 2. For a detailed discussion of the "model conquistador," see Pastor Bodmer, *The Armature of Conquest.*

30. AGI, Lima 159. "Relación que Iuan Recio de León," fol. 2.

31. The derogatory word "Chunchos" was frequently used by Spanish chroniclers and missionaries to refer collectively to the ethnic groups of Upper Peru's subtropical borderlands and adjoining tropical lowlands. Apparently of Aymara origin, the word was assimilated in Quechua as a synonym of "savages." See Saignes, *Los Andes orientales,* 51–54.

32. AGI, Lima 159. "Relación que Iuan Recio de León," fol. 2v.

33. While an Augustinian account of the frontier encounters in Recio's *relación* concurs with Recio's version in relation to the *caciques'* requests, it differs strikingly in that Recio, far from being portrayed as the principal Spanish protagonist, is not even mentioned. Instead, the discourse of both the native leaders and the Augustinian friars is directed toward the governor, Pedro de Leáegui. See Torres, *Crónicas augustinias,* 335.

34. AGI, Lima 159. "Relación que Iuan Recio de León," fol. 8.

35. AGI, Lima 159. "Relación que Iuan Recio de León," fol. 8.

36. Cárdenas, *Problemas, y secretos,* folios 83v–84. The belief that the equatorial regions of the Americas were particularly rich in gold and other precious minerals and stones may be traced back to the earliest era of European exploration in the New World. Basing his observations on the geographical origins of precious commodities, the cartographer Jaume Ferrer informed Columbus in 1495 that such commodities were especially abundant in hot climates. In the early sixteenth century the idea was discussed at length in Anghiera's *Decades* and was also used by later historians and chroniclers such as José de Acosta and Antonio de Herrera. See Pastor Bodmer, *The Armature of Conquest,* 154–55. As Cañizares-Esguerra notes, however, the alleged association between the sun and the formation of gold was disputed in the 1550s by the humanist Julius Caesar Scaliger, who argued that Brazil, despite its location beneath the tropical sun, was largely devoid of gold. See Cañizares-Esguerra, *Nature, Empire, and Nation,* 73. In the following century, the Spanish mining expert Alvaro Alonso Barba likewise expressed doubts about the influence of the sun and other heavenly bodies on the formation of metals. See Alonso Barba, *Arte de los metales,* 37.

37. The generative effects on gold that some early modern writers attributed to the sun were not, as a rule, extended to other metals. Cárdenas, for example, argued that while gold possessed an affinity with the sun, silver was attracted to "the cold and humidity of the abyss." Cárdenas, *Problemas, y secretos,* fol. 84.

38. Cárdenas, *Problemas, y secretos,* fol. 9.

39. Recio's request was not unusual. It was common for those who solicited or held commissions for colonizing ventures to also request a *corregimiento* in close geographical proximity to the areas to which they hoped to lay claim, on the grounds that this would facilitate the organization and deployment of the venture. In 1586 the *corregimiento* of Larecaja was awarded to Juan Alvarez Maldonado, governor of the as yet unpacified "Chunchos province," for one year, but he argued that he needed to hold the post for at least six years if the venture was to be carried out successfully. See documents relating to Juan Alvarez Maldonado, in Maúrtua, *Juicio de límites,* vol. 6, 126–35. In 1618 the Spanish inhabitants of Charazani, a settlement situated in Larecaja's eastern valleys, argued that the current *corregidor* of the province, don Diego de Lodeña, was the ideal person to lead an expedition to the Chunchos, precisely because he held this post: "as *corregidor . . .* no one has better access to assistance, manpower, food, and all the rest that is necessary for the said expedition." AGI, Lima 152. "Méritos y servicios de don Diego de Lodeña," fol. 153. By the mid-seventeenth century, Larecaja was one of the most desirable jurisdictions in Upper Peru in terms of the (illicit) profits that could be made by *corregidores,* due to the heavy migration of native people from the *altiplano* to the eastern valleys. By the 1680s it was one of the most populous regions in the *Audiencia* of Charcas. See Evans, "Migration Processes." See also Saignes, *Los Andes orientales.*

40. AGI, Lima 159. "Relación que Iuan Recio de León," fol. 9.

41. It is possible that the geographical description, or a different version of it, was written earlier, as Recio also mentions a geographical description that he submitted in Lima to the *audiencia.*

42. AGI, Lima 159. "Breve relación," fol. 5v.

43. AGI, Lima 159. "Breve relación," fols. 4–5v. As in many other Spanish reports, the kingdom of Paititi was associated in Recio's description with a nearby mountain range rich in silver and the proximity of the elusive Amazon women.

44. AGI, Lima 159. "Breve relación," fol. 4v.

45. AGI, Lima 159. "Breve relación," fol. 5.

46. This is a central feature, for example, in the journals and letters of Christopher Columbus. In his endeavor to make the New World correspond with his geographical image of it, he repeatedly sought to interpret

the human and physical geographies of the Caribbean in a way that would demonstrate the close proximity to his own location of the wealthy kingdoms of East Asia. See in particular Pastor Bodmer, *The Armature of Conquest,* chapter 1, and Zamora, *Reading Columbus.*

47. Where the search for El Dorado was concerned, for example, the arrival in Chachapoyas in 1549 of a group of Tupinambas who had migrated upriver from their Brazilian homelands and who bore news of rich provinces directly triggered the launching of Orsúa's ill-fated Amazon expedition in 1560. See Gil, *Mitos y utopías,* 209–19, for an overview of these events. MacCormack argues that the persuasive power of the legends centered on the Amazon basin derived from the fact that they were "rooted in information that had been gathered from Indians who were believed to understand 'the secrets' of their native land." See MacCormack, "Ethnography in South America," 143.

48. This venture is mentioned by Recio in a document presented in 1625; see Recio de León, "Otro memorial," 280. See also Gil, *Mitos y utopías,* 230. While Recio refers to the captain as Araña, in Gil his name appears as Arana. The latter is no doubt correct as it is taken from Arana's own papers.

49. Gil, *Mitos y utopías,* 229–30. The Dutch were especially active in Brazil in the early 1620s; by this time, Lynch writes, they may have secured as much as one half to two thirds of all trade between Brazil and Europe, and represented "the most serious contemporary threat to the Iberian empires." Lynch, *The Hispanic World,* 81 and 98.

50. See "Tres consultas del Consejo de Indias," 292.

51. Recio de León, "Otro memorial."

52. In 1628 the entire silver fleet from New Spain was captured by the Dutch in the Cuban harbor of Matanzos. Lynch, *The Hispanic World,* 103 and 252.

53. Phelan, *The Kingdom of Quito,* 12. These attempts, however, in the Pacific as well as elsewhere, were largely unsuccessful; as Lynch points out, the elements posed a far greater risk to the Spanish fleets than did pirate attacks. Lynch, *The Hispanic World,* 252.

54. Recio de León, "Otro memorial," 276.

55. Recio claimed, moreover, that this knowledge had been certified by a number authoritative individuals who were resident in the court; "Otro memorial," 276–77. One of these individuals, who is named in Recio's text, was the friar Antonio Vázquez de Espinosa, who in 1628–29 wrote his *Compendio y descripción de las Indias occidentales.*

56. Recio de León, "Otro memorial," 285.

57. Recio de León, "Otro memorial," 280.

58. Recio de León, "Otro memorial," 289.

59. AGI, Charcas 16, R. 6, N. 26.

60. See Gil, *Mitos y utopías,* 230. The idea of using the fluvial network of the Amazon basin for commercial traffic also resurfaced strongly in the late eighteenth century, a period when the colonial authorities sought to incorporate the Amazon regions within their sphere of control. See García Jordán, *Cruz y arado,* 39–40.

61. See Bolívar, "Relación de la entrada."

62. Bolívar, "Relación de la entrada," 219. The narrows on the Beni river to which Bolívar refers are almost certainly those now known as the Encañada de Bala, located immediately upstream of the town of Rurrenabaque in the Bolivian department of Beni.

63. The story of the friar's missionary activities on the frontiers of Upper Peru is a colorful one. Inspired by the reports of a *mestizo* named Diego de Ramírez, who claimed to have encountered numerous highland refugees in the jungle who wished to be reunited with the Catholic faith, Bolívar made his way to the piedmont regions beyond Larecaja, accompanied by Ramírez. However, the partnership soon broke down over Ramírez's endeavors to pass himself off as an Inca prince to the native people. See Gil, *Mitos y utopías,* 335–42, for a discussion of this episode.

64. See AGI, Lima 159. "El Maesse de Campo . . . dize, que la riqueza." It is worth noting that arguments for using the Amazon as a travel and transportation route between the Andes and Europe continued to be made in later decades. In 1639, for example, the Jesuit Christoval de Acuña suggested that the Amazon's potential to be used as an easier and cheaper route to Spain constituted one significant justification for carrying forward the pacification and colonization of the territories through which the river passed. See Acuña, *Nuevo descvbrimiento,* 46.

65. A detailed discussion of the creation of the Potosí labor draft and the complex reasons for its subsequent disintegration is provided by Cole, *The Potosí Mita.*

66. See, e.g., AGI, Lima 41, N. 5, lib. I, fols. 74–80; AGI, Lima 41, N. 3, lib. III, folios. 45–48v; AGI, Lima 41, N. 4, lib. IV, fols. 18–21.

67. Cole, *The Potosí Mita,* 48–50.

68. One of the three documents, entitled "El Maestro de Campo . . . dize: que los Indios," is dated 08.III.1627. The second, "El Maesse de Campo . . . dize, que la riqueza," is undated but appears to have been written in 1627, since it makes explicit reference to the collapse of the Cari Cari reservoir, which occurred in "the past year of 1626." There are no clear indications when the third—entitled "Iuan Recio de León . . . como persona que tiene bien entendida"—was written. All three are located in AGI, Lima 159. The closely related subject matter of all three, however, suggests that they were all written in 1627 and submitted together.

69. AGI, Lima 159. "El Maesse de Campo . . . dize, que el principal efecto."

70. AGI, Lima 159. "El Maestro de Campo . . . dize: que los Indios."

71. A letter dated 1621, for example, declared that the Indians "are so harassed . . . that their complete ruin and end becomes more evident every day, so that unless they are favored and compensated, in a few years, what happened in the Windward Islands and the mainland [central America] . . . will happen here." AGI, Lima 151. "El Licenciado Hernando Machado."

72. AGI, Lima 159. "El Maestro de Campo . . . dize: que los Indios," fol. 4.

73. Recio's claims may have contained some truth; a general census conducted in 1683–86 suggests that in Upper Peru the total population had not declined significantly since Toledo's *Visita General* of 1575: what had taken place was a dramatic redistribution of the population. See Evans, "Migration Processes," 62–63.

74. AGI, Lima 159. "El Maestro de Campo . . . dize: que los Indios," fol. 9.

75. AGI, Lima 159. "El Maestro de Campo . . . dize: que los Indios," fol. 3v.

76. AGI, Lima 159. "El Maestro de Campo . . . dize: que los Indios," fol. 9v.

77. In a letter to Viceroy Esquilache, the bishop warned that if attempts were made to return the *yanaconas* living in and around Huamanga to their reduction villages, "it is very believable that they will go to the Chunchos, Indian infidels who are nearby, as they did a few years ago when they were to be reduced by order of the viceroy Marqués de Montesclaros." The viceroy strongly rejected this, arguing that this was a rumor put about by those interested in preventing the reductions from being implemented. AGI, Lima 37, N. 34, lib. IV. Another opponent of the notion that implementation of the reductions would encourage Andeans to flee to the lowland peoples was Ortiz de Sotomayor, former *corregidor* of Potosí. Like Esquilache, he believed that the idea was promoted by those who were opposed to the reductions. See AGI, Charcas 54. "Don Raphael Ortiz de Sotomayor," fols. 21v–22v. Given this outlook, his apparent willingness to support Recio's petition is surprising, but is possibly explained by the fact that he believed colonizing ventures to be the best way of ridding Peru of "idle people." See AGI, Charcas 51. "Don Raphael Ortiz de Sotomayor."

78. While substantial migration to the warm valleys had occurred from the conquest onward (see Evans, "Migration Processes," and Saignes, *Los Andes orientales*), often to areas that were outside effective Spanish control, it seems that only a small proportion of the huge numbers who fled the reductions in the late sixteenth and early seventeenth centuries took up residence

among "unpacified" peoples of the piedmont and lowlands (Cole, *The Potosí Mita,* 125). Undoubtedly, however, it did occur. A document dated 1626, for example, provides testimonies of how a *cacique* of the Azángaro province, no longer able to provide *mitayos* for the mercury mines of Huancavelica, fled with his family to live among unsubjugated forest groups. See BNP, B1477, "Expediente sobre la petición."

79. AGI, Lima 159. "El Maestro de Campo . . . dize: que los Indios," fol. 9.

80. AGI, Lima 159. "El Maestro de Campo . . . dize: que los Indios," fol. 9v.

81. Recio was not alone in presenting the authorities with unlikely plans for reinstating the reductions. As early as 1598, a friar claimed to have found the key for "reducing" the native people and ensuring that they would never again flee. See AGI, Lima 321. "Fray Miguel de Monsalue a S. M." Referring to the many proposals and suggestions that individuals had sent in past years to the viceroy and king, an official in Potosí wrote that "some [were] impossible, others improbable, while others contained a mixture of pros and cons, and amidst such great variety the affair came to a halt." AGI, Charcas 54. "Don Luis de Ribera."

82. In 1641, Christoval de Acuña similarly suggested that the conquest of the Amazon could solve the demographic crisis in Peru. His reasoning, however, differed from Recio's. Pacification and conversion to Christianity, he argued, would bring an end to the wars that the native peoples of the Amazon continually conducted among themselves. As a result, they would multiply greatly and the excess population would be obliged to move out of the Amazon regions and settle in the Andes, where their labor could be put to good use. Acuña, *Nuevo descvbrimiento,* 45–45v.

83. Lynch, *The Hispanic World,* 116.

84. Recio de León, "Otro memorial," 294.

85. Recio de León, "Otro memorial," 294. Interestingly, Philip IV seemed more willing to give consideration to Recio's cause than the Council did; while approving its decision, he commented in a terse reply (295) that the opinions of the viceroys on many matters did not always coincide with the view from Madrid.

86. Recio de León, "Otro memorial," 296. In the end, and under pressure from the monarch, the Council offered Recio a minor appointment in the royal treasury in the port of Arica, on the Peruvian coast. See Recio de León, "Otro memorial," 297. It is not clear whether he accepted it or even returned to America.

87. See Latour, *Science in Action,* 216–33. It is unwise, however, to push this idea too far: as the failure of the Council of the Indies' efforts to obtain adequate responses to its geographical questionnaires (see chapter 3 of

this book) reflects, Madrid's status as a "center of calculation" was hesitant and flawed.

88. Elliott, "Philip IV of Spain," 170. It was in the early decades of the seventeenth century, Elliott comments, that the Spanish court took on the aura and attributes of a capital city.

89. Livingstone's observation that "the haphazard, the irregular, and the capricious were the enemy of knowledge circulation" is strikingly apt here. Livingstone, *Putting Science in Its Place,* 175. See also Latour, *Science in Action,* who argues that the effective organization and analysis of data is crucial if an emergent "center of calculation" is to become dominant.

90. For discussions of patronage systems in Spain, see Casey, "Some Considerations on State Formation"; Gunn, "War, Religion and the State." Both rulers and their councils, Gunn (118) suggests, were susceptible to competing courtly networks of patronage, which "threatened to destabilize the whole exercise of government."

91. See Recio de León, "Otro memorial," 277.

s i x .   Contested Frontiers and the Amazon/Andes Divide

1. Renard-Casevitz, Saignes, and Taylor, *L'inca, l'espagnol et les sauvages,* 360. These authors reject the notion of a seamless continuity between Andean and European perceptions of the Amazon regions. A similar point is also made by Taylor, who observes that early Spanish visitors to the western Amazon "had no notion of such a harsh and summary duality." Taylor, "The Western Margins of Amazonia," 196–97.

2. Renard-Casevitz, Saignes, and Taylor, *L'inca, l'espagnol et les sauvages,* 361.

3. Examples include Esvertit Cobes, "Los imaginarios tradicionales"; Santos-Granero, "Boundaries Are Made to Be Crossed"; Zárate Botía, "Movilidad y permanencia." Studies that focus specifically on the Republican era include García Jordán, *Cruz y arado*; Roux, *L'Amazonie Péruvienne.*

4. See, e.g., Santos-Granero, "Boundaries Are Made to Be Crossed." As Viola Recasens argues, this tendency is also reflected in the neat scholarly distinctions that have traditionally been made by anthropologists and ethnohistorians between "highland" and "lowland" groups—a tendency that "has contributed to the promotion of an image of their history which is as schematic as it is unreal." Viola Recasens, "La cara oculta de los Andes," 7.

5. See Rabasa, *Writing Violence,* chapter 2.

6. On colonial-era indigenous trade networks between Amazon and Andes, see Reeve, "Regional Interaction." See also Taylor, "The Western Margins."

7. Until 1570, Taylor observes, "the southern part of the equatorial piedmont of the Andes was in fact inhabited, urbanized, and administered to a greater degree than the corresponding Andean and coastal zones." After this date, however, the colonial frontier began to retract as Spanish settlers retreated to the highlands, largely due to the collapse of indigenous populations in the piedmont and the discovery of promising mines in the Andean regions. Another outcome of the collapse of native populations was the emergence of a growing gap between highlands and lowlands and a breakdown in the social and economic ties that interlinked them. See Taylor, "The Western Margins," 197 and 215–17.

8. The Omaguas were descendants of Tupi-Guarani groups. In the sixteenth century they controlled a portion of the Upper Amazon that stretched for over seven hundred kilometers. See Villamarín and Villamarín, "Chiefdoms," 616.

9. In the 1540s, Carvajal sent his account of Orellana's voyage to the historian Gonzalo Fernández de Oviedo and may have written it for this express purpose. Oviedo incorporated the account into book 50 of his vast *Historia general y natural de las Indias,* which was first published in full in 1851–55. A version of the account was also submitted to the Council of the Indies by Orellana, along with other documents relating to his voyage. It was also read by the historian Antonio de Herrera. Although it did not appear in print until the mid-nineteenth century, Carvajal's text was therefore known to a number of prominent individuals in the sixteenth and seventeenth centuries. See Toribio Medina, *The Discovery of the Amazon,* 7–11 and 383–89.

10. Carvajal, *La aventura del Amazonas,* 83. The crucial role of indigenous inhabitants in shaping Spanish perceptions and experiences of the landscape, discussed in chapter 2, is again evident in Carvajal's account. If the friar was able to envisage a future landscape of European crops, it was in part because the landscape *already* reminded him of Spain, as a result of indigenous agricultural practices that bore a likeness to those of his homeland: "the land is so good, so fertile and so like that of our Spain, for we entered it around the day of St. John and the Indians were already beginning to burn the fields." See Carvajal, *La aventura del Amazonas,* 83.

11. As MacCormack observes, "What drove the first Spaniards to see the Amazon and to make contact with indigenous peoples was primarily their need for food." MacCormack, "Ethnography in South America," 145.

12. Carvajal, *La aventura del Amazonas,* 44.

13. Carvajal, *La aventura del Amazonas,* 44–45.

14. On September 3, 1542, Pizarro wrote to the king to give an account of the events of the expedition and to denounce the actions of his lieutenant, Orellana. He stated that he had expressly instructed Orellana to return within twelve days, and that Orellana assured him that he would abide

by this arrangement. Carvajal's version of events is strikingly different. According to the friar, Orellana asked Pizarro not to wait for him if he failed to return within a few days, to which Pizarro responded that he should do whatever he thought was best. See Carvajal, *La aventura del Amazonas,* 42–45.

15. Cieza de León, *Crónica del Perú. Cuarta parte,* 333.

16. Cieza de León, *Crónica del Perú. Cuarta parte,* 341.

17. Cieza de León, *Crónica del Perú. Cuarta parte,* 341.

18. Pastor Bodmer, *The Armature of Conquest.*

19. See, e.g., AGI, Patronato 99, N. 1, R. 3, account of services of Luis Palomino, and AGI, Patronato 112, R. 3, account of services submitted by Pedro de León.

20. Cieza de León, *Crónica del Perú. Cuarta parte,* 299.

21. See Maldonado, *Descripción y calidades* and *Relación verdadera.* See also Gil, *Mitos y utopías,* 296–99, who briefly discusses Maldonado's expedition in the context of Spanish efforts to find Paititi from Cuzco.

22. The wealth that Maldonado described included the riches of Paititi, which lay, he claimed, just beyond the area that his expedition had reached. See Maldonado, *Descripción y calidades.*

23. Maldonado, *Relación verdadera,* 17.

24. Maldonado, *Relación verdadera,* 19.

25. Maldonado, *Relación verdadera,* 22.

26. As Saignes suggests, Maldonado's hyperbolic language vis-à-vis the dangers that his expedition faced may also have been deployed as a means of concealing its scant results in terms of material gain. See *Los Andes orientales,* 45.

27. Maldonado, *Relación verdadera,* 40.

28. Maldonado, *Relación verdadera,* 47.

29. On the Araona, an ethnic group that forms part of the Tacanan linguistic family, see Métraux, "Tribes of Eastern Bolivia," 438–49.

30. Maldonado, *Relación verdadera,* 59.

31. Maldonado, *Relación verdadera,* 40.

32. See chapter 18 in Taussig, *Shamanism.*

33. Andrés López's letter was included in a report written by José de Acosta on the state of the Jesuit missions in Peru in 1576. See Acosta, *Obras,* 275.

34. Torres, *Crónicas augustinias,* 352.

35. Torres, *Crónicas augustinias,* 307.

36. Torres, *Crónicas augustinias,* 384.

37. Viceregal as well as metropolitan rhetoric constantly emphasized the importance of "pacifying" uncolonized territories by means of religious preaching and conversion, yet often words did not translate into practical

assistance or funding. Torres (*Crónicas augustinias,* 335) relates, for example, that the Augustinian friar José García spent two whole years in Lima, attempting to secure further missionaries for the Amazon frontier, but obtained only promises.

38. The groups of the piedmont made circumstantial alliances with the Spanish with the aim of resolving their own conflicts; missionaries and other Spaniards, therefore, could only expect a good reception as long as an alliance was advantageous to those groups. Saignes, *Los Andes orientales,* 66–67.

39. Torres, *Crónicas augustinias,* 406. Torres provides a detailed chronology of missionary activities carried out by Augustinian and other religious orders in the piedmont regions between 1560 and the mid-seventeenth century.

40. Torres, *Crónicas augustinias,* 399.

41. Torres, *Crónicas augustinias,* 399.

42. See especially chapters 13, 16, 17, and 20 in Mendoza, *Chrónica de la provincia.*

43. Mendoza, *Chrónica de la provincia,* 118.

44. Mendoza, *Chrónica de la provincia,* 118.

45. Settlements such as Nuestra Señora de Guadalupe, founded by Pedro de Leáegui in the early seventeenth century, were established in what Renard-Casevitz, Saignes, and Taylor, *L'inca, l'espagnol et les sauvages,* 172, refer to as a "no-man's land" that was created, following the collapse of Inca rule, by the retreat of the Andean presence from the piedmont regions in the face of aggressive lowland groups. An attack carried out by unpacified groups on the frontier settlement of Coroico in 1603 features with particular prominence in the archival records. See official correspondence from 1603 in ABNB, CaCh-429 and CaCh-440. The prominence of this particular attack, however, appears to have less to do with its magnitude—five or six *yanaconas* and one Spaniard were killed—than with the viceroy's concerns that Juan Ferrán, the individual chosen to lead a punitive campaign, would exacerbate the hostilities rather than resolve them: the viceroy was unsure, he wrote, whether those who had been entrusted with the defense of the area "will turn out to be more harmful . . . than the very attacking Indians." ABNB, CaCh-446.

46. AGI, Lima 229, N. 12, fols. 1–1v.

47. A seminal study on colonial Latin American frontiers is provided by Hennessy, *The Frontier.* For more recent work on the nature and development of frontiers in the Americas, see Daniels and Kennedy, eds., *Negotiated Empires.* On colonial Spanish frontier strategy, see Slatta, "Spanish Colonial Military Strategy."

48. AGI, Charcas 138. "El Obispo a S. M."

49. AGI, Charcas 138. "El Obispo a S. M." Fears about communication between "unpacified" groups and those under colonial rule were still being expressed in the mid-eighteenth century, as reflected in a document that records the election of a new *maestre de campo* for the frontier regions beyond Larecaja. ABNB, MyCh-14, fol. 1v.

50. ABNB, MyCh-1, fol. 5.

51. ABNB, MyCh-1, fol. 5. Don Pascual lodged complaints in 1629 and again in 1630. See fols. 3–4.

52. *Discurso de la sucesión y gobierno de los Yngas,* 162.

53. *Discurso de la sucesión y gobierno de los Yngas,* 165.

54. AGI, Lima 152. "Relación del alzamiento." See also Mendoza, *Chrónica de la provincia,* 105. Describing the same uprising, he draws attention to "the known advantages that they [the natives] possess in those places where the mist is ever present and so dense that the native people can barely make out the paths and strangers easily become confused and lost among those forests and crags."

55. AGI, Lima 152. "Relación del alzamiento."

56. AGI, Lima 152. "Relación del alzamiento."

57. AGI, Chile 44, N. 2. In Diego de Mendoza's account of the rebellion, no mention is made of Ulloa's role. Don Diego de Lodeña, the *corregidor* of La Paz, was the overall coordinator of the military response to the uprising. See Mendoza, *Chrónica de la provincia,* chapters 16 and 17.

58. AGI, Lima 152. "Relación del alzamiento."

59. See Saignes, *Los Andes orientales,* esp. 86, 111–13, and 129.

60. Mendoza, *Chrónica de la provincia,* 100.

61. Above all, Mendoza blamed the *corregidor*'s deputy, Francisco Ortiz, and his hangers-on for provoking the uprising. See Mendoza, *Chrónica de la provincia,* 100.

62. Mendoza, *Chrónica de la provincia,* 100.

63. Piqueras Céspedes suggests that in issuing the *Ordenanzas,* the crown officially marked the end of an era of conquest and the initiation of a new era, characterized by an active policy of colonial consolidation. Piqueras Céspedes, "Antonio de Berrío," 235–36. As Rabasa writes, moreover, the *Ordenanzas* revised and rationalized what had gone before, promoting "developmentalist policies and pastoral forms of power." Rabasa, *Writing Violence,* 95–96.

64. *Ordenanzas sobre descubrimiento,* 498.

65. *Ordenanzas sobre descubrimiento,* 498.

66. Rabasa, *Writing Violence,* 107.

67. AGI, Lima 159. "Relación que Iuan Recio de León," fol. 3.

68. AGI, Lima 159. "Breve relación," fol. 1v.

69. The accounts of missionaries who followed the same route as Recio to the lowlands in the late nineteenth and early twentieth centuries also emphasized the harshness and difficulty of the route into the lowlands. Describing the route from Apolobamba to the Tuichi river, the missionary Nicolás de Armentia commented: "God knows if this deserves to be called a trail, let alone a pathway." Armentia, *Descripción del territorio,* 32.

70. AGI, Lima 159. "Breve relación," fols. 2–2v.

71. See AGI, Lima 159. "El Maestre de Campo . . . dize: que los Indios."

72. For a detailed account of the reprisals led by Lodeña, and of the Franciscans' role as mediators between the rebels and the colonial authorities in La Paz, see Mendoza, *Chrónica de la provincia,* chapters 16 and 17.

73. AGI, Lima 152. "Méritos y servicios de don Diego de Lodeña."

74. AGI, Lima 152. "Méritos y servicios de don Diego de Lodeña," fol. 151.

75. AGI, Lima 152. "Méritos y servicios de don Diego de Lodeña," fol. 153.

76. AGI, Lima 152. "Méritos y servicios de don Diego de Lodeña," fol. 153. Their assessment was rather more promising than that provided by the Aguachiles, who, on being asked about the products and resources of their lands, replied that they knew of no mineral deposits nor where they might be found. See fol. 151v.

77. Torres, *Crónicas augustinias,* 406.

78. AGI, Lima 166, Govierno no. 9.

79. AGI, Lima 166, Govierno no. 9.

80. For a summary of westward Portuguese expansion from the Brazilian coastal regions in the seventeenth and eighteenth centuries, see Burns, *A History of Brazil,* 48–61.

81. The Raches were a small ethnic group occupying the forested piedmont that now forms the Chapare region beyond Cochabamba. Like other small groups in the *yungas* and piedmont regions in the seventeenth century, they had been pushed eastward into these regions by the European invasion. Renard-Casevitz, Saignes, and Taylor, *L'inca, l'espagnol et les sauvages,* 180.

82. The savannah regions of the Beni were an object of desire not only for the Spanish but also for the Incas, who pressed eastward in search of the riches of the Moxos, and for the Tupi-guaraní from Paraguay, who in the early sixteenth century migrated westward in search of the mythical kingdom of Candire (Saignes, *Los Andes orientales,* 27–28). By the seventeenth century the search for Candire had become entangled with tales of Paititi, since descriptions of the latter were thought to correspond to the peoples of the Beni (Saignes, *Los Andes orientales,* 49–50). Spanish ventures to conquer the Moxos were carried out not only from the Andes but also from the

southeast; in 1561, Spanish settlers arriving from Paraguay founded Santa Cruz de la Sierra, which for many decades was the principal base for expeditions. In 1560 the unexplored regions to the north of Santa Cruz were designated the Province of Moxos by the viceroy of Peru. Over the next century, numerous unsuccessful expeditions were carried out; major, government-backed expeditions ended in the 1620s, but in the final decades of the seventeenth century, the region was brought under Jesuit control. See Denevan, *The Aboriginal Cultural Geography,* 29–30. For detailed discussions of Spanish expeditions to the region, see Denevan, *The Aboriginal Cultural Geography*; Gil, *Mitos y utopías*; Parejas Moreno, *Historia del oriente boliviano.* For a history of Jesuit missions in the Moxos regions, see especially Block, *Mission Culture.*

83. The testimonies, all made in 1644, are contained in two documents and accompany a letter sent by royal officials of Potosí to the Crown: AGI, Lima 166. "Los officiales reales a S. M." In these testimonies, a persistent motif in descriptions of the Moxos is that of a large town containing a street of silversmiths and goldsmiths, over a league in length, where all manner of silver and gold articles are made. Numerous witnesses expressed the belief that these populations were descended from Incas who had taken refuge in the lowlands following the conquest; as Saignes (*Los Andes orientales,* 49–50) points out, tales of Paititi and Candire, imposed upon the Beni regions, also became entangled in the seventeenth century with notions of a neo-Inca kingdom beyond the Andes. The indigenous inhabitants of the Moxos lacked the gold and silver to which the testimonies refer. However, recent research reveals that these areas once contained dense populations with sophisticated technology for the drainage and cultivation of the savannah environment. Denevan suggests that these chiefdoms may already have been in decline at the time Europeans arrived. Extensive networks of drainage channels and earthworks are still in evidence today (Denevan, *The Aboriginal Cultural Geography,* 1–2).

84. Testimony of General Francisco Rodrigues Peinado. AGI, Lima 166. "Don Phelipe por la gracia de dios," fol. 12v.

85. Testimony of General Francisco Rodrigues Peinado. AGI, Lima 166. "Don Phelipe por la gracia de dios," fol. 17v.

86. Testimony of Capitán don Sancho Abarca. AGI, Lima 166. "En la ciudad de plata," fol. 2.

87. Testimony of Capitán don Sancho Abarca. AGI, Lima 166. "En la ciudad de plata," fol. 3v.

88. Testimony of Alonso Franco. AGI, Lima 166. "Don Phelipe por la gracia de dios," fol. 23. The theme of the tantalizing accessibility of riches that lay just beyond the colonial frontier is expressed in a petition that was presented almost one hundred years later to request a license for the conquest of the "Gran Paititi" via Cuzco. ABNB, MyCh-8.

89. Testimony of don Juan de Liano. AGI, Lima 166. "Don Phelipe por la gracia de dios," fol. 76.

90. Testimony of General Rodrigues Peinado. AGI, Lima 166. "Don Phelipe por la gracia de dios," fols. 14v–15.

91. Testimony of General Rodrigues Peinado. AGI, Lima 166. "Don Phelipe por la gracia de dios," fol. 15.

92. Saignes, *Los Andes orientales*, 20.

93. AGI, Lima 166. "En la ciudad de plata," fol. 42. Despite the failure of the proposals of 1644 to secure royal approval, the very same arguments upon which they had been founded were embraced eight years later by Lorenzo Ruiz de Saabedra, in a further attempt to obtain backing for a colonizing venture in the lowlands beyond Cochabamba. From the time of the first conquistadors onward, he argued, knowledge had circulated about the existence of an opulent "new world" in the vicinity of Charcas, but the route by which it could be entered was not known. For twelve years he had endeavored to commence the *entrada* in order to serve the crown, and finally, he declared, "I have discovered a track, and pathway, by which it may be achieved." AGI, Lima 168. "Lorenzo Ruiz de Saabedra a S. M." Lima, 25.VIII.1652.

Conclusion: Mapping Peru in the Sixteenth and Seventeenth Centuries

1. Altuna, *El discurso colonialista de los caminantes*, 38–40.
2. Rose, "The Seductions of Resistance."
3. Stern, *Peru's Indian Peoples*, 104.

BIBLIOGRAPHY

ARCHIVAL SOURCES

Archivo Arzobispal de Lima (AAL)

Capítulos, I:16. "Causa de capítulos seguida por los caciques principales y por el promotor fiscal del Arzobispado don Fr. de los Ríos, contra el bachiller Alonso Osorio, sobre haberse ausentado de su doctrina . . . así mismo contiene otro auto, contra el maestro Julián de los Ríos, cura de Moyobamba, provincia de Checras sobre acusación que hace a los indios por hechiceros." 24.VI.1611.

Curatos (Huarochirí), XXX:2. "Autos seguidos por el bachiller Antonio Guerrero de Espinar . . . contra el lic. don Andrés de Mojica, sobre la agregación de la parcialidad de los indígenas de Quichas del pueblo de San Juan de Matucana." 1630.

Hechicerías e Idolatrías, I:8. "Ynformación secreta contra los visitadores de la ydolatría, hecha en la villa de Carrión de Velasco." Huaura, 1622.

Hechicerías e Idolatrías, IV:3. "Petición del cacique Francisco Yalliruco para que sus parcialidades sigan viviendo en el asiento de Cochas." Margos, 1615.

Papeles Importantes, III:13. "Los indios de la parcialidad del pueblo de Calaguaya, mandados reducir en el pueblo de Huarochirí, y los del ayllo de Chacacancha en el pueblo de Chorrillo solicitan no se les obligue a oir misa más que las fiestas de guardar por tener sus sementeras en los pueblos viejos, a cinco leguas de sus reducciones." Huarochirí, 1594/1617.

Visitas (Huarochirí), IX:6. "Visita del Br. Felipe de Medina, cura de Santa Inés." Huarochirí, 1631.

Visitas (Huarochirí), IX:10. "Doctrina de San Gerónimo de Surco, autos contra el cura Antonio Guerrero de Espinar." San Gerónimo de Surco, 1631.

Archivo General de Indias, Seville (AGI)

Audiencia de Charcas

16, R. 6, N. 26. "Como por otras tengo escrito no tengo de dexar a avisar a V. M." La Plata, 02. I.1566.

36. "Joseph Saez de Elorduy a S. M." Potosí, 20. V.1625.

40. "Antonio Ramírez Vázquez a S. M." Potosí, 10. I.1560.

51. "Don Raphael Ortiz de Sotomayor a S. M." Potosí, 18. II.1617.

54. "Don Luis de Ribera. Redución general de los indios del Pirú." Potosí, 15. III.1620.

54. "Don Raphael Ortiz de Sotomayor, sobre la mita del zerro de Potosí." Potosí, 1620.

138. "El Obispo a S. M. Da quenta a V. M. del estado en que halló la yglesia de La Paz y de como ha visitado aquel obispado." La Paz, 12. III.1635.

Audiencia de Chile

44, N. 2. "Información de servicios de don Luis de Ulloa y de los padres y abuelos de Doña Antonia de Bahamon su muger." 1631.

Lima

31, lib. 17, fols. 140–41. "Carta del virrey al rey." Callao, 23. XII.1586.

33, N. 32, lib. 1, fols. 13–14. "Virrey a S. M." Lima, 10. IV.1597.

34, N. 40, lib. V, fols. 311–14v. "La horden que se ha de guardar acerca de los indios de mita que van a Potosí." Lima, 10. IV.1603.

36, N. 1, lib. IV, fols. 150–50v. "Virrey a S. M." Lima, 08. IV.1611.

37, N. 15. "Virrey a S. M." Lima, 10. V.1616.

37, N. 34, lib. IV, fols. 27–28v. "Reducción de indios." Lima, 06. IV.1617.

37, N. 34, lib. IV, fols. 29–42v. "El virrey a todos los corregidores, en razón de la reducción de indios y de algunas que el obispo de Huamanga escribió sobre las dificultades de estas reducciones." 1616.

37, N. 34, lib. IV, fols. 176–77. "El virrey a S. M., descuido de los doctrineros en el empadronamiento." Lima, 10. IV.1617.

37, N. 34, lib. IV, fols. 200–201. "Rui Diaz de Guzman ba prosiguiendo en la entrada que estaua dada para los indios chiriguanaes." Lima, 06. IV.1617.

38, lib. III, fol. 293. "Entre las poblaciones." Lima, 16. IV.1618.

39, N. 10, lib. V, fols. 377–84v. "Razón de las culpas que resultan contra don Luis de Oznayo." Lima, 25. IV.1620.

41, N. 3, lib. III, fols. 45–48v. "El virrey a S. M. Mita de Potosí." Lima, 08. III.1627.

41, N. 4, lib. IV, fol. 11. "Virrey a S. M. Oidor para visitar la tierra." Lima, 15.III.1628.

41, N. 4, lib. IV, fols. 18–21. "El virrey a S. M. Reducción de los indios." Lima, 15.III.1628.

41, N. 5, lib. I, fols. 74–80. "El virrey a S. M. Mita de Potosí y reducciones." Lima, 24.V.1625.

44, N. 4, lib. IV, fols. 80–85v. "Parezer de la Real Audiencia de La Plata sobre la reducción general de los indios del Perú." La Plata, 01.XI.1632.

45, N. 4, lib. I, fols. 47–47v. "Virrey a S. M. Respuesta a la carta que escribió Juan de Porras Vallejo sobre la reducción de los indios." Lima, 08.XI.1633.

97. "La Audiencia de Lima a S. M." Lima, 06.V.1622.

99. "El Licenciado Luis Enrríquez a S. M." Lima, 31.V.1629.

118. "Probanza de Alvaro Muñoz, vezino de Granadilla." Lima, 24.III.1536.

118. "Información de méritos y servicios de Sebastián de Torres, uno de los primeros conquistadores." Lima, 24.V.1537.

118. "Probanza de Martín Salas, conquistador, que tomó parte en la defensa de Cuzco y la guerra contra los incas." Lima, 07.III.1539.

121. "Los caciques e yndios del Perú sobre que se quiten los corregidores." Lima, 10.I.1566.

123. "Don Xpobal Guacai, cacique principal de La Madalena, a S. M." Lima, 26.IV.1572.

126. "Don Juan Dáualos de Riuera. Información de servicios de su padre, Niculás de Ribera." Lima, 1582.

127. "Para que no se rreçiban ynformaçiones de seruiçios de ningún yndio." Lima, 02.IV.1585 (date of original document 24.X.1575).

135. "El Licenciado don Gerónimo Rodríguez de Herrera a S. M." Collaguas, 11.II.1601.

143. "Juan Velez, intérprete general del virrey, a S. M." Lima, 13.V.1613.

145. "Probanza de Juan Belez." Lima, 1615.

149. "El Doctor Alberto de Acuña a S. M." Lima, 20.IV.1619.

151. "El Licenciado Hernando Machado sobre los malos tratamientos que padecen los naturales, a S. M." Lima, 20.III.1621.

152. "Méritos y servicios de don Diego de Lodeña." Lima, 1621.

152. "Relación del alzamiento de los Indios de los pueblos de los Yungas, de la Prouincia de Larecaxa y su castigo, por el Maesse de Campo don Diego de Lodeña." 1624.

154. "Jorge de Fonseca a S. M." Lima, 30.IV.1623.

159. "Breve relación de la descripción y calidad de las tierras, y ríos de las Prouincias de Tipuane, Chunchos, y otras muchas que a ellas se siguen." Madrid, 19.X.1623.

159. "Relaciones de méritos y servicios del maestre de campo Juan Rojas [sic] de Leon." 1627.

159. "El Maestro de Campo . . . dize: Que los Indios." 08.III.1627.

159. "El Maesse de Campo . . . Dize, que el principal efecto." No date.

159. "El Maesse de Campo . . . dize, que la riqueza." No date.

159. "Iuan Recio de León . . . como persona que tiene bien entendida." No date.

159. "Relación que Iuan Recio de León . . . caminando desde los Reynos del Pirú." Madrid, no date.

161. "Juan de Porras Vallejo a S. M." Lima, 25.IX.1631.

162. "Ynformaçión de las palabras que dixo fray Pedro de Oña del orden de st. francisco." Cuzco, 23.VII.1635.

166, Govierno no. 9. "Señor: Con zédula de 22 de febrero." Lima, 20.I.1639.

166. "En la ciudad de plata en dos días del mes de henero de mill y sei-scientos y quarenta y quatro años." La Plata, 02.I.1644.

166. "Don Phelipe por la gracia de dios . . . a bos el nuestro corregidor." Salinas, 15.I.1644.

166. "Los officiales reales a S. M. Con vnos autos tocantes al descubrim-iento de las Prouincias de los Indios Raches." Potosí, 27.III.1644.

168. "Lorenzo Ruiz de Saabedra a S. M." Lima, 25.VIII.1652.

205, N. 7. "Probanza de méritos y servicios de Francisco Cusichaca, cacique principal de Hatun Xauxa." Lima, 05.IX.1561.

205, N. 16. "Información de parte y servicio de don Felipe Paucar, caçique principal de Jauja." Lima, 25.VI.1560.

229, N. 12. "Rodrigo de Herrera Hurtado, Informaciones. Corregidor de Larecaja y capitán de las fronteras de Larecaja." Lima, 1631.

270. "Licenciado Matienzo a S. M." La Plata, 21.I.1573.

301. "Arzobispo de Lima a S. M." Lima, 20.VI.1625.

302. "Arzobispo de Lima a S. M." Lima, 06.X.1626.

302. "Arzobispo de Lima a S. M." Lima, 08.X.1626.

302. "Arzobispo de Lima a S. M." Cuzco, 15.IV.1630.

308. "Francisco Verdugo a S. M." Huamanga, 01.II.1626.

313. "Domingo de Santo Tomas a S. M." Lima, 10.XII.1563.

313. "Frai Baltasar de Vargas al licenciado Lope García de Castro." Jauja, 06.IX.1566.

317. "Memorial de fray Joan Saborido." Lima, 10.XII.1587.

321. "Fray Miguel de Monsalue a S. M." Lima, 25.IV.1598.

326. "Información de servicio de Francisco de Avila en el descubrimiento de idolatrías en Guarocherí y Yauyos." Lima, 06.IV.1617.

569, lib. 11. "Para que dexen descubrir minas a los yndios." Monserrat, 31.I.1564.

570, lib. 14, fol. 132. "Para que se guarde . . . la çédula aquí ynscrita sobre los descubrimientos de minas en Potosí." 06.III.1575.

570, lib. 14, fols. 173v–174. "Al virrey y audiençia de la çiudad de los Reyes." 13.IX.1577.

570, lib. 16, fols. 108–108v. "Que ynforme sobre lo que se a aduertido açerca de lo que se podrá hazer porque los Indios descubriesen algunas rriquezas." 21.IX.1603.

570, lib. 16, fols. 190v–91. "Al virrey del Pirú con vna relaçión que se ha dado en el Consejo sobre los ritos de los Indios y las guacas que tienen para que se informe y auise." 05.VI.1607.

Patronato

29, R. 15, 1. "Copia de vn traslado de las ynstruçiones que el conde de nieba suele dar para nuevas poblaciones." 1561.

93, N. 4, R. 1. "Probanza de méritos y servicios de Alonso Brizeño de Figueroa y Joan de Céspedes de Figueroa, hijos de Rui Hernández Briceño, conquistador." 23.VI.1589.

99, N. 1, R. 3. "La muger e hijos del capitán alonso palomino difunto sobre que se les gratifiquen los seruicios hechos en el Pirú por el dicho capitán." Lima, 1556.

112, R. 3. "Lope de Herrera en nombre del capitán Pedro de León." Santiago de Chile, 1564.

150, N. 3, R. 2. "Información hecha a pedimento de algunos vecinos de la provincia de Tierra Firme. Sus servicios hechos en el descubrimiento de la Costa de Lebante, y otras cosas." 1528, Panama.

150, N. 6, R. 2. "Probanza de Luis Maça." Panama, 1534.

Archivo General de la Nación, Lima (AGN)

Derecho Indígena 4, C. 65. "Testimonio de las provisiones, cartas y otros documentos relativos a la visita y reducción que don Alonso de Mendoza Ponce de León, Corregidor y Justicia Mayor del Partido de Azángaro ó Sángaro, hizo por comisión del Príncipe de Esquilache en las dos provincias de Huamanga, que mitaban al servicio de las minas de Huancavelica." 1619.

Archivo y Biblioteca Nacionales de Bolivia, Sucre (ABNB)

CaCh-429. "Copia de carta de la Audiencia de la Plata al virrey del Perú. Comunica sobre: Que la situación de la jornada de los Mojos es incierta." 24.XI.1603.

CaCh-440. "Relación de lo que por carta al theniente de chuquiabo—y en la conduta de capitan Juan Ferrán—el virrey nro. Señor tiene ordenado." Lima, 01. XI.1603.

CaCh-446. "Virrey a la Audiencia de La Plata." Lima, 14. XII.1603.

MyCh-1. "Muy poderoso señor: El Protector de los naturales desta Provinçia." La Plata, 1640.

MyCh-8. "Representación a nombre de don Bartolomé de Oviedo y Correoso, sobre se le conceda licencia para el descubrimiento del Gran Paititi." La Plata, 1734.

MyCh-14. "Recurso a nombre de don Pedro de Hendara." La Plata, 1755.

Biblioteca Nacional de España, Madrid (BNE)

Manuscritos de América, Tomo de varios, N. 294, 3044. Papeles varios tocantes al Gobierno de Indias.

Biblioteca Nacional del Perú, Lima (BNP)

A332. "Cuentas que el Illtro. Señor Cristóbal Suárez de Angulo, Corregidor tomó a Diego de Avila Briceño su antecesor, de la Caja del repartimiento de Chaclla de la encomienda de Martín de Ampuero." Chaclla, 29. XI.1586. (Badly deteriorated.)

A620. Padre Jacinto Barrasa, *Historia eclesiástica de la provincia del Perú de la Compañía de Jesús*. 1598. Modern typed copy.

B57. "Vuestra Excelencia confirma y apruba las provisiones de los señores marqueses de Cañete y Salinas aquí insertas acerca de que la mita de Choclococha se entere cumplidamente." Lima, 27. V.1616.

B1477. "Expediente sobre la petición presentada por Cap. Fernando Carbajal y Córdova, Corregidor y Justicia Mayor de la provincia de Azángaro para que se le reciba información sobre la ausencia de mitayos en su jurisdicción." Huancavelica, 13. I.1626.

EARLY MODERN SOURCES

Acosta, José de. *Obras de José de Acosta*. Edited by Francisco Mateos. Biblioteca de Autores Españoles, vol. 73. Madrid: Ediciones Atlas, 1954 [1590].

Acuña, Christoval de. *Nuevo descvbrimiento del gran rio de las Amazonas*. Madrid, 1641.

Albornoz, Cristóbal de. "Instrucción para descubrir todas las guacas del Pirú y sus camayos y haciendas." Edited by Pierre Duviols. *Journal de la Société des Américanistes* 56, no. 1 (1967) [c. 1582]: 17–39.

Alonso Barba, Alvaro. *Arte de los metales, en que se enseña el verdadero beneficio de los de oro, y plata por azogue. El modo de fundirlos todos, y como se han de refinar, y apartar vnos de otros.* Madrid, 1729 [1640].

Andagoya, Pascual de. *Relación de los sucesos de Pedrarias Dávila en las provincias de Tierra Firme o Castilla del Oro, y de lo ocurrido en el descubrimiento de la mar del Sur y costas del Perú y Nicaragua.* In *Colección de los viajes y descubrimientos que hicieron por mar los españoles desde fines del siglo XV: con varios documentos inéditos concernientes a la historia de la marina castellana y de los establecimientos españoles en Indias.* Compiled by Martín Fernández de Navarrete. Vol. 3, 393–456. Madrid: Imprenta Nacional, 1829.

Armentia, Nicolás de. *Descripción del territorio de las misiones franciscanas de Apolobamba, por otro nombre frontera de Caupolicán.* La Paz, 1905.

Arriaga, Pablo J. de. *La extirpación de la idolatría en el Perú.* In *Colección de libros y documentos referentes a la historia del Perú,* series 2, vol. 1. Edited by Horacio H. Urteaga. Lima: Imprenta y Librería San Martín, 1920 [1621].

Bolívar, Fray Gregorio de. "Relación de la entrada del Padre fray Gregorio de Bolívar." In *Juicio de límites entre el Perú y Bolivia.* Edited by Víctor M. Maúrtua. Vol. 8, 205–37. Barcelona, 1906.

Cabello Valboa, Miguel. *Miscelanea antártica.* Lima: Ediciones del Instituto de Etnología, 1951 [1586].

Cabeza de Vaca, Diego. *Descripción y relación de la ciudad de La Paz* [1586]. In *Relaciones Geográficas de Indias: Perú.* Edited by Marcos Jiménez de la Espada. Biblioteca de Autores Españoles, vol. 183, 342–351. Madrid: Ediciones Atlas, 1965.

Canilleros, Conde de, ed. *Tres Testigos de la Conquista del Perú (Hernando Pizarro, Juan Ruiz de Arce y Diego de Trujillo).* Buenos Aires: Espasa-Calpe, 1953.

Carabajal, Pedro de. *Descripción fecha de la provincia de Vilcas Guaman por el illustre Señor don Pedro de Carabajal, corregidor y justicia mayor della . . .* [1586]. In *Relaciones Geográficas de Indias: Perú.* Edited by Marcos Jiménez de la Espada. Biblioteca de Autores Españoles, vol. 183, 205–19. Madrid: Ediciones Atlas, 1965.

Cárdenas, Juan de. *Problemas, y secretos marauillosos de las Indias.* Valladolid: Editorial Maxtor, 2003 [1591].

Carvajal, Gaspar de. *La aventura del Amazonas.* Edited by R. Díaz. Madrid: Historia 16, 1986 [1541–42].

Cieza de León, Pedro. *Crónica del Perú. Primera parte.* Edited by Franklin Pease G. Y. Lima: Pontificia Universidad Católica del Perú, 1984 [1553].

———. *Crónica del Perú. Segunda parte.* Edited by Francesca Cantù. Lima: Pontificia Universidad Católica del Perú, 1985 [before 1554].

———. *Crónica del Perú. Tercera parte.* Edited by Francesca Cantù. Lima: Pontificia Universidad Católica del Perú, 1987 [before 1554].

————. *Crónica del Perú. Cuarta parte.* Vol. 1, *Guerra de Las Salinas.* Edited by P. Guibovich Pérez. Lima: Pontificia Universidad Católica del Perú, 1991 [before 1554].

Códice de leyes y Ordenanzas nuevamente hechas por S. M. para la governación de las yndias [1571]. In *Colección de documentos inéditos relativos al descubrimiento, conquista y organización de las antiguas posesiones españolas de América y Oceania,* vol. 16, 409–10. Madrid: Real Academia de la Historia, 1871.

Concilios Limenses (1551–1772). Edited by Rubén Vargas Ugarte. 3 vols. Vol. 1. Lima: Tip. Peruana, S. A., 1951.

Dávila Briceño, Diego. *Descripción y relación de la provincia de los Yauyos toda, Anan Yauyos y Lorin Yauyos, hecha por Diego Dávila Briceño, corregidor de Guarocheri* [1586]. In *Relaciones Geográficas de Indias: Perú.* Edited by Marcos Jiménez de la Espada. Biblioteca de Autores Españoles, vol. 183, 155–65. Madrid: Ediciones Atlas, 1965.

The Discovery of the Amazon. Edited by José Toribio Medina. New York: Dover Publications, 1988.

Discurso de la sucesión y gobierno de los Yngas. In *Juicio de límites entre el Perú y Bolivia.* 12 vols. Edited by Víctor M. Maúrtua. Vol. 8, 149–65. Barcelona, 1906.

Documentos relativos a don Pedro de la Gasca y a Gonzalo Pizarro. Edited by Juan Pérez de Tudela Bueso. Madrid: Real Academia de la Historia, 1964.

Egaña, Antonio de, ed. *Monumenta Peruana.* 8 vols. Vol. 1. Rome: Monumenta Histórica Societatis Iesu, 1954.

Estete, Miguel de. *Noticia del Perú.* In *Biblioteca peruana: Primera serie.* Vol. 1, 345–402. Lima: Editores Técnicos Asociados, 1968 [1535?].

Fernández, Diego. *Historia del Perú.* Edited by Juan Pérez de Tudela Bueso. Biblioteca de Autores Españoles, vol. 164. Madrid: Ediciones Atlas, 1963 [1571].

Fornee, Niculoso de. *Descripción de la tierra del corregimiento de Abancay, de que es corregidor Niculoso de Fornee* [1586]. In *Relaciones Geográficas de Indias: Perú.* Edited by Marcos Jiménez de la Espada. Biblioteca de Autores Españoles, vol. 184, 16–30. Madrid: Ediciones Atlas, 1965.

Gasca, Pedro de la. *Descripción del Perú.* Edited by Josep M. Barnadas. Caracas: Universidad Católica 'Andrés Bello', 1976 [1553].

Gobernantes del Perú: Cartas y papeles, siglo XVI. Documentos del Archivo de Indias. Edited by Roberto Levillier. 14 vols. Madrid: Sucesores de Rivadeneyra, S. A., 1921–26.

Guaman Poma de Ayala, Felipe. *El primer nuevo corónica y buen gobierno.* Edited by John Murra and Rolena Adorno. 3 vols. Mexico: Siglo XXI Editores, 1980 [c. 1613].

Hanke, Lewis, ed. *Los virreyes españoles en América durante el gobierno de la Casa de Austria. Perú.* Biblioteca de Autores Españoles, vol. 280. Madrid: Ediciones Atlas, 1978.

Herrera y Tordesillas, Antonio de. *Historia general de los hechos de los castellanos en las islas y tierra firme del mar océano escrita por Antonio de Herrera y Tordesillas, cronista de Castilla de Mayor de las Indias. Descripción de las islas, y tierra firme que llaman Indias Occidentales.* Madrid, 1730.

Hijos de Pariya Qaqa: La tradición oral de Waru Chiri (mitología, ritual y costumbres). Transcribed, translated, and introduced by George L. Urioste. Syracuse: Syracuse University, 1983 [c. 1598].

Historia general de la Compañía de Jesús en la provincia del Perú. Crónica anónima de 1600 que trata del establecimiento y misiones de la Compañía de Jesús en los países de habla española en la América meridional. Edited by Francisco Mateos. Madrid: Consejo Superior de Investigaciones Científicas; Instituto Gonzalo Fernández de Oviedo, 1944.

The Huarochirí Manuscript: A Testament of Ancient and Colonial Andean Religion. Translated from Quechua by Frank Salomon and George L. Urioste. Austin: University of Texas Press, 1991 [ca. 1598].

Jiménez de la Espada, Marcos, ed. *Relaciones geográficas de Indias: Perú.* Biblioteca de Autores Españoles, vols. 183–85. Madrid: Ediciones Atlas, 1965.

Lizárraga, Reginaldo de. *Descripción breve de toda la tierra del Perú, Tucumán, Río de la Plata y Chile.* Edited by Mario Hernández Sánchez-Barba. Biblioteca de Autores Españoles, vol. 216. Madrid: Ediciones Atlas, 1968 [c. 1603–9).

López de Gomara, Francisco. *Historia general de las Indias. "Hispania Victrix."* Edited by Pilar Guibelalde and introduced by Emiliano M. Aguilera. Barcelona: Obras Maestras, 1954 [1553].

López de Velasco, Juan. *Geografía y descripción universal de las Indias.* Edited by Marcos Jiménez de la Espada. Biblioteca de Autores Españoles, vol. 248. Madrid: Ediciones Atlas, 1971 [1574].

Luís de Granada, Fray. *Introducción del símbolo de la fe.* Edited by José María Balcells. Madrid: Ediciones Cátedra S. A., 1989 [1583].

Maldonado, Juan Alvarez. *Descripción y calidades desta tierra llamada la Nueva Andalucía.* In *Juicio de límites entre el Perú y Bolivia.* Edited by Víctor M. Maúrtua. Vol. 6, 60–68. Barcelona, 1906.

———. *Relación verdadera del discurso y subceso de la jornada y descubrimiento que hize desdel año del 1567 hasta el de 69.* In *Juicio de límites entre el Perú y Bolivia.* Edited by Víctor M. Maúrtua. Vol. 6, 17–59. Barcelona, 1906.

Matienzo, Juan de. *Gobierno del Perú.* Edited by Guillermo Lohmann Villena. Paris and Lima: Institut Français d'études andines, 1967 [1567].

Maúrtua, Víctor M. *Juicio de límites entre el Perú y Bolivia.* 12 vols. Barcelona, 1906.

Mena, Cristóbal de (?). *La conquista del Perú llamada la nueva Castilla.* In *Las Relaciones Primitivas de la Conquista del Perú.* Edited by Raúl Porras Barrenechea, 79–101. Paris: Cuadernos de Historia del Perú, 1937 [1534].

Mendoza, Diego de. *Chrónica de la provincia de S. Antonio de los Charcas del orden de nuestro seraphico P. S. Francisco en las Indias Occidentales, reyno del Perú.* La Paz, 1976 [1665].

Molina, Cristóbal de. *Cosas acaescidas en el Perú.* In *Crónicas peruanas de interés indígena.* Edited by F. Esteve Barba. Biblioteca de Autores Españoles, vol. 209, 61–95. Madrid: Ediciones Atlas, 1968 [1552].

Monzón, Luis de. *Descripción de la tierra del repartimiento de Atunsora, encomendado en Hernando Palomino, jurisdición de la Ciudad de Guamanga* [1581]. In *Relaciones Geográficas de Indias: Perú.* Edited by Marcos Jiménez de la Espada. Biblioteca de Autores Españoles, vol. 183, 220–25. Madrid: Ediciones Atlas, 1965.

———. *Descripción de la tierra del repartimiento de los Rucanas Antamarcas de la Corona Real jurisdición de la Ciudad de Guamanga* [1586]. In *Relaciones Geográficas de Indias: Perú.* Edited by Marcos Jiménez de la Espada. Biblioteca de Autores Españoles, vol. 183, 237–48. Madrid: Ediciones Atlas, 1965.

———. *Descripción de la tierra del repartimiento de San Francisco de Atunrucana y Laramati, encomendado en don Pedro de Córdoba, jurisdición de la Ciudad de Guamanga* [1586]. In *Relaciones Geográficas de Indias: Perú.* Edited by Marcos Jiménez de la Espada. Biblioteca de Autores Españoles, vol. 183, 226–36. Madrid: Ediciones Atlas, 1965.

Ordenanzas sobre descubrimiento nuevo y población [1573]. In *Colección de documentos inéditos, relativos al descubrimiento, conquista y organización de las antiguas posesiones españolas de América y Oceania, sacados de los Archivos del Reino, y muy especialmente del de Indias.* Compiled by Luis Torres de Mendoza. Vol. 8. Madrid: Imprenta de Frias y Compañía, 1867.

Oviedo y Valdés, Gonzalo F. de. *Historia general y natural de las Indias.* Edited by Juan Pérez de Tudela Bueso. Biblioteca de Autores Españoles, vols. 117 and 121. Madrid: Ediciones Atlas, 1959 [1535–47].

Pizarro, Hernando. *Carta a los oidores de la Audiencia de Santo Domingo.* In *Biblioteca peruana: Primera serie,* vol. 1, 117–30. Lima: Editores Técnicos Asociados, 1968 [1533].

Ralegh, W. *The Discoverie of the Large, Rich, and Beutiful Empyre of Guiana by Sir Walter Ralegh.* Transcribed, annotated and introduced by Neil L. Whitehead. Manchester: Manchester University Press, 1997 [1595].

Recio de León, Juan. "Otro memorial de Juan Recio de León." In *Juicio de límites entre el Perú y Bolivia.* Edited by Víctor M. Maúrtua. Vol. 6, 272–90. Barcelona, 1906.

Recopilación de leyes de los reynos de las Indias. 4 vols. Preliminary study by Juan Manzano Manzano. Madrid: Ediciones Cultura Hispánica, 1973 [1681].

Relación de la ciudad de Guamanga y sus términos [1586]. In *Relaciones Geográficas de Indias: Perú.* Edited by Marcos Jiménez de la Espada. Biblioteca de Autores Españoles, vol. 183, 181–204. Madrid: Ediciones Atlas, 1965.

Relación francesa de la conquista del Perú [1534]. In *Las relaciones primitivas de la conquista del Perú.* Edited by Raúl Porras Barrenechea, 69–78. Paris: Cuadernos de Historia del Perú, 1937.

Relación Samano-Xerez [1527?]. In *Las relaciones primitivas de la conquista del Perú.* Edited by Raúl Porras Barrenechea, 63–68. Paris: Cuadernos de Historia del Perú, 1937.

Sancho de la Hoz, Pedro. *Relación para su Magestad.* In *Biblioteca peruana: Primera serie,* vol. 1, 275–343. Lima: Editores Técnicos Asociados, 1968 [1534].

Solórzano y Perreyra, Juan de. *Política Indiana.* Edited by M. Ochoa Brun. Biblioteca de Autores Españoles, vol. 252. Madrid: Ediciones Atlas, 1972 [1648].

Tercero catecismo y exposición de la doctrina christiana por sermones. Lima, 1773 [1585].

Toledo, Francisco de. *Disposiciones gubernativas para el virreinato del Perú, 1569–74.* Introduction by Guillermo Lohmann Villena. Seville: Escuela de Estudios Hispanoamericanos, 1986.

Torres, Bernardino de. *Crónicas augustinias del Perú.* Edited by M. Merino. Vol. 2. Madrid: Consejo Superior de Investigaciones Científicas, 1972.

"Tres consultas del Consejo de Indias sobre las pretensiones de Juan Recio de León." In *Juicio de límites entre el Perú y Bolivia.* Edited by Víctor M. Maúrtua. Vol. 6, 291–97. Barcelona, 1906.

Tudela Bueso, Juan de, ed. *Crónicas del Perú.* Biblioteca de Autores Españoles, vol. 164. Madrid: Ediciones Atlas, 1963.

Ulloa Mogollón, Joan de. *Relación de la provincia de los Collaguas para la descripción de las Indias que su Magestad manda hacer.* In *Relaciones Geográficas de Indias: Perú.* Edited by Marcos Jiménez de la Espada. Biblioteca de Autores Españoles, vol. 183, 326–33. Madrid: Ediciones Atlas, 1965.

Vega, Andrés de. *La descripción que se hizo en la provincia de Xauxa por la instrución de S. M. que a la dicha provincia se invió de molde.* In *Relaciones Geográficas de Indias: Perú.* Edited by Marcos Jiménez de la Espada. Biblioteca de Autores Españoles, vol. 183, 166–75. Madrid: Ediciones Atlas, 1965 [1582].

Xerez, Francisco de. *Verdadera relación de la conquista del Perú.* Edited by Concepción Bravo. Madrid: Historia 16, 1985 [1534].

Zárate, Agustín de. *Historia del descubrimiento y conquista de las provincias del Perú.* Seville, 1577 [1550].

MODERN SECONDARY SOURCES

Abercrombie, Thomas A. *Pathways of Memory and Power: Ethnography and History among an Andean People.* Madison: University of Wisconsin Press, 1998.

Acosta Rodríguez, Antonio. *El pleito de los indios de San Damián (Huarochirí) contra Francisco de Avila, 1607.* Separata de "Historiografía y bibliografía americanistas," vol. 23. Seville, 1979.

———. "Los doctrineros y la extirpación de la religión indígena en el Arzobispado de Lima, 1600–1620." *Jahrbuch für Geschichte von Staat, Wirtschaft und Gesellschaft Lateinamerikas* 19 (1982): 69–109.

Adorno, Rolena. *Guaman Poma: Writing and Resistance in Colonial Peru.* Austin: University of Texas Press, 1986.

———. "The Depiction of Self and Other in Colonial Peru." *Art Journal* 49, no. 2 (1990): 110–18.

———. "Images of Indios Ladinos in Early Colonial Peru." In *Transatlantic Encounters: Europeans and Andeans in the Sixteenth Century,* edited by Rolena Adorno, 232–70. Oxford: University of California Press, 1991.

———. "Reconsidering Colonial Discourse for Sixteenth- and Seventeenth-Century Spanish America." *Latin American Research Review* 28, no. 3 (1993): 135–45.

———. "The Indigenous Ethnographer: The "Indio Ladino" as Historian and Cultural Mediator." In *Implicit Understandings: Observing, Reporting and Reflecting on the Encounters between Europeans and Other Peoples in the Early Modern Era,* edited by Stuart Schwartz, 378–402. Cambridge: Cambridge University Press, 1994.

———, ed. *Transatlantic Encounters: Europeans and Andeans in the Sixteenth Century.* Oxford: University of California Press, 1991.

Ahern, Maureen. "'Llevando el norte sobre el ojo isquierdo': Mapping, Measuring, and Naming in Castañeda's *Relación de la jornada de Cíbola (1563).*" In *Mapping Colonial Spanish America,* edited by Santa Arias and Mariselle Meléndez, 24–50. Lewisburg, Pa.: Bucknell University Press, 2002.

Alonso, Martín. *Enciclopedia del idioma: Diccionario histórico y moderno de la lengua española (siglos XII al XX) etimológico, tecnológico, regional e hispanoamericano.* Madrid: Aguilar, 1958.

Altuna, Elena. *El discurso colonialista de los caminantes, siglos XVII–XVIII.* Berkeley, Calif.: Latinoamericana Editores, 2002.

Alvarez Peláez, Raquel. "El cuestionario de 1577: La 'Instrucción y memoria de las relaciones que se han de hacer para la descripción de las Indias' de 1577." In *Cuestionarios para la formación de las Relaciones Geográficas de Indias, siglos XVI/XIX,* edited by Francisco de Solano, xciii–cvi. Madrid: Centro de Estudios Históricos, 1988.

"The Americas before and after 1492: Current Geographical Research." Special issue edited by Karl Butzer. *Annals of the Association of American Geographers* 82, no. 3 (1992).

Andrien, Kenneth J. *Crisis and Decline: The Viceroyalty of Peru in the Seventeenth Century.* Albuquerque: University of New Mexico Press, 1985.

———. "Spaniards, Andeans and the Early Colonial State in Peru." In *Transatlantic Encounters: Europeans and Andeans in the Sixteenth Century,* edited by Rolena Adorno, 121–48. Oxford: University of California Press, 1991.

Arias Coello, Alicia. "La imagen mítica de América en la España del siglo XVI." In *Actas XXXIX Congreso del Instituto Internacional de Literatura Iberoamericana.* Barcelona: Promociones y Publicaciones Universitarias, 1994.

Arias, Santa, and Mariselle Meléndez, eds. *Mapping Colonial Spanish America.* Lewisburg, Pa.: Bucknell University Press, 2002.

Armas Medina, Fernando de. *Cristianización del Perú (1532–1600).* Seville: Escuela de Estudios Hispano-Americanos, 1953.

Arroyo Ilera, Fernando. "Las Relaciones Geográficas y el conocimiento del territorio en tiempos de Felipe II." *Estudios Geográficos* 59, no. 231 (1998): 169–99.

Ashcroft, Bill. *Post-colonial Transformation.* London: Routledge, 2001.

Barclay Rey de Castro, Frederica. "Olvido de una historia: Reflexiones acerca de la historiografía andino-amazónica." *Revista de Indias* 41, no. 223 (2001): 493–511.

Barnes-Karoz, Gwendolyn. "Religious Oratory in a Culture of Control." In *Culture and Control in Counter-Reformation Spain,* edited by Anne J. Cruz and Mary E. Perry, 51–77. Minneapolis and Oxford: University of Minnesota Press, 1992.

Barnett, Clive. "'Sing along with the Common People': Politics, Postcolonialism, and Other Figures." *Environment and Planning D: Society and Space* 15 (1997): 137–54.

Bassin, Mark. "Studying Ourselves: History and Philosophy of Geography." *Progress in Human Geography* 24, no. 3 (2000): 475–87.

Bauer, Brian S. *The Sacred Landscape of the Inca: The Cusco Ceque System.* Austin: University of Texas Press, 1998.

Bautista Lassègue, Juan. "Cabildo secular, justicia y doctrina en la reducción de Cotaguasi (1609–1616)." In *Catolicismo y extirpación de idolatrías: Siglos XVI–XVIII,* edited by Gabriela Ramos and Henrique Urbano, 293–345. Cusco: Centro de Estudios Regionales Andinos Bartolomé de Las Casas, 1993.

Bell, Morag, Robin Butlin, and Michael Heffernan, eds. *Geography and Imperialism 1820–1940.* Manchester and New York: Manchester University Press, 1995.

Bender, Barbara. *Landscape: Politics and Perspectives.* Oxford: Berg Publishers, 1995.

———. "Introduction." In *Contested Landscapes: Movement, Exile and Place,* edited by Barbara Bender and Margot Winer, 1–18. Oxford: Berg Publishers, 2001.

Berthe, Jean-Pierre. "Juan López de Velasco (ca. 1530–1598), cronista y cosmógrafo mayor del Consejo de Indias: Su personalidad y su obra geográfica." *Relaciones* 75, no. 19 (1998): 141–72.

Bhabha, Homi K. *The Location of Culture.* London and New York: Routledge, 1994.

———. "Of Mimicry and Man: The Ambivalence of Colonial Discourse." In *Tensions of Empire: Colonial Cultures in a Bourgeois World,* edited by Ann Laura Stoler and Frederick Cooper, 152–60. London: University of California Press, 1997.

Block, David. *Mission Culture on the Upper Amazon: Native Tradition, Jesuit Enterprise and Secular Policy in Moxos, 1660–1880.* Lincoln and London: University of Nebraska Press, 1994.

Blunt, Alison. *Travel, Gender, and Imperialism: Mary Kingsley and West Africa.* New York and London: Guilford Press, 1994.

Blunt, Alison, and Gillian Rose, eds. *Writing Women and Space: Colonial and Postcolonial Geographies.* New York: Guilford Press, 1994.

Bolaños, Alvaro F. "On the Issues of Academic Colonization and Responsibility When Reading and Writing about Colonial Latin America Today." In *Colonialism Past and Present: Reading and Writing about Colonial Latin America Today,* edited by Alvaro Félix Bolaños and Gustavo Verdesio, 19–49. Albany: State University of New York Press, 2002.

Boone, Elizabeth H. "Introduction: Writing and Recording Knowledge." In *Writing without Words: Alternative Literacies in Mesoamerica and the Andes,* edited by Elizabeth Boone and Walter Mignolo, 3–26. Durham, N.C., and London: Duke University Press, 1994.

Boone, Elizabeth H., and Tom Cummins, eds. *Native Traditions in the Postconquest World.* Washington, D.C.: Dumbarton Oaks Research Library and Collection, 1998.

Bowser, Frederick P. *The African Slave in Colonial Peru, 1524–1650.* Stanford: Stanford University Press, 1974.

Brading, David A. *The First America: The Spanish Monarchy, Creole Patriots, and the Liberal State, 1492–1867.* Cambridge: Cambridge University Press, 1991.

Bravo Guerrera, María C. "¿Fue Francisco de Xerez el autor de la Relación Samano? Anotaciones al viaje de descubrimiento del Perú." *Anuario de Estudios Americanos* 33 (1976): 33–55.

Brotton, Jerry. *Trading Territories: Mapping the Early Modern World.* London: Reaktion Books, 1997.

Bunn, David. "'Our Wattled Cot': Mercantile and Domestic Space in Thomas Pringle's African Landscapes." In *Landscape and Power,* edited by W. J. T. Mitchell, 127–73. London: University of Chicago Press, 2002.

Burke, Peter. *Popular Culture in Early Modern Europe.* Aldershot: Scolar Press, 1994.

Burkhart, Louise. *The Slippery Earth: Nahua-Christian Moral Dialogue in Sixteenth-Century Mexico.* Tucson: University of Arizona Press, 1989.

Burkholder, M. A., and Lyman Johnson. *Colonial Latin America.* New York and Oxford: Oxford University Press, 1994.

Burnett, Graham. *Masters of All They Surveyed: Exploration, Geography, and a British El Dorado.* Chicago: University of Chicago Press, 2000.

Burns, E. Bradford. *A History of Brazil.* New York: Columbia University Press, 1993.

Burns, Kathryn. *Colonial Habits: Convents and the Spiritual Economy of Cuzco, Peru.* Durham, N.C., and London: Duke University Press, 1999.

Bustamante, Jesús. "El conocimiento como necesidad de estado: Las encuestas oficiales sobre Nueva España durante el reinado de Carlos V." *Revista de Indias* 54, no. 218 (2000): 33–55.

Butzer, Karl W. "From Columbus to Acosta: Science, Geography, and the New World." *Annals of the Association of American Geographers* 82, no. 3 (1992): 543–65.

Campbell, J. A., and David N. Livingstone. "Neo-Lamarckism and the Development of Geography in the United States and Great Britain." *Transactions of the Institute of British Geographers* 8 (1983): 267–94.

Camps, Assumpta. "En pos del Dorado (mito y literatura en la conquista del Nuevo Mundo)." In *Espacio geográfico/espacio imaginario: El descubrimiento del Nuevo Mundo en las culturas italiana y española,* edited by María de las Nieves Muñiz Muñiz, 149–56. Cáceres: Universidad de Extremadura, 1993.

Cañedo-Argüelles Fabrega, Teresa. "La tenencia de la tierra en el sur andino: El valle de Moquegua, 1530–1825." *Revista de Indias* 51, no. 193 (1991): 481–503.

Cañizares-Esguerra, Jorge. *Nature, Empire, and Nation: Explorations of the History of Science in the Iberian World.* Stanford: Stanford University Press, 2006.

Capel Saez, Horacio. *La física sagrada. Creencias religiosas y teorías científicas en los orígenes de la geomorfología española, siglos XVII–XVIII.* Spain: Ediciones del Serbal, 1985.

Carcelén Reluz, Carlos G. "Las doctrinas de Chaclla-Huarochirí, siglos XVI y XVII: Organización y desarrollo de las parroquias rurales en el Perú colonial." Master's dissertation, Lima, 1996.

———. "Las doctrinas de Chaclla-Huarochirí en los siglos XVI y XVII." *Revista Andina* 16, no. 1 (1998): 99–118.

Carter, Paul. *The Road to Botany Bay: An Exploration of Landscape and History.*
New York: Alfred A. Knopf, 1988.
———. *The Lie of the Land.* London: Faber and Faber, 1996.
Casey, James. "Some considerations on State Formation and Patronage
in Early Modern Spain." In *Patronages et clientélismes, 1550–1750 (France,
Angleterre, Espagne, Italie),* edited by C. Giry-Deloison and R. Mettam,
103–15. Lille and London: Université Charles de Gaulle, 1995.
Castillero Calvo, Alfredo. "'La ciudad imaginada': Contexto ideológico-
emblemático y funcionalidad." *Revista de Indias* 59, no. 215 (1999): 143–69.
Castro-Klaren, Sara. "Huamán Poma y el espacio de la pureza." *Revista
Iberoamericana* 114–15 (1981): 45–67.
Certeau, Michel de. *The Practice of Everyday Life.* Berkeley and London: University of California Press, 1984.
Chang-Rodríguez, Raquel. *El discurso disidente: Ensayos de literatura colonial pe-
ruana.* Lima: Pontificia Universidad Católica del Peru, Fondo Editorial,
1991.
Chrisman, Laura. "The Imperial Unconscious? Representations of Imper-
ial Discourse." In *Colonial Discourse and Post-Colonial Theory: A Reader,* ed-
ited by Laura Chrisman and Patrick Williams, 498–516. Hemel Hemp-
stead: Harvester Wheatsheaf, 1993.
Christian, William A. *Apparitions in Late Medieval and Renaissance Spain.*
Princeton: Princeton University Press, 1981.
———. *Local Religion in Sixteenth-Century Spain.* Princeton: Princeton Uni-
versity Press, 1981.
Chueca Goitia, Fernando. *Planos de ciudades iberoamericanos y filipinas existentes
en el Archivo de Indias.* Madrid: Instituto de Estudios de Administración
Local–Seminario de Urbanismo, 1951.
Clayton, Daniel. *Islands of Truth: The Imperial Fashioning of Vancouver Island.*
Vancouver and Toronto: University of British Columbia Press, 2000.
———. "The Creation of Imperial Space in the Pacific Northwest." *Journal
of Historical Geography* 26, no. 3 (2000): 327–50.
Clendinnen, Inga. "Landscape and World View: The Survival of Yucatec
Maya Culture under Spanish Conquest." *Comparative Studies in Society and
History* 22 (1980): 374–93.
Cline, Howard F. "The *Relaciones Geográficas* of the Spanish Indies, 1577–1586."
Hispanic American Historical Review 44, no. 3 (1964): 341–74.
Cobarruvias, Sebastián de. *Tesoro de la lengua castellana o española.* Madrid:
Editorial Turner, 1977 [1610].
Cole, Jeffrey A. *The Potosí Mita, 1573–1700: Compulsory Indian Labor in the Andes.*
Stanford: Stanford University Press, 1985.
The Collins Spanish Dictionary. Glasgow: HarperCollins Publishers, 1992.

Comaroff, John L., and Jean Comaroff. *Of Revelation and Revolution.* Vol. 2, *The Dialectics of Modernity on a South African Frontier.* Chicago and London: University of Chicago Press, 1997.

Cook, Noble D. *Demographic Collapse: Indian Peru, 1520–1620.* Cambridge: Cambridge University Press, 1981.

———. "Population Data for Indian Peru: Sixteenth and Seventeenth Centuries." *Hispanic American Historical Review* 62, no. 1 (1982): 73–120.

———. "Migration in Colonial Peru: An Overview." In *Migration in Colonial Spanish America,* edited by David J. Robinson, 41–61. Cambridge: Cambridge University Press, 1990.

Cornejo-Polar, Antonio. "Los discursos coloniales y la formación de la literatura hispanoamericana." In *Actas XXIX Congreso del Instituto Internacional de Literatura Iberoamericana,* Universidad de Barcelona, 15–19 June 1992. Barcelona: Promociones y Publicaciones Universitarias, 1994.

Cosgrove, Denis E. *Social Formation and Symbolic Landscape.* London: University of Wisconsin Press, 1998.

———. "Introduction: Mapping Meaning." In *Mappings,* edited by Denis Cosgrove, 1–23. London: Reaktion Books, 1999.

———. "Landscape and the European Sense of Sight—Eyeing Nature." In *Handbook of Cultural Geography,* edited by Kay Anderson, Mona Domosh, Nigel Thrift, and Steve Pile, 249–68. London: Sage, 2003.

Cosgrove, Denis, and Stephen Daniels, eds. *The Iconography of Landscape.* Cambridge: Cambridge University Press, 1988.

Craib, Raymond B. "Cartography and Power in the Conquest and Creation of New Spain." *Latin American Research Review* 35, no. 1 (2000): 7–36.

———. *Cartographic Mexico: A History of State Fixations and Fugitive Landscapes.* Durham, N.C., and London: Duke University Press, 2004.

Cresswell, Timothy. "Falling Down: Resistance as Diagnostic." In *Entanglements of Power: Geographies of Domination/Resistance,* edited by Joanne Sharp, Paul Routledge, Chris Philo, and Ronan Paddison, 256–68. London: Routledge, 2000.

———. "Landscape and the Obliteration of Practice." In *Handbook of Cultural Geography,* edited by Kay Anderson, Mona Domosh, Nigel Thrift, and Steve Pile, 269–81. London: Sage, 2003.

Cruz, Anne J., and Mary E. Perry, eds. *Culture and Control in Counter-Reformation Spain.* Minneapolis and Oxford: University of Minnesota Press, 1992.

Cummins, Tom. "Forms of Andean Colonial Towns, Free Will, and Marriage." In *The Archaeology of Colonialism,* edited by Claire L. Lyons and John K. Papadopoulos, 199–240. Los Angeles: Getty Publications, 2002.

Cushner, Nicholas P. *Lords of the Land: Sugar, Wine and Jesuit Estates of Coastal Peru, 1600–1767.* Albany: State University of New York Press, 1980.

D'Altroy, Terence N. "Transitions in Power: Centralization of Wanka Political Organization under Inka Rule." *Ethnohistory* 34, no. 1 (1987): 78–102.

———. *The Incas.* Malden, Mass., and Oxford: Blackwell Publishers, 2002.

Daniels, Christine, and Michael V. Kennedy, eds. *Negotiated Empires: Centers and Peripheries in the Americas, 1500–1820.* New York and London: Routledge, 2002.

Davies, Keith A. *Landowners in Colonial Peru.* Austin: University of Texas Press, 1984.

Dedieu, Jean Pierre. "'Christianization' in New Castile: Catechism, Communion, Mass, and Confirmation in the Toledo Archbishopric, 1540–1650." In *Culture and Control in Counter-Reformation Spain,* edited by Anne J. Cruz and Mary E. Perry, 1–4. Minneapolis and Oxford: University of Minnesota Press, 1992.

Denevan, William M. *The Aboriginal Cultural Geography of the Llanos de Mojos of Bolivia.* Berkeley and Los Angeles: University of California Press, 1966.

———. "The Pristine Myth: The Landscape of the Americas in 1492." *Annals of the Association of American Geographers* 82, no. 3 (1992): 369–85.

Dirks, Nicholas B. "Colonial Histories and Native Informants: Biography of an Archive." In *Orientalism and the Postcolonial Predicament,* edited by Carol A. Breckenridge and Peter van der Veer, 279–313. Philadelphia: University of Pennsylvania Press, 1993.

Driver, Felix. "Geography's Empire: Histories of Geographical Knowledge." *Environment and Planning D: Society and Space* 10 (1992): 23–40.

———. "New Perspectives on the History and Philosophy of Geography." *Progress in Human Geography* 18, no. 1 (1994): 92–100.

———. *Geography Militant: Cultures of Exploration and Empire.* Oxford: Blackwell Publishers, 2001.

Dubow, Jessica. "From a View on the World to a Point of View in It: Rethinking Sight, Space and the Colonial Subject." *Interventions* 2, no. 1 (2000): 87–102.

Duncan, James S. *The City as Text: The Politics of Landscape Interpretation in the Kandyan Kingdom.* Cambridge: Cambridge University Press, 1990.

———. "Sites of Representation: 'Place, Time and the Discourse of the Other.'" In *Place/Culture/Representation,* edited by James Duncan and David Ley, 39–56. London: Routledge, 1993.

———. "Complicity and Resistance in the Colonial Archive: Some Issues of Method and Theory in Historical Geography." *Historical Geography* 27 (1999): 119–28.

———. "Dis-Orientation: 'On the Shock of the Familiar in a Far-away Place.'" In *Writes of Passage: Reading Travel Writing,* edited by James Duncan and Derek Gregory, 151–63. London: Routledge, 1999.

Duncan, James S., and Trevor Barnes, eds. *Writing Worlds: Discourse, Text and Metaphor in the Representation of Landscape.* London: Routledge, 1992.

Duncan, James S., and Nancy Duncan. "(Re)reading the Landscape." *Environment and Planning D: Society and Space* 6 (1988): 117–26.

Duncan, James S., and Derek Gregory, eds. *Writes of Passage: Reading Travel Writing.* London: Routledge, 1999.

Durán Estragó, Margarita. "The Reductions." In *The Church in Latin America, 1492–1992,* edited by Enrique Dussel, 351–62. Kent: Burns & Oates, 1992.

Durston, Alan. "Notes on the Authorship of the Huarochirí Manuscript." *Colonial Latin American Review* 16, no. 2 (2007): 227–41.

Duviols, Pierre. "Un inédit de Cristóbal de Albornoz: La instrucción para descubrir todas las guacas del Pirú y sus camayos y haciendas." *Journal de la Société des Américanistes* 56 (1967): 7–39.

———. *La lutte contre les religions autochtones dans le Pérou colonial: "L'extirpation de l'idôlatrie" entre 1532 et 1660.* Lima and Paris: Institut Français d'Etudes Andines, 1971.

Edwards, Clinton R. "Mapping by Questionnaire: An early Spanish Attempt to Determine New World Geographical Positions." *Imago Mundi* 23 (1969): 17–28.

Eliade, Mircea. *The Sacred and the Profane: The Nature of Religion.* San Diego and London: Harcourt Brace and Company, 1987.

Elliott, J. H. *The Old World and the New.* Cambridge: Cambridge University Press, 1971.

———. "Philip IV of Spain: Prisoner of Ceremony." In *The Courts of Europe: Politics, Patronage and Royalty, 1400–1800,* edited by A. G. Dickens, 169–89. London: Thames and Hudson, 1977.

———. "Spain and America in the Sixteenth and Seventeenth Centuries." In *The Cambridge History of Latin America,* Vol. 1, *Colonial Latin America,* edited by Leslie Bethell, 287–339. Cambridge: Cambridge University Press, 1984.

———. "Final Reflections: The Old World and the New Revisited." In *America in European Consciousness, 1493–1750,* edited by Karen Kupperman, 391–408. Chapel Hill and London: University of North Carolina Press, 1995.

Espinoza Soriano, Waldemar. "El alcalde mayor indígena en el virreinato del Perú." *Anuario de Estudios Americanos* 17 (1960): 183–300.

———. "La guaranga y la reducción de Huancayo: Tres documentos inéditos para la etnohistoria del Perú." *Revista del Museo Nacional* 31 (1963): 8–80.

———. "Los señoríos étnicos de Chachapoyas y la alianza hispano-chacha." *Revista Histórica* 30 (1967): 224–332.

————. "Los huancas aliados de la conquista: Tres informaciones inéditas sobre la participación indígena en la conquista del Perú." *Anales Científicos* 1 (Huancayo-Lima, 1971): 9–410.

————. *Enciclopedia Departamental de Junín,* vol. 1. Huancayo: Editorial San Fernando, 1973.

Esvertit Cobes, Natalie. "Los imaginarios tradicionales sobre el Oriente ecuatoriano." *Revista de Indias* 41, no. 223 (2001): 541–71.

Ette, Otmar. "Funciones de mitos y leyendas en textos de los siglos XVI y XVII sobre el Nuevo Mundo." In *De conquistadores y conquistados: Realidad, justificación, representación,* edited by Karl Kohut, 131–52. Frankfurt am Main: Vervuert Verlag, 1992.

Evans, Brian. "Migration Processes in Upper Peru in the Seventeenth Century." In *Migration in Colonial Spanish America,* edited by David J. Robinson, 62–85. Cambridge: Cambridge University Press, 1990.

Fernández-Armesto, Felipe. *Philip II's Empire: A Decade at the Edge.* London: Hakluyt Society, 1999.

Fossa, Lydia. "The Discourse of History in Andean America: Europeans Writing for Europeans." Ph.D. dissertation, University of Michigan, 1996.

Foucault, Michel. *Discipline and Punish: The Birth of the Prison.* London: Penguin Books, 1977.

Fraser, Valerie. *The Architecture of Conquest: Building in the Viceroyalty of Peru, 1535–1635.* Cambridge: Cambridge University Press, 1990.

Friede, Juan. "La censura española del siglo XVI y los libros de historia de América." *Revista de Historia de América* 47 (1959): 45–94.

————. "Las Casas and Indigenism in the Sixteenth Century." In *Bartolomé de Las Casas in History: Toward an Understanding of the Man and His Work,* edited by Juan Friede and Benjamin Keen, 127–234. DeKalb: Northern Illinois University Press, 1971.

Gade, Daniel W. "Landscape, System and Identity in the Post-Conquest Andes." *Annals of the Association of American Geographers* 82, no. 3 (1992): 460–77.

Gade, Daniel W., and Mario Escobar. "Village Settlement and the Colonial Legacy in Southern Peru." *The Geographical Review* 74, no. 4 (1982): 430–39.

Gakenheimer, Ralph A. "The Peruvian City of the Sixteenth Century." In *The Urban Explosion in Latin America: A Continent in Process of Modernization,* edited by Glenn H. Beyer, 33–56. Ithaca and New York: Cornell University Press, 1967.

García Cabrera, Juan C., ed. *Ofensas a Dios. Pleitos e injurias. Causas de idolatrías y hechicerías. Cajatambo, siglos XVII–XIX.* Cusco: Centro de Estudios Regionales Andinos Bartolomé de las Casas, 1994.

García Jordán, Pilar. *Cruz y arado, fusiles y discursos: La construcción de los Orientes en el Perú y Bolivia, 1820–1940.* Lima: Instituto de Estudios Peruanos, 2001.

Gerbi, Antonello. *Caminos del Perú.* Lima: Banco de Crédito del Perú, 1944.

Gibson, Charles. *Spain in America.* New York: Harper and Row, 1966.

Gil, Juan. *Mitos y utopías del descubrimiento.* Vol. 3, *El Dorado.* Madrid: Alianza Editorial, 1989.

Ginzburg, Carlo. *The Cheese and the Worms: The Cosmos of a Sixteenth-Century Miller.* London: Penguin Books, 1992.

Glave Testino, Luís. *Trajinantes: Caminos indígenas en la sociedad colonial, siglos XVI/XVII.* Lima: Instituto de Apoyo Agrario, 1989.

Godlewska, Anne, and Neil Smith, eds. *Geography and Empire.* Oxford and Cambridge, Mass.: Blackwell Publishers, 1994.

Goldberg, David T. "Heterogeneity and Hybridity: Colonial Legacy, Post-colonial Heresy." In *A Companion to Postcolonial Studies,* edited by Henry Schwarz and Sangeeta Ray, 72–86. Oxford: Blackwell Publishers, 2000.

Gomez Rivas, León. *El Virrey del Perú don Francisco de Toledo.* Madrid: Instituto Provincial de Investigaciones y Estudios Toledanos, 1994.

González Sánchez, Carlos A. "La cultura del libro en el Virreinato del Perú en tiempos de Felipe II." *Colonial Latin American Studies* 9, no. 1 (2000): 63–80.

Goodman, David C. *Power and Penury: Government, Technology and Science in Philip II's Spain.* Cambridge: Cambridge University Press, 1988.

Graubart, Karen B. "Indecent Living: Indigenous Women and the Politics of Representation in Early Colonial Peru." *Colonial Latin American Review* 9, no. 2 (2000): 213–35.

Greenblatt, Stephen. *Marvelous Possessions: The Wonder of the New World.* Chicago: University of Chicago Press, 1991.

———, ed. *New World Encounters.* Oxford: University of California Press, 1993.

Griffiths, Nicholas. *The Cross and the Serpent: Religious Repression and Resurgence in Colonial Peru.* Norman and London: University of Oklahoma Press, 1996.

Gruzinski, Serge. *The Conquest of Mexico.* Translated by Eileen Corrigan. Cambridge: Polity Press, 1993.

Gunn, Steven. "War, Religion and the State." In *Early Modern Europe: An Oxford History,* edited by Euan Cameron, 102–33. Oxford: Oxford University Press, 1999.

Gutiérrez, Gustavo. *Dios o el oro en las Indias. Siglo XVI.* Lima: Instituto Bartolomé de Las Casas, 1989.

Guy, Donna J., and Thomas E. Sheridan, eds. *Contested Ground: Comparative Frontiers on the Northern and Southern Edges of the Spanish Empire.* Tucson: University of Arizona Press, 1998.

Hampe Martínez, Teodoro. "El trasfondo personal de la 'extirpación': La carrera y la formación intelectual de Francisco de Avila y Fernando de Avendaño." *Colonial Latin American Review* 8, no. 1 (1999): 91–111.

Hanke, Lewis. "Viceroy Francisco de Toledo and the Just Titles of Spain to the Inca Empire." *The Americas* 3, no. 1 (1946): 3–19.

———. *All Mankind Is One.* DeKalb: Northern Illinois University Press, 1974.

———. *Guía de las fuentes en el Archivo General de Indias para el estudio de la administración virreinal española en México y en el Perú: 1535–1700,* vol. 3. Köln and Wien: Böhlau Verlag, 1977.

Hardoy, Jorge E. "Las formas de las ciudades coloniales en la América Española." *Revista de Indias* 131–38 (1973–74): 315–44.

———. *Cartografía urbana colonial.* Buenos Aires: Instituto Internacional de Medio Ambiente, 1991.

Harley, J. B. "Rereading the Maps of the Columbian Encounter." *Annals of the Association of American Geographers* 82, no. 3 (1992): 522–42.

———. "Maps, Knowledge and Power." In *The Iconography of Landscape: Essays on the Symbolic Representation, Design and Use of Past Environments,* edited by Denis Cosgrove and Stephen Daniels, 277–312. Cambridge: Cambridge University Press, 1994.

———. *The New Nature of Maps: Essays in the History of Cartography.* Baltimore and London: Johns Hopkins University Press, 2001.

Harris, Olivia. "'The Coming of the White People'; Reflections on the Mythologisation of History in Latin America." *Bulletin of Latin American Research* 14, no. 1 (1995): 9–24.

Hemming, John. *The Conquest of the Incas.* London: Macmillan & Co., 1970.

Hennessy, Alistair. *The Frontier in Latin American History.* London: Edward Arnold, 1978.

Hirsch, Eric, and Michael O'Hanlon, eds. *The Anthropology of Landscape: Perspectives on Place and Space.* Oxford: Clarendon Press, 1995.

Holland, Dorothy, William Lachicotte Jr., Debra Skinner, and Carole Cain. *Identity and Agency in Cultural Worlds.* Cambridge, Mass., and London: Harvard University Press, 1998.

Hulme, Peter. *Colonial Encounters: Europe and the Native Caribbean, 1492–1797.* London and New York: Routledge, 1992.

Hyland, Sabine. *The Jesuit and the Incas: The Extraordinary Life of Padre Blas Valera, S.J.* Ann Arbor: University of Michigan Press, 2003.

Hyslop, John. *The Inka Road System.* Orlando and London: Academic Press, 1984.

———. *Inka Settlement Planning.* Austin: University of Texas Press, 1990.

Ingold, Tim. *The Perception of the Environment: Essays on Livelihood, Dwelling and Skill.* London and New York: Routledge, 2000.

Jacobs, Jane M. *Edge of Empire: Postcolonialism and the City.* London and New York: Routledge, 1996.

Jamieson, Ross W. *Domestic Architecture and Power: The Historical Archaeology of Colonial Ecuador.* New York and London: Kluwer Academic/Plenum Publishers, 2000.

Julien, Catherine J. "History and Art in Translation: The Paños and Other Objects Collected by Francisco de Toledo." *Colonial Latin American Review* 8, no. 1 (1999): 61–89.

Kagan, Richard L. *Urban Images of the Hispanic World, 1493–1793.* New Haven and London: Yale University Press, 2000.

Kamen, Henry. *Spain, 1469–1714: A Society of Conflict.* London and New York: Longman, 1983.

Kinsbruner, Jay. *The Colonial Spanish American City: Urban Life in the Age of Atlantic Capitalism.* Austin: University of Texas Press, 2005.

Klor de Alva, J. Jorge. "The Postcolonization of (Latin) American Experience: A Reconsideration of 'Colonialism,' 'Postcolonialism,' and 'Mestizaje.'" In *After Colonialism: Imperial Histories and Postcolonial Displacements,* edited by Gyan Prakash, 241–75. Princeton: Princeton University Press, 1995.

Larson, Brooke. *Cochabamba, 1550–1900: Colonialism and Agrarian Transformation in Bolivia.* Durham, N.C., and London: Duke University Press, 1998.

Latin American Subaltern Studies Group. "Founding Statement." *boundary 2* 20, no. 3 (1993): 110–21.

Latour, Bruno. *Science in Action: How to Follow Scientists and Engineers through Society.* Milton Keynes: Open University Press, 1987.

Lavallé, Bernard. *Las promesas ambiguas: Criollismo colonial en los Andes.* Lima: Pontificia Universidad Católica del Perú, 1993.

Lehman, Kathryn. "Geography and Gender in the Narrative of Argentinean National Origin: The "Pampa" as Chronotope." *Revista de Estudios Hispánicos* 32 (1998): 3–28.

Leibsohn, Dana. "Colony and Cartography: Shifting Signs on Indigenous Maps of New Spain." In *Reframing the Renaissance: Visual Culture in Europe and Latin America, 1450–1650,* edited by Claire Farago, 265–81. New Haven and London: Yale University Press, 1995.

Leonard, Irving A. *The Books of the Brave; Being an Account of Books and Men in the Spanish Conquest and Settlement of the Sixteenth-Century New World.* Cambridge, Mass.: Harvard University Press, 1949.

Lester, Alan. "'Otherness' and the Frontiers of Empire: The Eastern Cape Colony, 1806–c. 1850." *Journal of Historical Geography* 24, no. 1 (1998): 2–19.

Lestringant, Frank. *Mapping the Renaissance World: The Geographical Imagination in the Age of Discovery.* Cambridge: Polity Press, 1994.

Levillier, Roberto. *Don Francisco de Toledo, Supremo Organizador del Perú.* Madrid: Espasa-Calpe, 1935.

———. *El Paititi, El Dorado y las Amazonas.* Buenos Aires: Emecé Editores, 1976.

Livingstone, David. *Putting Science in Its Place: Geographies of Scientific Knowledge.* Chicago and London: University of Chicago Press, 2003.

Lockhart, James. *Spanish Peru, 1532–1560.* Milwaukee and London: University of Wisconsin Press, 1968.

———. *The Men of Cajamarca: A Social and Biographical Study of the First Conquerors of Peru.* Austin and London: University of Texas Press, 1972.

———. *Of Things of the Indies: Essays Old and New in Early Latin American History.* Stanford: Stanford University Press, 1999.

Lohmann Villena, Guillermo. *El corregidor de indios en el Perú bajo los Austrias.* Madrid: Ediciones Cultura Hispánica, 1957.

Loomba, Ania. *Colonialism/Postcolonialism.* London: Routledge, 1998.

López Piñero, José M. *Ciencia y técnica en la sociedad española de los siglos XVI y XVII.* Barcelona: Editorial Labor S. A., 1979.

Lovell, W. George. "The Real Country and the Legal Country: Spanish Ideals and Mayan Realities in Colonial Guatemala." In *Nature and Identity in Cross-Cultural Perspective,* edited by Anne Buttimer and Luke Wallin, 151–61. Dordrecht: Kluwer Academic Publishers, 1999.

Lux, David S., and Harold J. Cook. "Closed Circles or Open Networks? Communicating at a Distance during the Scientific Revolution." *History of Science* 36 (1998): 179–211.

Lynch, John. *The Hispanic World in Crisis and Change, 1598–1700.* Oxford and Cambridge, Mass.: Blackwell Publishers, 1992.

———. "The Institutional Framework of Colonial Spanish America." *Journal of Latin American Studies* 24 (1992): 69–81.

MacCormack, Sabine. *Religion in the Andes: Vision and Imagination in Early Colonial Peru.* Princeton: Princeton University Press, 1991.

———. "Ethnography in South America: The First Two Hundred Years." In *The Cambridge History of the Native Peoples of the Americas.* Vol. 3, *South America,* Part I, edited by Frank Salomon and Stuart Schwartz, 96–187. Cambridge: Cambridge University Press, 1999.

Mackenthun, Gesa. *Metaphors of Dispossession: American Beginnings and the Translation of Empire, 1492–1637.* Norman and London: University of Oklahoma Press, 1997.

MacLeod, Murdo J. "The *Relaciones de Méritos y Servicios* and Their Historical and Political Interpretation." *Colonial Latin American Historical Review* 7, no. 1 (1998): 25–42.

Málaga Medina, Alejandro. "Las reducciones en el Perú durante el gobierno del Virrey Francisco de Toledo." *Anuario de Estudios Americanos* 31 (1974): 819–42.

———. "Las reducciones en el Perú (1532–1600)." *Historia y Cultura* 8 (1974): 141–72.

———. "Las reducciones en el Perú durante el gobierno del Virrey Francisco de Toledo." *Separata del Tomo XXXI del Anuario de Estudios Americanos.* Seville, 1976.

———. *Reducciones toledanas en Arequipa.* Arequipa, Peru: PUBLIUNSA, 1989.

Mallon, Florencia E. "The Promise and Dilemma of Subaltern Studies: Perspectives from Latin American History." *American Historical Review* 99, no. 5 (1994): 1491–515.

Martínez Val, José María. "El paisaje geográfico en los historiadores de Indias." *Revista de Indias* 6, no. 19 (1945): 289–322.

Martins, Luciana L. "A Naturalist's Vision of the Tropics: Charles Darwin and the Brazilian Landscape." *Singapore Journal of Tropical Geography* 21, no. 1 (2000): 19–33.

Matless, David. "Introduction: The Properties of Landscape." In *Handbook of Cultural Geography,* edited by Kay Anderson, Mona Domosh, Nigel Thrift, and Steve Pile, 227–32. London: Sage, 2003.

McAlister, Lyle N. *Spain and Portugal in the New World, 1492–1700.* Minneapolis: University of Minnesota Press, 1984.

McClintock, Anne. *Imperial Leather: Race, Gender and Sexuality in the Colonial Contest.* New York and London: Routledge, 1995.

McEwan, Cheryl. "Paradise or Pandemonium? West African Landscapes in the Travel Accounts of Victorian Women." *Journal of Historical Geography* 22, no. 1 (1996): 68–83.

———. "Cutting Power Lines within the Palace? Countering Paternity and Eurocentrism in the 'Geographical Tradition.'" *Transactions of the Institute of British Geographers* 23 (1998): 371–84.

Métraux, Alfred. "Tribes of Eastern Bolivia and the Madeira Headwaters." In *Handbook of South American Indians.* Vol. 3, *The Tropical Forest Tribes,* edited by Julian H. Steward, 381–454. Washington: Government Printing Office, 1948.

Métraux, Alfred. "Tribes of the Eastern Slopes of the Bolivian Andes," In *Handbook of South American Indians.* Vol. 3, *The Tropical Forest Tribes,* edited by Julian H. Steward, 465–506. Washington: Government Printing Office, 1948.

Mignolo, Walter D. "Cartas, crónicas y relaciones del descubrimiento y la conquista." In *Historia de la literatura hispanoamericana.* Vol. 1, *Epoca colonial,* edited by Luis Iñigo Madrigal, 57–116. Madrid, 1982.

————. "El mandato y la ofrenda: La *Descripción de la ciudad y provincia de Tlaxcala,* de Diego Muñoz Camargo, y las relaciones de Indias." *Nueva Revista de Filología Hispánica* 35, no. 2 (1987): 451–79.

————. "Colonial Situations, Geographical Discourses and Territorial Representations: Towards a Diatopical Understanding of Colonial Semiosis." *Dispositio* 14, nos. 36–38 (1991): 93–140.

————. *The Darker Side of the Renaissance: Literacy, Territoriality and Colonization.* Ann Arbor: University of Michigan Press, 1995.

————. "Human Understanding and (Latin) American Interests—The Politics and Sensibilities of Geohistorical Locations." In *A Companion to Postcolonial Studies,* edited by Henry Schwarz and Sangeeta Ray, 180–202. Oxford: Blackwell Publishers, 2000.

Millones Figueroa, Luís, and Domingo Ledezma, eds. *El saber de los jesuitas, historias naturales y el Nuevo Mundo.* Frankfurt and Madrid: Vervuert and Iberoamericana, 2005.

Mills, Kenneth. *Idolatry and Its Enemies: Colonial Andean Religion and Extirpation, 1640–1750.* Princeton: Princeton University Press, 1997.

Mills, Sara. *Discourse.* London: Routledge, 1997.

Mishra, Vijay, and Bob Hodge. "What is Post(-)colonialism?" In *Colonial Discourse and Post-Colonial Theory: A Reader,* edited by Laura Chrisman and Patrick Williams, 276–90. Hemel Hempstead: Harvester Wheatsheaf, 1993.

Mitchell, Don. *The Lie of the Land: Migrant Workers and the California Landscape.* Minneapolis and London: University of Minnesota Press, 1996.

————. "The Lure of the Local: Landscape Studies at the End of a Troubled Century." *Progress in Human Geography* 25, no. 2 (2001): 269–81.

Mitchell, Timothy. *Colonising Egypt.* Cambridge: Cambridge University Press, 1988.

Mitchell, W. J. T., ed. *Landscape and Power.* Chicago and London: University of Chicago Press, 1994.

Moliner, María. *Diccionario de uso del español.* Madrid: Editorial Gredos, 1966.

Molinié Fioravanti, Antoinette. "El simbolismo de frontera en los Andes." *Revista del Museo Nacional* (Lima) 47 (1986–87): 251–86.

Molloy, Sylvia. "Alteridad y reconocimiento en los Naufagios de Alvar Nuñez Cabeza de Vaca." *Nueva Revista de Filología Hispánica* 35 (1987): 425–49.

Moore, Jerry. *Architecture and Power in the Ancient Andes: The Archaeology of Public Buildings.* Cambridge: Cambridge University Press, 1996.

Moore-Gilbert, Bart. *Postcolonial Theory: Contexts, Practices, Politics.* London: Verso, 1997.

Morphy, Howard. "Colonialism, History and the Construction of Place: The Politics of Landscape in Northern Australia." In *Landscape: Politics and Perspectives,* edited by Barbara Bender, 205–44. Oxford: Berg Publishers, 1995.

Muir, Richard. "Landscape: A Wasted Legacy." *Area* 30, no. 3 (1998): 263–71.

Mundy, Barbara. *The Mapping of New Spain: Indigenous Cartography and the Maps of the Relaciones Geográficas.* Chicago: University of Chicago Press, 1996.

Muñiz Muñiz, María de las Nieves, ed. *Espacio geográfico/espacio imaginario: El descubrimiento del Nuevo Mundo en las culturas italiana y española.* Cáceres: Universidad de Extremadura, 1993.

Murphy, Robert C. "The Earliest Spanish Advances Southward along the West Coast of South America." *Hispanic American Historical Review* 21 (1941): 2–28.

Murra, John V. "Andean Societies before 1532." In *The Cambridge History of Latin America.* Vol. 1, *Colonial Latin America,* edited by Leslie Bethell, 59–90. Cambridge: Cambridge University Press, 1984.

———. "'Nos Hazen Mucha Ventaja': The Early European Perception of Andean Achievement." In *Transatlantic Encounters: Europeans and Andeans in the Sixteenth Century,* edited by Kenneth J. Andrien and Rolena Adorno, 73–89. Berkeley and London: University of California Press, 1991.

Myers, Garth A. "Colonial Geography and Masculinity: Eric Dutton's Kenya Mountain." *Gender, Place and Culture* 9, no. 1 (2002): 23–38.

Myers, Kathleen A. "Writing of the Frontier: Blurring Gender and Genre in the Monja Alférez's Account." In *Mapping Colonial Spanish America,* edited by Santa Arias and Mariselle Meléndez, 181–201. Lewisburg, Pa.: Bucknell University Press, 2002.

Nash, June. *We Eat the Mines and the Mines Eat Us: Dependency and Exploitation in Bolivian Tin Mines.* New York: Columbia University Press, 1979.

Naylor, Simon. "Discovering Nature, Rediscovering the Self: Natural Historians and the Landscapes of Argentina." *Environment and Planning D: Society and Space* 19 (2001): 227–47.

Newson, Linda A. *Life and Death in Early Colonial Ecuador.* Norman and London: University of Oklahoma Press, 1995.

Noreña, Carlos G. *Studies in Spanish Renaissance Thought.* The Hague: Martinus Nijhoff, 1975.

Nutall, Zelia. "Royal Ordinances Concerning the Laying Out of New Towns." *The Hispanic American Historical Review* 4, no. 4 (1921): 743–53.

Orlove, Benjamin. "Mapping Reeds and Reading Maps: The Politics of Representation in Lake Titicaca." *American Ethnologist* 18, no. 1 (1991): 3–38.

Ortiz Rescanière, Alejandro. *Huarochirí, 400 años después.* Lima: Pontificia Universidad Católica, 1980.

Ortner, Sherry B. "Resistance and the Problem of Ethnographic Refusal." *Comparative Studies in Society and History* 37, no. 1 (1995): 173–93.

Padrón, Ricardo. *The Spacious Word: Cartography, Literature, and Empire in Early Modern Spain.* Chicago: University of Chicago Press, 2004.

Pagden, Anthony. "Identity Formation in Spanish America." In *Colonial Identity in the Atlantic World, 1500–1800,* edited by Nicholas Canny and Anthony Pagden, 51–93. Princeton: Princeton University Press, 1987.

———. *European Encounters with the New World.* New Haven and London: Yale University Press, 1993.

———. "Heeding Heraclides: Empire and Its Discontents, 1619–1812." In *Spain, Europe and the Atlantic World: Essays in Honour of John H. Elliott,* edited by Richard L. Kagan and Geoffrey Parker, 316–33. Cambridge: Cambridge University Press, 1995.

———. *Lords of All the World: Ideologies of Empire in Spain, Britain and France c.1500–c.1800.* New Haven and London: Yale University Press, 1995.

Parejas Moreno, Alcides J. *Historia del oriente boliviano: Siglos XVI y XVII.* Santa Cruz: Universidad Gabriel René Moreno, 1980.

Parry, J. H. *The Spanish Theory of Empire.* Cambridge: Cambridge University Press, 1940.

———. *The Age of Reconnaissance: Discovery, Exploration and Settlement 1450–1650.* London: Weidenfeld and Nicolson, 1963.

Pastor Bodmer, Beatriz. *The Armature of Conquest: Spanish Accounts of the Discovery of America, 1492–1589.* Stanford: Stanford University Press, 1992.

———. *El jardín y el peregrino: Ensayo sobre el pensamiento utópico latinoamericano, 1492–1695.* Amsterdam: Rodopi, 1996.

Pease G.Y., Franklin. "Las visitas como testimonio andino." In *Historia, problema y promesa: Homenaje a Jorge Basadre,* edited by Francisco Miró Quesada C., Franklin Pease G.Y., and D. Sobrevilla A., 437–53. Lima: Pontificia Universidad Católica del Perú, 1978.

———. *Las crónicas y los Andes.* Lima: Pontificia Universidad Católica del Perú, 1995.

———. *Curacas, reciprocidad y riqueza.* Lima: Pontificia Universidad Católica del Perú, 1999.

Phelan, John L. *The Kingdom of Quito in the Seventeenth Century: Bureaucratic Politics in the Spanish Empire.* Madison and London: University of Wisconsin Press, 1967.

Phillips, Richard. *Mapping Men and Empire: A Geography of Adventure.* London and New York: Routledge, 1997.

Piqueras Céspedes, Ricardo. "Antonio de Berrío y las Ordenanzas de 1573." *Boletín Americanista* 39, no. 49 (1999): 233–44.

———. *Entre el hambre y El Dorado: Mito y contacto alimentario en las huestes de conquista del XVI.* Seville: Diputación de Sevilla, 1997.

Ponce Leiva, Pilar. "Las cuestionarios oficiales: ¿Un sistema de control de espacio?" In *Cuestionarios para la formación de las Relaciones Geográficas de*

Indias, siglos XVI/XIX, edited by Francisco de Solano, xxix–xxxvi. Madrid: Centro de Estudios Históricos, 1988.

————. "Las Ordenanzas sobre descripciones (1573): su aplicación en la Real Audiencia de Quito." In *Cuestionarios para la formación de las Relaciones Geográficas de Indias, siglos XVI/XIX,* edited by Francisco de Solano, lxxix–xci. Madrid: Centro de Estudios Históricos, 1988.

Poole, Deborah. *Vision, Race and Modernity: A Visual Economy of the Andean Image World.* Princeton: Princeton University Press, 1997.

Porras Barrenechea. *Las Relaciones primitivas de la conquista del Perú.* Paris: Cuadernos de Historia del Perú, 1937.

————. *Catálogo de la mapoteca, del siglo XVI al siglo XX.* Lima: Ministerio de Relaciones Exteriores, 1957.

————. *Cartas del Perú (1524–1543).* Lima: Edición de la Sociedad de Bibliófilos Peruanos, 1959.

————. *Fuentes históricas peruanas.* Lima: Instituto Raúl Porras Barrenechea, 1963.

————. *Los cronistas del Perú (1528–1650) y otros ensayos.* Lima: Editorial e Imprenta DESA, 1986.

Poupeney Hart, Catherine. "La crónica de Indias entre 'historia' y 'ficción.'" *Revista Canadiense de Estudios Hispánicos* 15, no. 3 (1991): 503–15.

Powers, Karen V. *Andean Journeys: Migration, Ethnogenesis, and the State in Colonial Quito.* Albuquerque: University of New Mexico Press, 1995.

Prakash, Gyan, ed. *After Colonialism: Imperial Histories and Postcolonial Displacements.* Princeton: Princeton University Press, 1995.

Pratt, Mary L. *Imperial Eyes: Travel Writing and Transculturation.* London: Routledge, 1992.

Prien, Hans-Jürgen. *Die Geschichte des Christentums in Lateinamerika.* Göttingen: Vandenhoeck & Ruprecht, 1978.

Rabasa, José. *Inventing America: Spanish Historiography and the Formation of Eurocentrism.* Norman and London: University of Oklahoma Press, 1993.

————. *Writing Violence on the Northern Frontier: The Historiography of Sixteenth-Century New Mexico and Florida and the Legacy of Conquest.* Durham, N.C., and London: Duke University Press, 2000.

Radcliffe, Sarah A. "Marking the Boundaries between the Community, the State and History in the Andes." *Journal of Latin American Studies* 22, no. 3 (1990): 575–94.

————. "Different Heroes: Genealogies of Postcolonial Geographies." *Environment and Planning A* 29 (1997): 1331–33.

Rafael, Vincente L. *Contracting Colonialism: Translation and Christian Conversion in Tagalog Society under Early Spanish Rule.* Durham, N.C., and London: Duke University Press, 1993.

Raffles, Hugh. *In Amazonia: A Natural History.* Princeton and Oxford: Princeton University Press, 2002.

Rama, Angel. *La ciudad letrada.* Hanover, N.H.: Ediciones del Norte, 1984.

Ramírez, Susan E. *The World Upside Down: Cross-Cultural Contact and Conflict in Sixteenth-Century Peru.* Stanford: Stanford University Press, 1996.

Ramos, Demetrio. "La crisis indiana y la Junta Magna de 1568." *Jahrbuch für Geschichte von Staat, Wirtschaft und Gesellschaft Lateinamerikas* 23 (1986): 1–61.

Ramos, Gabriela, and Henrique Urbano, eds. *Catolicismo y extirpación de idolatrías, siglos XVI–XVIII.* Cusco: Centro de Estudios Regionales Andinos Bartolomé de Las Casas, 1993.

Ramos Pérez, Demetrio. *El mito del Dorado: Su génesis y proceso.* Caracas: Academia Nacional de la Historia, 1973.

Rappaport, Joanne, and Tom Cummins. "Between Images and Writing: The Ritual of the King's Quillca." *Colonial Latin American Review* 7, no. 1 (1998): 7–32.

Reeve, Mary-Elizabeth. "Regional Interaction in the Western Amazon: The Early Colonial Encounter and the Jesuit Years: 1538–1767." *Ethnohistory* 41, no. 1 (1993): 106–38.

Renard-Casevitz, France M., Thierry Saignes, and A. C. Taylor. *L'Inca, l'espagnol et les sauvages: Rapports entre les sociétés amazoniennes et andines du Xve au XVIIe siècle.* Paris: Éditions recherche sur les civilisations, 1986.

Restall, Matthew. *Seven Myths of the Spanish Conquest.* Oxford: Oxford University Press, 2003.

Richards, Thomas. *The Imperial Archive: Knowledge and the Fantasy of Empire.* London and New York, 1993.

Rivera-Ayala, Sergio. "Riding High, the Horseman's View: Urban Space and the Body in *México en 1554.*" In *Mapping Colonial Spanish America,* edited by Santa Arias and Mariselle Meléndez, 251–74. Lewisburg, Pa.: Bucknell University Press, 2002.

Robinson, David J. "La ciudad colonial hispanoamericana: ¿Símbolo o texto?" In *Ciencia, vida y espacio en Iberoamérica,* edited by José Luis Peset, 249–80. Madrid: Consejo Superior de Investigaciones Científicas, 1989.

———. "The Language and Significance of Place in Latin America." In *The Power of Place,* edited by John A. Agnew and James S. Duncan, 157–84. London: Unwin Hyman, 1989.

Romero, Carlos. "Idolatrías de los Indios Huachos y Yauyos." *Revista Histórica* 6 (Lima 1918): 180–97.

Roosevelt, Anna, ed. *Amazonian Indians from Prehistory to the Present: Anthropological Perspectives.* Tucson and London: University of Arizona Press, 1994.

Rose, Mitchell. "Landscapes and Labyrinths." *Geoforum* 33 (2002): 455–67.

————. "The Seductions of Resistance: Power, Politics and a Performative Style of Systems." *Environment and Planning D: Society and Space* 20 (2002): 383–400.

Rosenzvaig, Eduardo. "La ostra abierta o la segunda conciencia espacial Americana." In *Espacio geográfico/espacio imaginario: El descubrimiento del Nuevo Mundo en las culturas italiana y española,* edited by María Muñiz Muñiz, 69–80. Cáceres: Universidad de Extremadura, 1993.

Rostworowski de Diez Canseco, María. *Señorías indígenas de Lima y Canta.* Lima: IEP Ediciones, 1978.

————. *History of the Inca Realm.* Cambridge: Cambridge University Press, 1999.

Roux, Jean-Claude. *L'Amazonie Péruvienne: Un El Dorado dévoré par la fôret, 1821–1910.* Paris: Harmattan, 1994.

Ryan, Michael T. "Assimilating New Worlds in the Sixteenth and Seventeenth Centuries." *Comparative Studies in Society and History* 23 (1981): 519–38.

Ryan, Simon. *The Cartographic Eye: How Explorers Saw Australia.* Cambridge: Cambridge University Press, 1996.

Said, Edward W. *Orientalism: Western Conceptions of the Orient.* London: Penguin Books, 1978.

Saignes, Thierry. *Caciques, Tribute and Migration in the Southern Andes: Indian Society and the 17th Century Colonial Order.* London: Institute of Latin American Studies, 1985.

————. *Los Andes orientales: Historia de un olvido.* Cochabamba: Ediciones CERES, 1985.

Sallnow, Michael J. *Pilgrims of the Andes: Regional Cults in Cuzco.* Washington, D.C., and London: Smithsonian Institution Press, 1987.

Salomon, Frank. "Vertical Politics on the Inka Frontier." In *Anthropological History of Andean Polities,* edited by John V. Murra, Nathan Wachtel, and Jacques Revel, 89–117. Cambridge: Cambridge University Press, 1986.

————. "Introductory Essay: The Huarochirí Manuscript." In *The Huarochirí Manuscript: A Testament of Ancient and Colonial Andean Religion.* Translated from Quechua by F. Salomon and G. L. Urioste, 1–38. Austin: University of Texas Press, 1991 [ca. 1598].

Sánchez Bella, Ismael. "El gobierno del Perú 1556–1564." *Anuario de Estudios Americanos* 17 (1960): 407–524.

Santos-Granero, Fernando. "Boundaries Are Made to Be Crossed: The Magic and Politics of the Long-lasting Amazon/Andes Divide." *Identities: Global Studies in Culture and Power* 9 (2002): 545–69.

Sauer, Carl Ortwin. *The Early Spanish Main.* Berkeley and London: University of California Press, 1966.

Schäfer, Ernesto. *El Consejo Real y Supremo de las Indias: Su historia, organización y labor administrativa hasta la terminación de la Casa de Austria,* 2 vols.

Seville: Publicaciones del Centro de Estudios de Historia de América, 1935.

Schwartz, Stuart. *Implicit Understandings: Observing, Reporting and Reflecting on the Encounters between Europeans and other Peoples in the Early Modern Era.* Cambridge: Cambridge University Press, 1994.

Schwarz, Bill. "Conquerors of Truth: Reflections on Postcolonial Theory." In *The Expansion of England: Race, Ethnicity and Cultural History,* edited by Bill Schwarz, 9–31. London: Routledge, 1996.

Scott, Heidi V. "Contested Territories: Arenas of Geographical Knowledge in Early Colonial Peru." *Journal of Historical Geography* 29, no. 2 (2003): 166–88.

———. "A Mirage of Colonial Consensus: Resettlement Schemes in Early Spanish Peru." *Environment and Planning D: Society and Space* 22 (2004): 885–99.

———. "Más allá del texto: Recuperando las influencias indígenas en las experiencias españolas del Perú." In *Más allá de la dominación y la resistencia: ensayos de historia peruana,* edited by Paulo Drinot and Leo Garófalo, 23–47. Lima: Instituto de Estudios Peruanos, 2005.

———. "Rethinking Landscape and Colonialism in the Context of Early Colonial Peru." *Environment and Planning D: Society and Space* 24 (2006): 481–96.

Scott, James C. *Seeing Like a State: How Certain Schemes to Improve the Human Condition Have Failed.* New Haven: Yale University Press, 1998.

Seed, Patricia. "Colonial and Postcolonial Discourse." *Latin American Research Review* 26, no. 3 (1991): 181–200.

———. "More Colonial and Postcolonial Discourses." *Latin American Research Review* 28, no. 3 (1993): 146–52.

———. *Ceremonies of Possession in Europe's Conquest of the New World, 1492–1640.* Cambridge: Cambridge University Press, 1995.

Sempat Assadourian, Carlos. "Los señores étnicos y los corregidores de indios en la conformación del estado colonial." *Anuario de Estudios Americanos* 44 (1987): 325–426.

———. "Los derechos a las tierras del Ynga y del sol durante la formación del sistema colonial." In *Reproducción y transformación de las sociedades andinas,* edited by Segundo Moreno Yánez and Frank Salomon, vol. 1, 215–84. Quito: Abya-Yala, 1991.

———. *Transiciones hacia el sistema colonial andino.* Lima: Instituto de Estudios Peruanos, 1994.

Sharp, Joanne, Paul Routledge, Chris Philo, and Ronan Paddison. "Entanglements of Power: Geographies of Domination/Resistance." In *Entanglements of Power: Geographies of Domination/Resistance,* edited by Joanne Sharp, Paul Routledge, Chris Philo, and Ronan Paddison, 1–42. London: Routledge, 2000.

Sidaway, James D. "The (Re)making of the Western 'Geographical Tradition': Some Missing Links." *Area* 29, no. 1 (1997): 72–80.

Silverblatt, Irene. "Becoming Indian in the Central Andes of Seventeenth-Century Peru." In *After Colonialism: Imperial Histories and Postcolonial Displacements,* edited by Gyan Prakash, 279–98. Princeton: Princeton University Press, 1995.

Slatta, R.W. "Spanish Colonial Military Strategy and Ideology." In *Contested Ground: Comparative Frontiers on the Northern and Southern Edges of the Spanish Empire,* edited by Donna J. Guy and Thomas E. Sheridan, 83–96. Tucson: University of Arizona Press, 1998.

Sluyter, Andrew. "Colonialism and Landscape in the Americas: Material/Conceptual Transformations and Continuing Consequences." *Annals of the Association of American Geographers* 91, no. 2 (2001): 410–28.

———. *Colonialism and Landscape: Postcolonial Theory and Applications.* Oxford: Rowman and Littlefield, 2002.

Solano, Francisco de. "Urbanización y municipalización de la población indígena." *Revista de Indias* 127–30 (1972): 241–68.

———, ed. *Cuestionarios para la formación de las Relaciones Geográficas de Indias, siglos XVI/XIX.* Madrid: Centro de Estudios Históricos, 1988.

Someda, Hidefuji. *El imperio de los Incas: Imagen del Tahuantinsuyu creada por los cronistas.* Lima: Pontificia Universidad Católica del Perú, 1999.

Sopher, David E. *Geography of Religions.* Eaglewood Cliffs, N.J.: Prentice-Hall, 1967.

Spalding, Karen. *Huarochirí: An Andean Society under Inca and Spanish Rule.* Stanford: Stanford University Press, 1984.

Spivak, Gayatri. "Can the Subaltern Speak?" In *Marxism and the Interpretation of Culture,* edited by Cary Nelson and Lawrence Grossberg, 271–313. Basingstoke: Macmillan Education, 1988.

Spurr, David. *The Rhetoric of Empire: Colonial Discourse in Journalism, Travel Writing, and Imperial Administration.* Durham, N.C., and London: Duke University Press, 1993.

Stanislawski, Dan. "Early Spanish Town Planning in the New World." *The Geographical Review* 37 (1947): 94–105.

Stavig, Ward. "Ambiguous Visions: Nature, Law and Culture in Indigenous-Spanish Land Relations in Colonial Peru." *Hispanic American Historical Review* 80, no. 1 (2000): 77–111.

Stern, Steve. *Peru's Indian Peoples and the Challenge of Spanish Conquest: Huamanga to 1640.* Madison and London: University of Wisconsin Press, 1982.

Stevenson, Edward L. "The Geographical Activities of the Casa de la Contratación." *Annals of the Association of American Geographers* 17, no. 2 (1927): 39–59.

Stoler, Ann L. "Rethinking Colonial Categories: European Communities and the Boundaries of Rule." In *Colonialism and Culture,* edited by Nicholas Dirks, 319–52. Ann Arbor: University of Michigan Press, 1992.

Stoler, Ann L., and Frederick Cooper. "Between Metropole and Colony: Rethinking a Research Agenda." In *Tensions of Empire: Colonial Cultures in a Bourgeois World,* edited by Ann L. Stoler and Frederick Cooper, 1–58. London: University of California Press, 1997.

Tau Anzoátegui, Víctor. "El 'Gobierno del Perú' de Juan de Matienzo: En la senda del humanismo jurídico." In *De conquistadores y conquistados: Realidad, justificación, representación,* edited by Karl Kohut, 168–87. Frankfurt am Main: Vervuert Verlag, 1992.

Taussig, Michael T. *The Devil and Commodity Fetishism in South America.* Chapel Hill: University of North Carolina Press, 1980.

———. *Shamanism, Colonialism and the Wild Man.* Chicago: University of Chicago Press, 1987.

Taylor, Anne Christine. "The Western Margins of Amazonia from the Early Sixteenth to the Early Nineteenth Century." In *The Cambridge History of the Native Peoples of the Americas.* Vol. 3, *South America,* Part I, edited by Frank Salomon and Stuart Schwartz, 188–256. Cambridge: Cambridge University Press, 1999.

TePaske, John J. *Research Guide to Andean History: Bolivia, Chile, Ecuador and Peru.* Durham, N.C.: Duke University Press, 1981.

Thomas, Nicholas. *Colonialism's Culture: Anthropology, Travel and Government.* Cambridge: Polity Press, 1994.

Tiffin, Chris, and Alan Lawson. "Introduction: The Textuality of Empire." In *De-scribing Empire: Postcolonialism and Textuality,* edited by Chris Tiffin and Alan Lawson, 1–11. London and New York: Routledge, 1994.

Todorov, Tzvetan. *The Conquest of America: The Question of the Other.* New York: Harper and Row, 1984.

Tord Nicolini, Javier. "El corregidor de indios del Perú: Comercio y tributos." *Historia y Cultura* (Lima) 8 (1974): 173–214.

Triff, Soren. "La crítica de las crónicas y la crisis de la crítica." In *Actas XXIX Congreso del Instituto Internacional de Literatura Iberoamericana,* Universidad de Barcelona, 15–19 June 1992. Barcelona: Promociones y Publicaciones Universitarias, 1994.

Vargas Ugarte, Rubén. "Mapas y planos del Perú, 1590–1905." *Revista del Museo Nacional* 22 (1953): 104–12.

———. *Historia de la Compañía de Jesús en el Perú.* Burgos: Imprenta de Aldecoa, 1963.

Varón Gabai, Rafael. *Francisco Pizarro and His Brothers: The Illusion of Power in Sixteenth-Century Peru.* Norman and London: University of Oklahoma Press, 1997.

Verdesio, Gustavo. "Las representaciones territoriales del Uruguay colo-nial: Hacia una hermenéutica pluritópica." *Revista de Crítica Latinoameri-cana* 23, no. 46 (1997): 135–61.

Villamarín, Juan, and Judith Villamarín. "Chiefdoms: The Prevalence and Persistence of 'Señoríos Naturales,' 1400 to European Conquest." In *The Cambridge History of the Native Peoples of the Americas.* Vol. 3, *South America,* Part I, edited by Frank Salomon and Stuart Schwartz, 577–667. Cambridge: Cambridge University Press, 1999.

Vindel, Francisco. *Mapas de América en los libros españoles, 1503–1798.* Madrid, 1955.

Viola Recasens, Andreu. "La cara oculta de los Andes: Notas para una redefinición de la relación histórica entre sierra y selva." *Boletín Ameri-canista* 33, nos. 42–43 (1992–93): 7–22.

Vives, Pedro. Las "Indias del Rey y las colonias de España, siglos XVI y XVII." *Rábida-Huelva* 11 (1992): 9–21.

Wachtel, Nathan. *The Vision of the Vanquished: The Spanish Conquest of Peru through Indian Eyes, 1530–1570.* Translated from French by Ben and Siân Reynolds. Sussex: Harvester Press, 1977.

Wheatley, Paul. *The Pivot of the Four Quarters: A Preliminary Enquiry into the Origins and Character of the Ancient Chinese City.* Edinburgh: Edinburgh University Press, 1971.

White, Richard. *The Middle Ground: Indians, Empires, and Republics in the Great Lakes Region, 1650–1815.* Cambridge: Cambridge University Press, 1991.

Wightman, Ann M. *Indigenous Migration and Social Change: The Forasteros of Cuzco, 1570–1720.* Durham, N.C., and London: Duke University Press, 1990.

Wintle, Michael. "Renaissance Maps and the Construction of the Idea of Europe." *Journal of Historical Geography* 25, no. 2 (1999): 137–65.

Withers, Charles J. "Writing in Geography's History: *Caledonia,* Networks of Correspondence and Geographical Knowledge in the Late Enlight-enment." *Scottish Geographical Journal* 120, nos. 1–2 (2004): 33–45.

Wood, Denis. *The Power of Maps.* London: Routledge, 1992.

Zamora, Margarita. "Historicity and Literariness: Problems in the Literary Criticism of Spanish American Colonial Texts." *Modern Language Notes* 102, no. 2 (1987): 334–46.

———. *Reading Columbus.* Berkeley and London: University of California Press, 1993.

Zárate Botía, Carlos G. "Movilidad y permanencia en la frontera amazónica colonial del siglo XVIII." *Journal de la Société des Américanistes* 84, no. 1 (1998): 73–98.

Zuidema, Rainer Tom. *The Ceque System of Cuzco: The Social Organisation of the Capital of the Inca.* Leiden: E. J. Brill, 1964.

INDEX

questionnaires: and the extirpation of idolatry, 101, 103–4
questionnaires, geographical, 49–52, 184n.67; and meanings for indigenous respondents, 67; and metropolitan anxiety, 51; utilitarian categories, 54
quipus, 31, 33

Rabasa, José, 44, 111–12, 134, 150–51; on the invention of America, 51
Raches, 155, 211n.81
Raffles, Hugh: on Guiana, 30, 37
Ramírez, Diego de, 203n.63
Ramírez, Susan, 182n.32; on *huaca* looting, 185n.79
Ramos, Gabriela, 189n.21
Recio de León, Juan, 14–15; accounts of services, 113–21; proposed solutions to depopulation, 125–28; proposed solutions to silver transport, 122–24; tactics of discourse, 151–52, 157, 160–61
reciprocity, 33
reducciones: decline of, 71, 205n.81; effects of, 56; in Huarochirí, 78–79, 84, 92–94; 193n.59, and the Jesuits, 89; and mining, 124–25, 187n.94; and the *RG*s, 70–71, 73; Viceroy Toledo's creation of, 69–70, 75
Relación Samano-Xerez, 1
relaciones de servicios. See accounts of services
Relaciones Geográficas, 14; and Christianization, 57–59; interpretation of, 52, 54; and knowledge of landscape, 159–60; and resistance, 164.

See also specific RG(s) under Collaguas; Huamanga; Jauja; La Paz; Mexico
religious practices, Andean, 58–59
resettlement. *See reducciones*
resistance, 14, 164–65; to the *reducciones,* 69–74
Restall, Matthew, 17
*RG*s. *See Relaciones Geográficas*
rhizome, as image for colonialism, 188n.6
Ribera, Nicolás de: *relación de servicios,* 26–27, 175n.26; as witness, 177n.42, 177n.49
rivalries: within Huanca communities, 34
Rodrigues Peinado, Francisco, 155–57
Rose, Mitchell, 60, 73
routes between Andes and Amazon, 151–52, 155–57

sacred geographies, 160; in Huarochirí, 94, 99–106; proliferation of, 101; in the *RG*s, 57–59, 63, 67; and the subterranean, 100–101
Sahagún, San Juan de, 114, 117, 151
settlements, colonial: foundation of, 44–46
settlements, precolonial: northern Peru, 1–2
Sharp, Joanne, et al., 60, 73
silver: transport routes to Spain, 121–24
Sluyter, Andrew, 5–6
Songo rebellion, 147–49, 152
Songonchi, San Pedro de, 57, 181n.29
Soquicancha, San Bartolomé de, 81–82, 84

HEIDI V. SCOTT

is Lecturer in Human Geography at the Institute of Geography and Earth Sciences, University of Wales, Aberystwyth. She is currently doing research on Franciscan missions in the Apolobamba region of colonial Bolivia.